PLEASURES
&PASTIMES

IN TUDOR
ENGLAND

ALISON SIM

To Jane and Geoff,
with love

First published in 1999
This edition first published in 2009

The History Press
The Mill, Brimscombe Port
Stroud, Gloucestershire, GL5 2QG
www.thehistorypress.co.uk

British Library Cataloguing in Publication Data.
A catalogue record for this book is available from the British Library.

ISBN 978 0 7524 5031 5

Typesetting and origination by The History Press
Printed in Great Britain

Contents

Acknowledgements

Thanks to the following people for providing specialist knowledge: Richard Burnip, Chris Gidlow, Robert and Jane Hugget, Caroline Johnson, Martin Pope and Roy Porter.

Thanks as usual to Margaret Peach for editing and making comments in her own inimitable style.

Last but not least, thanks to Malcolm and Moira Lewin, and Janet and Keith Waldock for chocolate, gin and sympathy.

Introduction

The sixteenth century in England was an age of change. The government became more centralised and powerful, changing the way the bureaucracy worked and the way the aristocracy behaved. The cultural changes of the Renaissance and the politics of the time became entwined so that the Church, the bedrock of medieval society, was weakened by the dissolution of the monasteries and by the religious tensions which eventually split the Roman Catholic and Protestant Churches. This in turn altered much that was so familiar to people of the time, even down to the way that the passing of the seasons was celebrated. The pleasures and pastimes of the English would never be the same again.

The centralisation of the state affected the way in which even the most powerful people behaved. Success at court became more important than ever before as the monarch became more powerful. The king was the man with the best rewards to hand out, whether in terms of jobs, lands or financial rewards like pensions. More than ever, careers were made or broken by royal favour or displeasure. Even the greatest lords no longer had the power they had once enjoyed. There was no 'Warwick the Kingmaker', who could literally decide the fate of kings, in the sixteenth century as there had been in the fifteenth.

In the Middle Ages a king, or a great lord, needed above all things to be a successful soldier. The force of law was not always maintained and you might find yourself having to defend your lands from other people by force. Land was the most secure form of wealth at the time, so there was always someone keen to take your land away from you. The fifteenth-century letters of the Paston family mention several disputes over the ownership of land, in particular one over the ownership of Caister Castle and another over the ownership of the manor of Gresham. Both properties changed hands by force several times during the dispute.[1]

This sort of behaviour was not tolerated by the Tudors. Henry VII outlawed all private armies except the royal bodyguard, so nobles no longer had the resources to flaunt the law in this way. Henry VIII was also determined to be absolutely in control of his realm. Disputes were to be settled in the law courts, not by private individuals fighting it out with no reference to the royal will.

The land disputes did not stop. There was no land registry at this time so it was often was a complicated business deciding who exactly owned what. The difference was that disputes now took place in the courts. This meant that landholders needed an education, in order to cope with the legal system. Most heirs to estates would henceforth finish their education at the Inns of Court, the legal schools. This meant more work for lawyers too, making the law a profitable career.

Henry VIII's determination to control his realm also meant a bigger bureaucracy, resulting in more career opportunities in the Tudor equivalent of the civil service. The changed atmosphere of the court also meant that if government office did come your way, a good education was necessary to carry it out effectively. Unlike his medieval predecessors, Henry VIII didn't have to look to the Church to provide educated administrators. There were plenty of secular men with the necessary training. Cardinal Wolsey was the last of the great prelate-administrators. All of these factors together meant that a good academic education, and not just training in military skills, became necessary for the successful Tudor.

This new emphasis on education meant that the pleasures of the aristocracy were changing. The Renaissance had well and truly arrived in England by the sixteenth century and with it had come the idea of the courtier as all round 'Renaissance man', as expressed in Castiglione's *Book of the Courtier*.[2] This was first published in Italy in 1528 and, although it was not published in

England until 1561, the ideas expressed in it were already current in English court circles before then.

Castiglione's courtier is everything from a warrior to a diplomat. He knows how to make elegant conversation on a wide range of topics, he has a knowledge of drawing and appreciates painting and sculpture, and he is a skilled musician who plays several instruments. He has an intimate knowledge of the classics, he is a good sportsman; in fact, he can do everything. Castiglione's courtier is, of course, an ideal. How many Tudor courtiers lived up to this picture of perfection is a matter of debate, but at least the ideal was there. The contrast with the behaviour of the knights of the round table in Malory's *Morte d'Arthur* (finished in 1469 and first printed by Caxton in 1485) is startling. Malory's knights spend all their time feasting, getting involved in very bloody fights of one kind or another, going to mass and dallying with their various ladies. They are heroes in the medieval tradition. They would hardly have been welcomed at the refined court of Urbino, where Castiglione's book is set. Times had definitely changed.

The new view of what constituted an ideal courtier led to new ideas in education. To be successful as a newcomer to the court you needed a patron, someone who knew the monarch personally and who could mention your name to him or her at the vital moment. A good way of gaining access to these exclusive circles was to become the kind of person who could make interesting conversation, dance elegantly and match the king at sport. Part of Henry's affection for Thomas More was based on the fact that they used to study astronomy together. Henry is recorded as having enjoyed singing with courtiers such as Sir Peter Carew. If you wanted to educate your son for life at court, he would have to study more than the arts of war.

The Tudor determination to dominate and shine changed not only the atmosphere of the court, but also its physical appearance. Henry VII had fought his way to the throne and spent most of his reign building up the royal finances and making sure that the English nobility knew that the Tudors were here to stay. England was kept out of expensive wars. Henry VIII came to the English throne in 1509 at the age of seventeen. His father had left him a fortune, admittedly not as large as is often stated[3] but enough to give him ambition. He was determined that his country should no longer be a backwater, but that it should be pulled into the centre of European affairs. As a sign of this, Henry VIII wanted to surround himself with a glittering court. The result was a new interest in the arts, interior design and even gardening.

Art occupied a very important place in Renaissance courts. The presence of the finest craftsmen and thinkers, together with wonderful displays of art, added considerably to the prestige of a nation at this time. This was why the Italian states vied with each other for the services of these men, and why families such as the Medici and the Gonzagas adorned their houses with the finest artwork available. Henry VIII was determined to follow suit.

The Renaissance led to a new, secular interest in the classical world, and brought with it a new regard for art, sculpture, music and debate of matters philosophical. In the classical world artists and sculptors had enjoyed high social status, but during the Middle Ages such men were seen as mere craftsmen. This was not to say that their work was not appreciated, but that it was seen more in terms of decoration than of being of value in its own terms. Gothic art was more concerned with putting across a message than presenting an image of the real world. For example, the most important people in a picture, such as a king or a bishop, were often drawn much larger than the other figures. Colours were used because of their symbolic value or simply because they looked good.

Renaissance art took a very different view of the world. Artists began to study classical art which presented the human figure as it really is, or at least an idealised form of it. As a result the study of anatomy became vital for the artist and there was a new interest in depicting people as individuals rather than as types. In addition colour began to be used more realistically, to represent the effects of light. The revived interest in the classical world did not result in a desire to copy slavishly the principles of either its people or its art, but rather to take the best of these and to apply them to what was then the modern world so as to create the perfect state.[4]

The arts were seen as playing an important role in this. Architecture could create the ideal setting for this new society. Painting could inspire men to great things. Leon Battista Alberti, whose book *On Painting* (published in 1435) very much influenced Renaissance art, commented, 'We should also consider it a very great gift to men that painting has represented the gods they worship, for painting has contributed considerably to the piety which binds us to the gods, and to filling our minds with sound religious beliefs.'[5] The arts were seen as necessary to the improvement of mankind.

The royal Tudors saw the political possibilities of this revived interest in art and made full use of them. One of the most obvious was that it could be used to create the most sumptuous settings for the court, reminding everyone of the wealth and power of the king. The Tudors were nothing like as secure on the throne as we often imagine them to be. Henry VII's defeat of Richard III in 1485 meant that the throne had changed hands by force six times in eighty-six years. The Tudors needed to convince their subjects of their dynasty's permanence and building was a good way of doing that. In an age when most buildings were still wooden, a large brick or stone palace was an important symbol.

Henry VIII was the greatest royal builder England has ever seen, so people tend to forget that his father also knew the value of architecture. Henry VII rebuilt the old palace of Sheen, and renamed it Richmond Palace as the Tudor family were Earls of Richmond before they came to the throne. The palace was greatly admired. He also built Greenwich Palace, rebuilt Baynard's Castle in London (which was more of a palace than a castle) and carried out work at the Tower of London and Windsor Castle. Henry VIII built or improved even more palaces and soon those wealthy enough were following suit, building or improving their houses in the style set by the king.[6]

Now that artists were portraying the world more realistically portraits became more of a fashion. As Alberti put it 'through painting, the faces of the dead go on living for a very long time'.[7] Portraits were of course not unknown in the Middle Ages, but people were usually shown kneeling at prayer beside their favourite

saints as part of a religious scene. Now there was a new emphasis
on showing people as individuals for their own sake. Portraits
remained a luxury for the wealthy and, like other luxuries, the
royal Tudors used them to good political effect. They helped to
build up the royal image, presenting the monarch in the way in
which he or she wished to be seen. Portraits could even be used
to remind people of certain facts about the monarch. The famous
Tudor *Dynasty* portrait at Hampton Court looks at first like a
simple portrait of Henry VIII and his family. It is, however, rather
more than that. This portrait was painted at the end of Henry's
life, at a time when he was almost paranoid about the succession.
He was forty-six when his son Edward was born and he knew
that it was unlikely that he would live to see Edward a grown
man. It was a political gamble to leave the throne to a young
boy – the last such to inherit the throne had been Edward V,
one of the two little princes who so famously disappeared. There
was also fear of invasion as the Pope called for loyal Catholic
monarchs to invade England. The initial threat in 1539 faded
away but it was a possibility which hung over England for the rest
of the century, particularly famously at the time of the Armada
in 1588. Henry saw it as enough of a threat to set about wiping
out what remained of the old Yorkist lords, however flimsy the
evidence against them. His cousin Henry Courtenay and the
elderly Margaret Pole were among the victims. The portrait shows
Henry sitting in state under his royal canopy, at Whitehall Palace,
the official seat of government. Henry is stating that he is the
King. His arm is around his son Edward, his heir, while Jane
Seymour, Edward's mother, sits on his left. Jane had been dead
for six or seven years by this time but she appears as she was, as
far as Henry was concerned, his first true wife. He had annulled
his first two marriages, considering neither to have been valid. The
picture is therefore a statement of Henry's power and of his son's
right to the throne.

Despite the many differences between the courtly pleasures of
the Middle Ages and those of the sixteenth century, there were
also striking similarities. Many of the pleasures of the former
period continued into the latter. Wealthy people in the sixteenth

century loved hunting every bit as much as their medieval ancestors and the young king Henry could spend as long as ten hours a day in the saddle. His excessive zeal for the sport led to a number of quite serious accidents. When he was out hawking in 1525 he pole-vaulted over a stream while following his hawk. The pole broke and the king landed head-first in the mud and nearly drowned. Fortunately someone was able to jump in and lift up his head which had become quite stuck in the clay at the bottom of the stream.[8]

Training for war was still seen as central to an aristocratic boy's education. Castiglione himself not only studied Latin and Greek at the university of Milan, but also jousting, fencing and wrestling.[9] The aristocracy were the natural leaders of society and therefore it fell to them to lead the army. Two very influential books on the education of boys were Sir Thomas Elyot's *Book Named the Governor* and Roger Ascham's *The Schoolmaster* and both make this very clear. Sir Philip Sidney, the famous Elizabethan poet, was himself also very much a soldier and even died in battle.

The tastes of the court could still be rather rough and ready by modern standards. Whitehall, Henry VIII's largest palace, boasted a very fine cockpit for housing cock-fights. The king himself enjoyed them very much, despite his fine education. Bear- and bull-baiting were popular pastimes enjoyed by rich and poor alike. Animal welfare lay a long way in the future but perhaps this was only to be expected in a society where public executions drew large crowds.

Despite this, the new tastes of the court inevitably filtered down through society and the new vogue for learning also affected the middle classes. The merchant classes had long been interested in at least basic education as boys had to be able to read, write and do basic figures in order to be apprenticed to the more prestigious trades. Merchants' daughters were also often taught to do basic figures and to read, as they often played an active part in helping to run their husbands' businesses.[10] Merchants were often away from home on business and many felt able to trust their wives with information in letters that they wouldn't trust a mere servant with.

They might also want to keep in touch with affairs at home, so would be happy for their wives to write as well as read. Certainly Sabine Johnson, whose husband was a merchant at the Staple in Calais, wrote often to her husband.[11]

The middle classes were also well placed to benefit from the new printing press. Hand-written books had been very expensive indeed but printed ones were within their reach and they bought them on a wide range of subjects, from housewifery manuals to books on religion. This new market for books led to the development of new types of writing, opening the way eventually for the development of the novel in the seventeenth and eighteenth centuries. One reason for this was the new regard for writing literature in English. Earlier generations had seen English as barbaric, preferring to write in the true scholar's language, Latin. This habit had been useful in creating a kind of international literature which could be read by learned men from many different countries, but it meant that access to learning was closed to those who did not have the time or the means to become fluent in Latin. As a result, those who chose to write in English sometimes felt the need to apologise for doing so. Sir Thomas Elyot, writing his health manual *The Castel of Helth* explained in the introduction that he had written in English as he wanted as many people as possible to be able to read it. Others, fortunately, took a different view. Roger Ascham felt it quite acceptable to take all the care over English prose and poetry that you might take with Latin. 'He that will write well in any tongue must follow the counsel of Aristotle, to speak as the common people do, to think as wise men do, and so should every man understand him . . .'[12]

The subjects that were taught and the way teaching took place also altered. Attitudes were very gradually moving away from the idea of merely accepting the ideas of previous generations. Learning in the Middle Ages had been very much based on ancient writings, whether on those of philosophers like Aristotle or of doctors such as the Greek physician Galen (born in AD 129).[13] Over time the wisdom of these ancients had come to be seen rather in the light of divine revelation, that is to say, something which was not to be questioned, but merely accepted. Now people began to question, but they had to do so cautiously and with considerable tact if they wished to avoid punishment.

A good case in point is the science of medicine. In the early sixteenth century medicine was taught as a purely academic subject. The Tudors believed that everything was made up of the four elements of earth, air, fire and water. The earth was considered dry, water was moist, fire was hot and air was cold. Blends of these elements made up the four basic character types which were recognised as sanguine (hot and moist), phlegmatic (cold and moist), choleric (hot and dry) and melancholic (cold and dry). These ideas dated back to the time of Aristotle.

The famous ancient Greek doctor Hippocrates had had very similar ideas, saying that the body was made up of four 'humours' or liquids which were blood, phlegm, yellow bile and black bile. These two ideas became mixed up together as time went on so that a sanguine man was considered to have blood as the dominant humour in his constitution, while a phlegmatic one had, of course, phlegm. The choleric man's dominating humour was yellow bile and the melancholic man's, black bile.[14] The theory was very appealing because it was used to explain everything from what we would now call depression to fevers and aches and pains. If the resulting remedies didn't work too successfully that wasn't too much of a problem. In the sixteenth century, you didn't necessarily expect a doctor to cure you, you merely hoped he could.

The fact that the moon controlled the tides suggested to people that the stars also affected the four humours and so a university-trained doctor spent much of his time studying astrology. He might also diagnose a disease simply by looking at a patient's urine, and might never even meet a patient at all. If a body were dissected before medical students the actual cutting of the body was done by a junior colleague of the professor, who sat up on a high chair reading his lecture on anatomy. The students watched, rather than getting an opportunity to dissect the body themselves.[15] This gradually changed as the century progressed. In 1543 a Flemish professor of anatomy at Padua university published a book on anatomy called *De Humani Corporis Fabrica* based on dissections which he had done personally.[16] It was a sign that the age of purely theoretical medical training was drawing to a close. Dissection gained official approval in England in 1540 when Henry VIII granted the Royal College of Surgeons four dead bodies from the Tyburn gallows each year.

It also became more acceptable to challenge the theories of the ancient writers. This had to be done with care: as late as 1559 Dr John Geynes was cited before the Congregated College of Physicians for suggesting that Galen's ideas were not infallible.[17] The sixteenth century was not particularly an age of dramatic scientific discovery in medicine, rather it was a time when doctors slowly developed a more practical and questioning attitude to their subject. This paved the way for the scientific discoveries of later generations.

The new spirit of questioning, rather than just accepting received wisdom, was also creeping into education at the most basic level, that of teaching young children. Roger Ascham's influential book *The Schoolmaster* shows this. Ascham was tutor to both Edward VI and Elizabeth I and very much advocated a gentle approach to education. He considered it better to praise children often and to be patient with their mistakes, rather than to beat them for getting things wrong, which was the usual practice in education at the time. 'For I assure you there is no such whetstone to sharpen a good wit and encourage a will to learning as his [the schoolmaster's] praise' is how he put it.[18] He also championed the idea of making education as interesting as possible, making it a joy rather than a grim necessity.

The scholar of the Middle Ages was encouraged to learn by heart what his master told him, but Ascham's scholar is not. 'Let your scholar be never afraid to ask you any doubt, but use discreetly the best allurements you can to encourage him to the same, lest his overmuch fearing of you drive him to seek some misorderly shift, as to seek to be helped by some other book or to be prompted by some other scholar, and so go about to beguile you much, and himself more.'[19] Ascham saw no point in a scholar so afraid of his teacher that he had to pretend to understand. Learning to question was part of this new education.

The Renaissance might have changed life for the well-to-do, but how far did it change the lives of more ordinary people? The answer is that, it altered everyone's lives, rich or poor, important or unimportant. The Church affected the lives of everyone, so the new form of religion touched the entire population. Most people in Tudor England lived in the countryside where there wasn't a great deal of entertainment. Organised entertainments took place mainly at the various festivals which marked the passing of the year. Most of these celebrations were based on religious festivals, so that the social and religious lives of communities were all bound up together. The sixteenth century changed this round of entertainments for ever. Some festivals were banned altogether and were no longer even kept as holidays. Some were greatly modified. None were exactly as they had been.

The church buildings themselves changed too. The parish church was very much the central focus of life. The carved and painted rood screens, the statues of saints and many other familiar objects were taken away. The 825 monasteries were dissolved, leaving their buildings to decay or to be torn apart for the value of their brick and stone.[20] The monasteries had been part of life in both town and countryside for centuries in many cases and the ruins of these once-splendid buildings must have been a very visual symbol of the power of the State over the Church. Some were pleased to see this and others deplored it, but nobody was unaffected by it.

The present book offers an overview of how these profound changes altered the lives of people in the sixteenth century with regard to their leisure time and the pleasure they gained from the objects around them. This is a very wide subject: alone, the art of the Renaissance and Reformation has produced a huge number of books. The present author can only attempt an introduction to the subject and guide the reader to further, more detailed sources through the notes and additional reading list.

ONE
The Perfect Setting

The sixteenth century was a time for building. Food prices were rising, so that landowners, who produced the food, were doing well. They had the money to improve their houses, or even to build new ones. At the top end of the scale the aristocracy were building huge houses like William Cecil, Lord Burghley's Theobalds or Sir John Thynne's Longleat, but people lower down the scale were improving their more modest houses too. Many of the gentry were constructing comfortable, if not necessarily magnificent, manor houses and even yeomen were building houses with comforts like wall-mounted fireplaces and chimneys. Architecture became a fashionable subject for conversation.

To study what they were building it is necessary first to look at how people were using their houses. In the Middle Ages, houses had tended to consist of a hall, which was a general purpose living/dining/bedroom for most of the household, and then a private room or rooms for the family who owned the house and their guests. This was true not only for grand houses but also for quite humble ones. The Boarhunt cottage was built in the fifteenth century for a yeoman family, and consists of a hall and private room.

In the late fifteenth and sixteenth centuries this began to change. Houses were built with much more emphasis on privacy, and communal life in the hall became a thing of the past. Henry VIII did construct a magnificent new great hall at Hampton Court, but this was done with politics in mind. Continuing the ancient tradition of the great hall was aimed deliberately at giving a feeling of continuity with the past, which was yet another way of asserting the Tudor claim to the throne. At some of his other palaces, where he felt free just to follow fashion, Henry VIII divided the great hall up into smaller rooms.[1] Lower down the scale the same sort of thing was happening. Pendean, a house built for a yeoman family in the sixteenth century, now at the Weald and Downland Museum, was designed as several smaller rooms, rather than around a hall.

In the wealthiest circles, these changes were due in part to the issues discussed in the introduction. The Tudors' more centralised government meant that great lords no longer needed large numbers of retainers as a private army to protect their interests. Success was based on gaining the favour of the monarch which meant concentrating resources on the court.

Court life was formidably expensive. Chapter 2 gives an indication of the kind of clothes needed and how much they could cost. The letters of the family of Lord Lisle, Henry VIII's governor of Calais, tell of the other costs involved. One expense was the necessary gift-giving. Endless presents had to be sent to the right people when the Lisles needed help, as Tudor courtiers did not use their influence for free. The Lisle's presents ranged from quail, which Lady Lisle sent to Jane Seymour,[2] to hunting dogs and even a pet monkey which was almost sent to Anne Boleyn; fortunately someone warned Lady Lisle in time that Anne hated such animals.[3] This, of course, was not counting the expensive gift every important person was expected to give the monarch at New Year. Few people could afford both the court and their retainers. A great hall was no longer needed to house retainers, but suitably magnificent and moderately private rooms were necessary to entertain key courtiers.

It is possible to over-emphasise this change. Great lords lived in considerable estate right up to the end of the century. In the 1580s the Earl of Derby's household was still operating much as it had done a century earlier and there were still between 115 and 140 people in the household, excluding the family. Self-made men like Lord Chancellor Ellesmere lived in the same kind of style.[4] Even so, the emphasis in grand people's houses moved away from the great hall and into the great chamber.

The greater amount of privacy found in well-to-do houses was partly made necessary by the increasing formality of life at court. The royal Tudors tried to create a mystique around the monarch by putting a greater distance between themselves and their courtiers and surrounding themselves with great ceremony. More formal etiquette came into use at court, which in turn meant that people needed private areas where they could escape from such pressures. This new formality worked its way into the lives of the grander courtiers, creating a greater need in their houses for formal areas where important people could be entertained in suitable style and private areas where the family and their friends could relax.

The great chamber became the most important room in the house. It was used for everything from formal meals in the presence of important guests and the lying-in of corpses of members of the family, to dancing, music and family prayers. It was often the most richly decorated room in the house. There was usually a withdrawing-room off the great chamber, at the end of which lay either the best bedchamber or the owner of the house's bedchamber. This meant that another layer of privacy had been added, as in the Middle Ages a bedroom was also used as a sitting-room. Now the withdrawing-room was the private sitting-room for whoever used the bedchamber while bigger houses also had one or more parlours where the family could dine informally or sit and chat. Longleat had no fewer than three of them.[5]

Another important feature of such houses was the staircase. The chamber was usually on the first floor and now that it was the most important room, the route up to it had to be impressive. At first these staircases tended to be made of stone but when joinery techniques improved in the early seventeenth century, open-well staircases became the fashion. They were usually elaborately carved and painted.

It was not only the layout of houses that was changing, but also the style in which they were built. In the Middle Ages houses had been constructed with the idea of making them defensible. This was such a habit that larger houses were built around courtyards and surrounded by moats into the sixteenth century, even though the need for this had faded.

Medieval houses were often added to over the years in a very haphazard way, so that the result was anything but orderly. The Renaissance idea of symmetry drove this idea quite out of fashion, leading to buildings like Henry VII's Richmond Palace, which was still based around courtyards but was a carefully planned symmetrical building. There was very much a change of spirit in building. Inward-looking courtyard houses were gradually replaced by outward-looking houses which were compressed into a single block. Windows became larger and the grander apartments were often pushed up to first- or second-floor level, so as to enjoy the view. A taller, more compact house also gave a better impression of wealth and power, which is of course what building was all about in the highest circles.

The new interest in things classical was to bring about yet more changes in architecture. Classical ideals of architecture were reconsidered and buildings, particularly in Italy, began to be designed according to classical principles. A number of influential books were written on the subject, such as Serlio's *Tutte L'Opere D'Architettura et Prospetiva*, the first volume of which was published in 1537.[6] Classical works on architecture, such as those of Vitruvius,[7] were also translated into modern languages. The idea was that to design a building in truly classical style you needed to understand the principles and spirit behind the original buildings rather than just slavishly copy them. These classical ideals were known in England in the sixteenth century, but building in true classical style only began in the early seventeenth century. It is of note that the first English book on architecture known, John Shute's *First and Chief Groundes of Architecture*, was only published in 1563. It did not contain any new ideas, and was probably intended to be the first in a series of books. The rest were never written, or at least never published, due to Shute's death. To most English builders, such ideas were considered to be just a fashion, so that classical styles of decoration were often used in houses that were not built to classical ideals. The reason why these ideals took so long to reach England lies in how buildings were designed at the time.[8]

The term 'architect' was rather vague in the sixteenth century.

It usually meant a surveyor of the works, the person who oversaw the various craftsmen working on a building. Architects were simply seen as workmen and not as equals by their employers, unlike the gentlemen architects of the seventeenth century. Some were reasonably educated men who owned books and collected architectural plans, but this was not always the case. Towards the end of the sixteenth century, architects began to emerge as an independent class of men who knew about the practical side of building and could oversee the workforce, but who were also capable of designing a building. Smaller country houses seem to often have been built by such men. Walter Hancock, who died in 1599, was one such man. He is known to have worked as a craftsman on Candover Hall in Shropshire and also to have worked for Sir Francis Newport who built High Ercall and Eyton-on-Severn.

Such designers were all very well for a modest country house but the nobility had rather different ideas. They often had strong feelings about what they did and did not want, and some of them had read widely on architectural theory. Some had travelled and seen new buildings in France or Italy. Sir Richard Weston, who built Sutton Place in Surrey, was one such man. He had travelled in France where classical ideas were taken up sooner than in England. Sutton Place was one of the first English houses to be decorated in the new style.

A problem arose because most courtiers were too busy with court business to be on the site of their new house very much. They might also not be skilled in drawing up plans to show their builders, so that very often the final design of the house was a compromise between the thoughts of the building's owner and those of the master mason supervising the workforce. Sir John Thynne's first version of Longleat seems to have been built this way, with Sir John knowing in general terms what he wanted but with individual features being considered as and when they arose. Sir John was, however, no standard client. He rebuilt Longleat no fewer than four times until he was happy with the building. His mason Robert Smythson and the French sculptor Allen Maynard both greatly influenced the final design, but there was no doubt that Sir John was a man who knew what he wanted. Other clients seem to have been happy to leave the detail to the mason, who in most cases did not understand the theories of classical architecture. The result was that Tudor buildings tended to be a mixture of styles and tastes, built according to the needs of the person paying for the building. This attitude to architecture gave sixteenth-century buildings a rather pleasant individual streak.

The sixteenth century was a time when people were fascinated by symbols and puzzles which had to be worked out by the viewer. They liked the idea of needing to think about what they had seen in order to work out the meaning behind it. This element ran through everything from the symbolism used at court entertainments to choices in jewellery design. It was also used in architecture.

Several plans which survive from the time show this love of playing with ideas. The surveyor John Thorpe designed a house in the form of his initials IT (I was often used as a J at this time) although it was never built.[9] Sir Thomas Tresham built his famous Triangular Lodge to announce his Catholic faith at a time when it was not easy to do so openly. It represents the Trinity and the measurements of the Lodge are all based on the number 3.

On the other hand, there were plenty of people who agreed with Francis Bacon who started his essay *Of Building* with a piece of practical advice: 'Houses are built to Live in, and not to Looke on: Therefore let Use bee preferred before uniformitie; Except where both may be had. Leave the Goodly Fabrickes of Houses, for Beautie only, to the Enchanted Palaces of the Poets: Who build them with small cost.[10] Many sixteenth-century houses were designed on a practical basis, with flights of fancy found only in the choice of decoration, or in the fancy banquet houses in the gardens which will be discussed later.

Classical ideals also tended to take a back seat as English masons never got the chance to travel to Italy to see the original buildings or the new ones built on classical principles. Instead they looked to other English buildings for inspiration. Before starting to construct the hall at Trinity College, Cambridge, the supervisor of the works took the carpenter to London to see various different halls, which they surveyed and measured. The final result was exactly the same dimensions as the hall of the Middle Temple.[11]

The same was also true for decoration. It is quite common to find features such as fireplaces and friezes copied several times in a small geographical area. For example, in North Devon the same plaster frieze appears in houses at Bideford, Weare Gifford and Barnstaple. This probably points to families of craftsmen working in a local area and using the same designs in several places, but doubtless local people also visited each other's houses and copied ideas just as happens today.[12]

Sixteenth-century interior design, whether copied or original, was a riot of colour and complicated designs. The *Dynasty* portrait of Henry VIII and his family shows what is believed to be an actual room in the king's apartments at Whitehall, and demonstrates the type of effect people aspired to. Every available inch of a public room would be decorated, if the owner could afford it.

This is how William Harrison describes the interior of an English house:

> The walls of our houses on the inner sides in like sort be either hanged with tapestry, arras work, or painted clothes, wherein either divers histories, or herbs, beasts, knots and suchlike be stained, or else they are ceiled [i.e. panelled] with oak of our own wainscot brought hither out of the East countries, whereby the rooms are not a little commended, made warm and much more close than otherwise they would be.[13]

As he says, panelling was a favourite form of decoration as it was practical as well as beautiful. The panelling was not left as plain wood, as we usually see it today, but was often painted in bright colours or even gilded, as the royal panelling is in the *Dynasty* picture.[14] Elaborate plasterwork was also very fashionable, although as an alternative to plaster leather-mâché might be used. This was made of shredded leather mixed with size and brick dust. Once it was dry it could be painted and even gilded. It was frequently used in Henry VIII's palaces to make the thousands of yards of decoration needed to grace the royal walls.

There were a number of sources of inspiration for the design of interiors. One fashionable form of decoration was grotesque work. At the end of the fifteenth century people began to explore the remains of Nero's Golden House which were to be found underground on the Esquiline Hill in Rome and to copy the decoration of them. This style became known as 'grotesque', as the underground rooms were known as grottoes, or as 'antique work' because of its classical origins. The grotesque style was a mixture of small figures with intertwining foliage, vases, masques, weaponry and just about anything else.

There was also a fashion for allegory, such as the five senses and various allusions to classical subjects. The fireplace in the High Chamber in Elizabethan Chatsworth (now at Hardwick Hall) shows Orpheus surrounded by the nine muses, a suitable subject for a room in which music and dancing often took place.

The possibilities for designs were so many and various that pattern books began to be produced. A complete royal pattern book survives, which is a French treatise on geometry owned by Henry VIII. It is illustrated with the five orders of architecture.[15] This pattern book is hand-written but there were also printed books available and there is evidence that these were used. The chapel ceiling at St James's, made for Henry VIII in 1540, is identical to a plate in the fourth book of Serlio's *Regole generali di architettura* published in Venice in 1537.[16]

It was not only pattern books that provided inspiration, but well-known works by artists too. A favourite subject for decoration particularly in the later sixteenth century was the 'Nine Worthies'. These were three Jewish heroes, (Joshua, David and Judas Maccabeus), three pagan heroes (Alexander the Great, Hector and Julius Caesar) and three Christian ones (King Arthur, Charlemagne and Godfrey of Bouillon). They were seen as symbols of valour and virtue. The Flemish artist Nicholas de Bruyn designed some cast medallion heads of the Worthies, which seem to have caught the Elizabethan imagination. Designs based on these medallions can be found in a number of places, such as in the State Room in the Old Palace, Bromley-by-Bow (now in the Victoria and Albert Museum), at Balcarres House in Scotland and at Mapledurham.[17]

Despite the fact that full-blown classical architecture took some time to reach England, designs from abroad reached the country remarkably quickly. Inspiration from the Low Countries arrived in the form of imported furniture. Edward Hall comments that the Dutch brought over cupboards, stools, tables and chests among other items, all of which would have been decorated. Large amounts of decorated German pottery were also imported in the sixteenth century, giving another source of inspiration.[18]

Foreign craftsmen were also often employed in England in large numbers and brought the styles of their homelands with them. As the quality of their work was high, many people were keen to employ them. For example, since the mid-fifteenth century Flemish bricklayers had been favoured and Henry VIII's great royal building programme also included the use of a number of foreign workmen. Flemings and Germans (who went under the collective title of 'Doche' at the time) did much of the royal carving and also much of the royal glazing. Henry also employed a number of Italians, such as his Serjeant Painter Toto del Nunziata. England was certainly not a cultural backwater at the time.[19]

Plasterwork and panelling were expensive options. A wall painting was a cheaper alternative. Many of these have not survived: the damp English climate is not good for them and they were in any case intended to be used in the way we use wallpaper, as a rather temporary form of decoration. When the paintings got a bit shabby or out of date, they were often painted over. Fortunately enough have survived to give an impression of what a painted room of the time looked like. Rooms were painted freehand and with stencils, or sometimes with a mixture of both. They were not necessarily done in bright colours, as there were three rooms painted in black and white in a small one-storeyed house known as Campions in Saffron Walden. An upper room in the same house was painted in bright colours.[20] The designs used were sometimes quite simple geometrical ones, like the black and white designs here. Sometimes they were much more complicated, like the early seventeenth-century paintings in Stodmarsh, Kent, which show the signs of the zodiac, the months and Jupiter, Venus and Mercury. Sir Richard Clement, a gentleman of the Privy Chamber to Henry VIII, had a design of royal heraldry painted at his house, Ightam Mote. Others, like those decorating the walls of the Priest's House in West Hoathly, copy the designs found on expensive Italian cut velvets of the time.

Copying the designs found on expensive fabric on to walls was a logical choice. The most expensive way of covering walls at the time was to hang rich fabrics, such as fine silks or tapestry. A wall painting which survives in Pittleworth Manor in Hampshire is designed to create the impression of a room hung with a rich fabric decorated with a pomegranate design.[21] Tapestry was very expensive, as it was hand-woven by professional weavers and was usually imported, which of course increased the price still further. It was far quicker, and therefore far cheaper, to paint a design on a piece of cloth, hence the 'painted cloths' described by Harrison. These seem to have been used even in quite humble homes. Thomas Hill, an Oxfordshire mason who died in 1588, lived in only two rooms but one of them was decorated with a painted cloth.[22]

Wall paintings were not only found in less wealthy houses. Royal palaces were also decorated with them. Henry VIII had a mural in his private chamber at Whitehall which showed his father and mother, Henry VII and Elizabeth of York, in the background and Henry himself with Jane Seymour in the foreground.[23]

Rooms might also be both panelled and painted, as is the case with the Wolsey Closet at Hampton Court. The paintings were moved from elsewhere in the palace but do seem to have originated in the building and were intended for use in this way. They may perhaps be the ones from Henry's study of 1529 where joiners worked upon five 'tables of waynscoting to be paynted.'[24]

The Wolsey Closet also shows the kind of elaborate ceiling that was fashionable in the early sixteenth century, as does the *Dynasty* portrait. Ceilings were given exactly the same kinds of treatment as the walls, if the owner could afford it. The timbers which made up the ceiling's structure were often exposed and decorated with paint, mouldings or carvings to add to the opulent atmosphere. Hammer beam ceilings, which had been very popular in the fourteenth and fifteenth centuries, were going out of fashion but Henry VIII provided his hall at Hampton Court with a fine one. As already discussed, this was done for political reasons to show continuity with the past, but Henry could not resist having it decorated with the latest fashionable antique work.

The fashion for elaborate ceilings continued throughout the century. A German visitor to Theobalds commented that some rooms had 'very beautiful and costly ceilings, which are skilfully wrought in joiner's work and elegantly coloured . . .'.[25] A ceiling might also be decorated with elaborate plasterwork, which was a cheaper alternative to carving. As with friezes, the plaster ceiling was often painted in bright colours, although sometimes it was left white, or it might be a mixture of both, with certain features picked out in strong colour and the background left white.

Floors were given a variety of treatments at the time. Many ordinary people's houses still had trodden earth floors at ground-floor level, but these were dusty and difficult to keep clean. The most usual alternatives in wealthier houses were bricks set on edge or flagstones. Tiles were another option, but they were expensive. Suspended timber floors were usual on upper levels, although tiles were sometimes used there too. However, tiles were quite heavy, so the building had to be designed to take the extra weight of the floor. This problem didn't stop Henry VIII installing a tiled floor in his great hall at Hampton Court, which is on the first floor.

Many of the floors in Henry VIII's palaces were quite simple, consisting of oak boards covered with plaster of Paris. The floors might also be covered with a sprinkling of rushes but rush matting became a more common alternative as the century progressed. This needed constant replacement, as the royal accounts show. Maintaining the matting in royal palaces was a very profitable business, so great was the demand, and in 1539 John Cradocke was given a monopoly for life to provide matting for all the royal lodgings within twenty miles of London.[26] Such matting was by

no means a royal luxury, but simply a standard floor covering of
the time. The plaster on the royal floors was not always covered
with matting. Instead it might be painted in imitation of marble,
like the floor in the *Dynasty* picture.

Carpets were known in the sixteenth century but they were a
great luxury. The word 'carpet' was used at the time to describe
a wide range of coverings made of everything from velvet and
embroidery to the kind of knotted pile fabrics which we would
call carpets today. Inventories talk not only of 'foot carpets' but
of table carpets, window carpets, etc., so by no means all carpets
were intended for use on the floor. They might equally be used to
cover a window seat or a cupboard.[27] A carpet can be seen draped
over the top shelf in Holbein's *Ambassadors*.

Carpets were used on floors in important rooms and on
important occasions. Henry VIII had a huge collection of over
eight hundred carpets, the bulk of which were oriental ones of one
kind or another. The inventory that was made on the king's death
in 1547 listed fifty or sixty 'great carpets' which were 15 feet by
30 feet. There were seventeen of these at Hampton Court, which
suggests that several of the rooms there were carpeted.[28] This was
royal splendour on display and certainly not the norm in English
houses of the time.

Another item we take for granted today is window glass, but
by no means all windows were glazed in the sixteenth century.
Pendean might have been built with wall-mounted fireplaces and
a chimney but it did not originally have glazed windows. William
Harrison noted in his *Description of England* (first published in
1577) that the use of glazing was increasing. 'Glass is come so
plentiful and within a very little so good cheap'[29] that more people
than ever were using it. He also comments that much of this glass
was imported from Burgundy, Normandy and Flanders, but that
glass was also made in England. He complains of the quality of
English-made glass, saying that 'it would be so good as the best
if we were diligent and careful to bestow more cost upon it'.[30]
Fortunately English glass-making was improving in both standard
and quantity at the time. The industry expanded after Jean Carre
obtained a patent to make glass in the Weald and brought over

glass-makers from Lorraine and Normandy.[31] Even so, some people still insisted on using imported glass. The windows of the chapel at Trinity College, Cambridge, were furnished with Burgundy glass while Normandy, Burgundy and Rhenish glass were used at Grafton Manor in 1576.[32]

Despite the increase in its use, glass was still a valued commodity and was often carefully re-used. Faulty pieces of glass were not discarded, but used in garret windows even in well-to-do establishments. The Hall of the Carpenters' Company in London was extended in 1572 and the glazier not only used 41 feet of new glass but also re-used 36 feet of old glass.[33]

The increased use of glass led to the development of much larger windows which did not always make houses better to live in. Francis Bacon commented 'You shall have sometimes Faire Houses so full of Glasse, that one cannot tell, where to become, to be out of the Sunne or Cold . . .'.[34] The big windows, for all they made the houses much lighter, must also have made them colder in winter and hotter in summer.

The truly wealthy were not content with even the best-quality clear glass, but also incorporated stained or painted glass into their houses. Elaborate windows showing human figures were generally restricted to the chapel, but heraldry was often used in other rooms, with panels of coloured glass showing the arms of the family set into clear glass windows. This gave the best of both worlds, the clear glass letting in the light and the coloured glass showing off the wealth of the owner of the house.[35] Henry VIII's palaces contained a wealth of heraldic glass, although very little survives today. The choice of heraldic subjects proved to be an expensive one in Henry's case. Henry married his last five wives in the ten years from 1533 to 1543 and every time he remarried new glass was needed.

Once the interior of a house was finally settled, it still required furnishing. Houses of the time would have seemed very sparsely furnished by modern standards. The industrial revolution brought mass-produced and therefore cheap furniture, so that we are used to rooms crammed with furniture. This was certainly not the case in the sixteenth century. The only moveables that the King's

Chamber at Arundel Castle contained in 1580 were a bed, a table and a chair. This would not have been unusual.[36]

Chairs were status symbols at this time and were usually reserved for the master of the house or an important guest. Sir William More's parlour at Losely contained six stools but only one chair. The parlour was evidently used as a sitting-room as it contained a main table, side table and other small tables, plus various footstools, a pair of virginals, a base lute and a guitar.[37]

This lack of chairs, and sometimes also of stools meant that even grand people sat on the floor on cushions. The picture of Queen Elizabeth receiving Dutch emissaries shows court ladies sitting on the floor. The other people are standing up out of respect for the Queen. The preliminary sketch for Holbein's painting of Thomas More's family also survives, even though the painting itself is now lost. Some of the ladies are again sitting on the floor.[38]

Sitting on the floor was perhaps not as bad as it sounds. The chairs and stools were not necessarily very comfortable. Sir William More's parlour stools had embroidered cushions and some very grand chairs were upholstered in fine fabrics like velvet. Generally, though, such furniture as people owned was made of unupholstered wood and, if there wasn't a cushion to use with it, it must have been very hard if you were sitting for a long time.

Tables of the time were often trestle tables, designed to come apart so that they could be moved around easily. By the mid-sixteenth century more fixed tables were being produced and extendable dining tables were often found in parlours. They were not always made of plain wood either. Wealthy people's furniture could be as magnificent as the imagination of the joiner could make it. The same German visitor who admired the ceilings at Theobalds also noticed 'tables of inlaid-work and marble of various colours, all of the richest and most magnificent description', a world away from the simple trestle tables that many people had in their great halls.[39]

Another important piece of furniture was the buffet, which was a kind of sideboard. It is also sometimes referred to as a 'cupboard'.[40] In some ways they were practical pieces of furniture where you could keep plate, candlesticks and other such items, but when it came to formal dining they showed off the family's wealth. The banking system was still in its infancy in sixteenth-century England and many people therefore chose to invest large sums of money in plate. This could easily be sold if money were needed quickly, or even taken to the local mint and made into coin. Plate was therefore a status symbol, and the buffet was the place where it was displayed on formal occasions. The number of shelves a buffet had was an important point, as it showed off the owner's rank. Descriptions of court celebrations always mention not only the buffet, but also how many shelves it had. Cardinal Wolsey's 'cupboard' when he entertained the French ambassadors in 1527 had six shelves 'full of gilt plate, very sumptuous and of the newest fashions'.[41] On occasions of state, Henry VIII's buffet had no less than twelve shelves.[42]

The most prestigious item of furniture was not the buffet, though, but the bed. The best bed in the house was a status symbol and was as fine as the owner's purse could make it. The bed frame of a top-quality bed was richly carved and sometimes painted too, while the hangings might be richly embroidered. Some beds had summer and winter hangings, as did a bed belonging to Jane Seymour.[43] These beds were substantial pieces of furniture but even so they were designed to come to pieces easily. This was because wealthy people might move round a great deal, and some of their furniture was designed to travel with them.

The court moved constantly and at least some of the royal furniture went with it. Courtiers' furniture had to be moved too, as lodgings provided at court were not furnished. The Office of Works merely maintained the structure of the lodgings; everything else from cleaning upwards was the problem of the person to whom they were allocated. A courtier's lodgings would also be his office when he was at court so they needed not only a bed but also a table to work at. You could not come to court without your furniture.[44] Moving was such a common thing that the more delicate furniture had special protection made for it when on the move. Henry VIII's own bedposts had leather cases lined with cotton to keep them safe when they were travelling, as did those belonging to Cardinal Wolsey.[45] Such elaborate beds were hardly the norm, even at court. Many good-quality beds of the time had smaller, much simpler beds on castors which tucked away neatly underneath them, for a personal attendant to sleep in. Lower down the social scale the bed would be made of plain wood with whatever hangings the owner could afford.

Chests were the general-purpose storage of the day. They could be very plain and serviceable but they could also be exotic creations elaborately carved and painted or inlaid with valuable woods. They were a practical form of storage as they could be moved easily. The more elaborate chests were often provided with protective leather cases to preserve their fine decoration.[46]

A fine house with all the correct furnishings was one thing, but to complete the effect you also needed to have a suitably magnificent garden. Great houses and castles had always had their pleasure gardens but now a new stress was put on garden design. Slowly architects began to design not only houses but gardens and the statues, fountains, etc. which adorned them.

The new ideas in gardening, like those in architecture, had their roots in classical antiquity. In Italy people began to read what the classical writers had to say about garden design and began to copy their ideas. In 1452 Alberti's book *De Re Aedificatoria* was published in Italy, which brought together all the references to gardens made in the classical texts which were known to people at the time and slowly a new type of garden developed.[47] As with architecture, the idea as conceived in Italy took a long time to reach England, where it was the early seventeenth century before such ideas were fully put into practice. However, garden design did change radically in England, even if not necessarily along true classical lines.

The basis of gardens at the time was the knot. This was a medieval idea, but one which was much loved in the sixteenth century. The usual knot consisted of a symmetrical design divided into quarters. An 'open' knot had the design marked out in plants such as rosemary, thyme or hyssop with the spaces in between the plants filled in with different coloured earths. A 'closed' knot had the spaces within the design filled in with flowers of one colour. The general effect that both styles of knot created can be seen in the illustration from *The Gardener's Labyrinth*, a popular gardening book of the time. Knots could be in any design the gardener could think of and in consequence they grew more and more elaborate as the century progressed. John Parkinson, in his book *Paradisi in Sole* published in 1620, commented that he had only included a few designs for knots as 'it would be almost endlesse to expresse so many as might bee conceived and set downe for that every man may invent other farre differing from these, or any other can be set forth. Let every man therefore, if he like of these, take what may please his mind, or out of these or his own conceit frame any other to his fancy or cause others to be done as he liketh best. . . .'[48]

Francis Bacon, however, writing in the early seventeenth century, was bored with over-complicated knots: 'As for the Making of knots or Figures with Divers Coloured Earths, that they may lie under the Windowes of the House, on that Side, which the Garden stands, they be but Toyes: You may see as good Sights, many times, in Tarts.'[49] Food was elaborately decorated at the time and tarts were often made in fancy designs with different coloured fruits, jams, etc., so Bacon's comparison is understandable.

One of the problems of studying sixteenth-century gardens is that no English garden of the period survives. There is not even a great deal in the way of descriptions of the earlier gardens, so working out what a grand garden looked like at the time is a matter of detective work. This is certainly the case with Henry VIII's garden at Hampton Court.

The Hampton Court garden was an innovation. It was a heraldic garden, which was an English idea. With the Tudors' rather weak claim to the throne, the heraldic garden was seen as another way of reminding people that Henry VIII was the king and that he had every intention of remaining so.

The garden was a very formal one and contained topiaries, which were found in both classical and medieval English gardens. The German Thomas Platter visited Hampton Court in 1599 and described what he saw:

There were all manner of shapes, men and women, half men and half horse, sirens, serving-maids with baskets, French lilies and delicate crenellations all round made from dry twigs bound together and the afore-said evergreen quick set shrubs, or entirely of rosemary, all true to the life, and so cleverly and amusingly interwoven, mingled and grown together, trimmed and arranged picture-wise that their equal would be hard to find.[50]

It might have been that some of the topiaries had changed since Henry's time, but they sound like the kind Henry was likely to have had. The 'French lilies' were often used by Henry, who believed himself to be King of France as well as England, a claim which went back to the Hundred Years War in the fourteenth century. Classical subjects like centaurs (the half-men half-horse figures) and sirens were also fashionable in Henry's time.

The main feature of Henry's garden was the heraldry. Wooden heraldic beasts were set up on poles painted in the Tudor colours of green and white. These creatures can just be seen in the garden at Whitehall through the doors in the *Dynasty* portrait.

Another feature was the Mount Garden which was by the river. It contained a mount crowned by the South or Great Round Arbour, which was almost entirely made of glass, topped with a lead cupola surmounted by the king's beasts and a great gilded crown. The path up to it was flanked with the king's heraldic beasts, displayed proudly on the tops of poles. The arbour was placed on the mount so as to give a pleasant view. On one side you could see the river and watch all the traffic going up and down. On the other you could see the garden, which was best appreciated by being viewed from above. The arbour would have been used as a banqueting house.

Banqueting was a great fashion of the sixteenth century. The word 'banquet' did mean a large meal, as today, but it also had a secondary meaning of the final course of a larger meal. It would consist of expensive delicacies, most of which contained sugar which was a great luxury at the time. The idea was that a small, select company of people would withdraw to a private room or banqueting house to enjoy fine food, fine wine and good conversation.[51] Entertainments tended to take place in daylight hours at this time, so banqueting houses were often placed to take advantage of a fine view. Both Longleat and Hardwick had banquet houses on the roof and visitors could walk out on to the leads and enjoy the view all around. Sir William Sharington also built a banqueting house at Lacock Abbey from which guests could walk out on to the roof.

The sixteenth-century taste for puzzles and conceits was as evident in the design of the garden as in that of the house. Banqueting houses were perfect vehicles for these ideas and all sorts of fantasy creations were built. The Triangular Lodge mentioned above was also intended partly for use as a banqueting house. Robert Smythson, the master mason who worked on houses like Longleat and Hardwick Hall, designed a mock-castle banquet house for Sir Gervase Clifton, showing just how wide the variety of banqueting houses was.[52] John Parkinson even mentions one at Lord Cobham's house in Kent, where a lime tree had been trained to form a famous banqueting house. It was three storeys high and reached by wooden stairs. According to Parkinson the bottom two storeys were capable of holding 'halfe an hundred men at the least' so it must have been very impressive.[53]

As the century progressed entire gardens were sometimes laid out with a hidden meaning to them, which the visitor was supposed to be able to interpret. There was a symbolic meaning to many flowers and so all kinds of complicated ideas could be expressed. Sir Robert Cecil, the younger son of William Cecil, used this idea in laying out his garden in homage to Queen Elizabeth. The three graces were represented by pansies and the nine muses by nine different types of flower.[54]

The choice of garden ornaments was sometimes influenced by this idea of symbolism. At Lord Burghley's house, Theobalds, there was the 'Venusberg', a small round hill at one end of a wood. It was surrounded by a maze, so that you had to work out the maze in order to reach it. This might have been to symbolise the successes and setbacks of courtly love, or could even have been in homage to Queen Elizabeth who was sometimes represented as Venus.[55]

Another development in garden design at the time was the increasing use of water as a feature. In the middle ages gardens had often contained fountains and many houses had been surrounded by moats, but now water features became increasingly elaborate. The Earl of Leicester's garden at Kenilworth included a marble fountain eight feet high in the form of two athletes back to back supporting a ball which spouted water into a basin beneath. At Theobalds, rather than a moat, there was a decorative canal, an idea which had come from France. Paul Hentzner, another German visitor, visited the garden and noted the waterworks:

. . . from this place one goes into the garden, encompassed with a ditch full of water, large enough for one to have the pleasure of going in a boat, and rowing between the shrubs: here are a great variety of trees and plants, labyrinths made with a great deal of labour, a jet d'eau, with its basin of white marble and columns and pyramids of wood and other materials up and down the garden. After seeing these, we were led by the gardener into the summer-house in the lower part of which, built semicircularly are the twelve Roman emperors in white marble and a table of touchstone, the upper part of it is set round with cistern of lead, into which the water is conveyed through pipes, so that fish may be kept in them, and in summer time they are convenient for bathing . . .[56]

The use of water was also much recommended by Francis Bacon, although he was quick to point out that under certain circumstances it could make a garden unpleasant. Stagnant water in pools was unattractive and encouraged flies and frogs. Water was also not intended to look natural. Bacon recommends water 'without Fish or Slime or Mud', and likes his water not in natural-style pools or streams but in large containers with paved bottoms. He also speaks highly of elaborate fountains. The idea that a garden should imitate nature lay far in the future.

A garden was intended to be a delight to the senses as well as to the mind. Francis Bacon starts his essay *On Gardens* with the words 'God Almightie first Planted a Garden. And indeed, it is the Purest of Humane pleasures. It is the Greatest Refreshment to the Spirits of Man; Without which, Buildings and Pallaces are but Grosse Handy-works'.[57] It was important to appeal to all the senses and not just the eye. Scented plants were used as far as possible so that the air would be full of their perfume. Francis Bacon provides a list of these and also explains the circumstances under which they best give off their scent. For example, he recommends burnet, wild thyme and mint as the best to plant alleys with, as their scent will be released when trodden underfoot.

There would of course be natural birdsong to entertain the ear but this was evidently not enough for the Tudors. The Earl of Leicester's garden at Kenilworth contained an elaborate aviary on a raised bank.[58] The idea of a garden aviary was common enough for Bacon to comment on it. He did not like aviaries unless they were big enough for the birds to fly around in. He also liked them to be turfed and set with plants to give a natural look and to allow the birds to nest properly. The Tudor love of birdsong was so strong that they often wanted it inside the house too. Both Henry VIII and Elizabeth had songbirds in cages hung inside the windows of their private apartments, as can be seen in the picture of Elizabeth meeting the Dutch emissaries.

It was also important to provide shade in the garden. Ladies would not want to risk their fashionably pale complexions by walking in the full sun and it would have been uncomfortably hot to do so in Tudor clothing anyway. Walkways covered with vines and shaded arbours were considered vital parts of the design. Bacon suggested shaded alleys to the side of the main garden in which to walk on hot days, but to have the main garden open for use in cooler weather.

Having described what the Tudors considered to be the perfect setting, it should be said that elaborate interiors and fine gardens were luxuries for a very few in the sixteenth century. Today it is not necessary to be wealthy to have a choice in the way you decorate your house, but things were different in Tudor England. The very social conditions which were making landowners wealthier were also making life harder for those who held no land. Most people of the period had neither the time nor the money for interior design, unless perhaps to chose the odd painted cloth.

Garden design was also for the few. For most people, their garden was a place to grow vegetables, fruit and herbs. It might also contain a few chickens and the family pig, but it was hardly likely to contain a knot or a fountain. The idea of cottage gardens full of flowers is a romantic nineteenth-century idea, although even at that time practical cottage gardeners concentrated on growing vegetables. For most Tudors interior design and garden planning were the stuff of daydreams.

TWO
Clothing and Fashion

In 1516 Thomas More described clothing in his ideal country, which he called *Utopia*:

> They have no tailors or dressmakers, since everyone on the island wears the same sort of clothes – except that they vary slightly according to sex and marital status – and that fashion never changes. These clothes are quite pleasant to look at, they allow free movement of the limbs, they're equally suitable for hot and cold weather – and the great things is, they're all home made.[1]

Thomas More's attitude to fashion was certainly not typical of his time and such an attitude to clothes would have seemed rather eccentric to wealthy Tudors. Clothes were a badge of rank to the Tudors and the sixteenth century was a status-conscious age. Those who had money flaunted it by wearing the most luxurious of clothes, so that a single gown could cost more than an average annual income.

Castiglione in his *Book of the Courtier* believed that in clothing 'one should adapt oneself to the custom of the majority' and that extremes of fashion should be avoided. He regarded both the overdressed French and the underdressed Germans to be rather vulgar in their choice of clothes.[2] The English court certainly followed his ideas in other areas, but in clothing they liked nothing better than excess.

Clothes were such an important symbol of rank that there were sumptuary laws which governed what men were supposed to wear. They were surprisingly detailed. The laws passed in 1533, in Henry VIII's reign, stated that only those with an income of £40 a year could wear any silk velvet at all, even a purse or hat; those with an income of £200 a year (or status as a knight or the son of a lord) could wear a voluminous gown of silk velvet; and only noblemen could wear scarlet, crimson or blue silk velvet. The idea was that you could tell someone's position in society simply from the way they were dressed.[3]

In practice the laws do not seem to have been enforced. For one thing, people with the money to flaunt the laws usually had friends in high places, making a prosecution unlikely. This problem is well illustrated by the fact that the Lord Mayor of London found himself in hot water trying to enforce the sumptuary laws in 1580.

Elizabeth had tried to stop ruffs becoming excessively large and so the Lord Mayor had criticised Mr Hewson, son-in-law of the Lord Chief Baron, for wearing 'excess of Ruffs, in the open street'. Mr Hewson bluntly refused to change his ways, and the Lord Mayor took the matter further. This enraged the Lord Chief Baron to such an extent that the Lord Mayor was forced to write a letter to the Lord Treasurer, begging for his help in making up the quarrel. In the face of this sort of opposition it was no surprise that the laws were quietly ignored.[4] It was in any case perfectly understandable that a wealthy Tudor should want to ignore sumptuary legislation. It was absolutely vital to have the right clothes to gain access to the highest circles. The whole point of going to court was to attract the attention of the right people and to try to gain the friendship of those in the inner circles surrounding the monarch. This meant that starting out on a career at court was an expensive undertaking, not to be taken lightly. When Arthur Throckmorton first came to court in 1583 he had to sell part of his land and borrow his brother's legacy in order to finance his new wardrobe. He was still paying the interest on the loan years later.[5] Success at court would have paid back the cost of the clothing many times over but it is easy to see how some people ruined themselves if their court career never took off.

The image of the Tudor courtier is so strong that most people forget how exceptional courtier's clothing was. Portraits, which provide the most memorable image of Tudor clothes, were expensive luxuries and were often painted to celebrate a wedding, a promotion at court or some similar event. This means that the clothing shown in portraits is particularly luxurious, even by the standards of very wealthy people. In fact the majority of people had very simple wardrobes indeed.

Perhaps it is best to start by describing sixteenth-century clothing. Fashion, of course, changed throughout the period. However, it is not the intention to give a survey of the changes here, rather simply to describe the main articles of clothing worn at the time.[6]

At this stage it is necessary to include a warning. Very little sixteenth-century clothing survives, for reasons explained below. The result is that today we have an incomplete picture of exactly how clothes at that time were made. Sometimes even costume experts differ over what certain garments were, as the only details are given in financial accounts. In this case a garment is usually named but not described in any great detail. The study of sixteenth-century costume is therefore far from simple. The words used to describe items also sometimes change with fashions, so that men's upper stocks might also be called breeches or slops. For simplicity the number of different terms used here has been kept to a minimum.

Underwear was made of linen for both sexes. Linen was practical as it was easy to wash. These linen garments were generally known as a shirt for a man and a smock for a woman. Men also wore linen drawers although these were not generally worn by women until the nineteenth century.

The next layer for a woman is a matter for debate. Not very much is known about Tudor underwear generally and of course underwear had to change with fashion in order to give women the right shape. 'Pairs of bodies' or corsets are mentioned in various places. They may have been attached to skirts to form a full-length undergarment. At first the bodies were stiffened with 'bents', a type of stiff, hollow-stemmed grass which grows on sand dunes, but later whalebone was introduced. However they were made, red was a favourite colour for them.[7]

The next layer was a kirtle, which for most women would be made of wool. It would be a garment like a dress, often with short sleeves or with longer sleeves which laced so that they could be rolled up for work. On top of this went the final layer, the gown, which was like a second, looser complete dress worn rather the same way we wear a coat.

A great lady's clothes were slightly different. She would wear her sumptuous gown at all times, so that all that was ever seen of her kirtle was the forepart. The effect can be seen in the *Dynasty* portrait. The ladies' foreparts are all red. The red sleeves would be attached to the gown.

Men's clothing is best introduced by this small section of dialogue taken from a textbook designed for teaching French which was published in 1566.[8] Modern parents will doubtless recognise the scene as Francis, the reluctant schoolboy, is being woken by Margaret, the maid:

Margaret: Ho Francis rise, and get you to schoole: you shalbe beaten, for it is past seven: make you self readie quickly, say your prayers, then you shall have your breakefast.

Francis: Margerite, geeve memy hosen: dispatche I pray you: where is my doublet? brygn my garters, and my shooes: geeve mee that shooyng horne.

Margaret: Take first a cleane shirte, for yours is fowle.

Francis: Make haste then, for I doo tarie too long.

Despite its sixteenth-century spelling the dialogue gives the basic idea of what men wore. The hose or breeches went from the waist to just above the knees and then the nether hose, which were stockings, covered from the knees down to and including the feet. The garters mentioned were used to keep the nether hose from falling down. Above the hose came a doublet, which covered the top of the body rather like a jacket. Sometimes it was the fashion to wear a jerkin over the doublet, as shown by Jean de Dinteville, the gentleman on the left in Holbein's *The Ambassadors*. Over all this a wealthy gentleman might wear a loose garment called a gown in the earlier half of the century (again see *The Ambassadors*), but this was later replaced by a cloak.

In talking of men's hose it is impossible not to mention that most famous of sixteenth-century items of dress, the codpiece. It was worn by all classes of men, rich and poor alike, as it was an essential, practical item: a decorated flap which fastened by means of laces to the upper hose to allow easy access.

It is of note that Margaret is careful to send Francis off to school in a clean shirt. The Tudors were a good deal fussier about cleanliness than modern people often realise. Clean linen was a sign of being a respectable person. George Whetstone in his *Heptameron of Civil Discourses* states that a women wearing dirty linen 'shal neither be prazed of strangers nor delight her husband'. The book is full of hints for having a successful marriage and cleanliness was a basic principle.[9]

Wealthy people had large amounts of linen and washerwomen to do the washing for them. Henry VIII's shirt coffer contained thirty-three shirts when the king died in 1547.[10] Further down in society it was harder to keep clean. There is no real indication of how many shirts or smocks a more ordinary person possessed but a tiny glimpse of the situation can be seen in wills. Clothing was so expensive that it was often specifically willed to certain people and sometimes smocks and shirts are mentioned. Information taken from wills proved in Essex at the end of the sixteenth century shows that those naming shirts mention between three and six of them. This suggests that even fairly ordinary people had enough underwear to see them through a week, wearing each one once or twice before washing it. Essex was a wealthy county, though, and it would be interesting to see the results of research done on a wider basis.[11]

Wealthy people's underwear was often richly embroidered, as shown in the portrait of Bess of Hardwick. Ladies did embroider such garments themselves, but by no means all the elaborate needlework which appears on sixteenth-century clothing was done by amateurs. Professional embroiderers had existed since the Middle Ages and they were much patronised by the wealthy. Embroidery was very expensive. One of the New Year's gifts presented to Elizabeth I in 1568 was 'two patrons for slevis drawen upon Cameryke'. 'Cameryke' or cambric was a fine quality linen. The present was given by a Mr Adams, who was the schoolmaster to the Queen's pages. He could probably not afford to pay an embroiderer to complete the sleeves. The present seems to have been entirely acceptable even so.[12]

Fine embroidered items were treated with great care even in the highest circles. The records of Queen Elizabeth I's wardrobe show that professional embroiderers were paid not only to work new items, but also to re-use old ones. Embroidered sections of old gowns were cut away and sewn onto new ones.[13] Embroidery done in gold or silver thread could also be unpicked and the thread used again.

A woman's underwear might also include a farthingale. This was an item rather like a crinoline which was designed to make a lady's skirts fall in a certain shape. There were two main types of farthingale: the Spanish farthingale, which became fashionable mid-century and gave a bell-shaped silhouette to the skirt, and the wheel farthingale, fashionable from the 1590s, which gave a more angular outline. The original Spanish farthingales used in Spain had been stiffened with the twigs taken from coppicing trees, but in England the usual stiffening seems to have been either rope or tightly rolled strips of material. Farthingales were fashionable items that were time-consuming to make, which made them expensive. Their use was confined to wealthier ladies.[14]

People's outer garments varied very much according to their wealth and social status. The vast majority of people wore wool, so that the word 'cloth' in the sixteenth century was a general term for woollen cloth.

Wool was not necessarily a down-market fabric. Scarlet, the finest quality wool, was used by the wealthiest people. Thomasine Petre, daughter of Henry VIII's private secretary

William Petre had some made for her wedding trousseau.[15] It was a favourite for petticoats as it was both soft and warm. It was certainly an expensive option. The 1¼ yards bought for Thomasine cost 36s 8d a yard, while the scarlet bought for her sister's trousseau cost 17s per yard.

The wealthy merchant John Johnson also had several pairs of fustian upper hose which were lined with linen.[16] Fustian was made of either worsted or flax and cotton or wool, depending on the period and where the fabric came from. It had a pile so that it looked rather like velvet, but would have been much harder wearing, making such hose ideal everyday wear for a well-to-do man. The fustian for one pair cost him 3s 2d plus 10d for the linen lining. It cost 8d to have the garments made up, bringing the total cost to 4s 8d. The Johnson family also owned various clothes made of silk, but these would have been kept for best.[17]

There was a huge variety of wool on the market and even the very wealthy did not just wear it as underwear. 'I heartily desire you to send me some demi-worsted for a gown . . .' Anne Basset wrote to her mother Lady Lisle in May 1534.[18] Thomasine Petre was also supplied with two new gowns when she went off to live in the household of the Marchioness of Exeter. One was made of worsted, a woollen fabric, and the other of black damask, a fine quality silk. Doubtless the damask was for best and the worsted for everyday.[19]

Lower down the scale was broadcloth, which was the kind of fabric that people might buy to make liveries for their servants, and kersey, which was a cheaper kind of wool worn by the less well off.

It was not only the cloth that varied in price but also the colour. Bright colours, like very bright reds, were expensive dyes to produce, as were dark colours, especially black. The more expensive dyes also gave an even colour all over the fabric. Ordinary people's clothes were therefore of much more subdued colours, like the clothes worn in Pieter Brueghel's pictures. The picture known as *The Peasant Wedding Feast*, of course shows everyone in their best clothes. A few wealthier guests wear black or bright red, but most cannot afford these, even for best.

Work clothes were often 'white', that is to say, undyed, the wool remaining the colour of the sheep it came from which might really have been black or brown. This black would have been nothing like as impressive as the deep black produced by dye. Wealthier country people, like yeomen, generally chose black for their 'holy day' clothes. Black was the perfect colour. It was an expensive dye, but practical in that it looked dignified and did not show the dirt.[20]

It is often assumed that everyone who wasn't incredibly wealthy made their own clothes, right down to weaving the linen and wool. As the quote above from *Utopia* shows, this was not the case. Most people simply did not have enough land to make this practical. The priority was to produce food, and space which could be devoted to flax must have been limited, if available at all. They may have done a little spinning and weaving with what they could produce but homespun fabrics were more likely to be made into sheets and blankets than clothes. People who had larger amounts of land aspired to something better than homespun clothing. If they could afford new clothes, most people had their outer garments made up by a tailor. Cloth would be bought either at a mercer's (for expensive fabrics like silks) or a draper's (for woollen fabrics and linen).

Buying fabric must have been quite complicated as different types of fabrics were sold in different widths. Broadcloths were 1¾ yards wide, kersey 1 yard wide and silks generally 20 to 22 inches wide. Some materials, such as russets, came in broad and narrow widths.[21] There were also no set prices, so shoppers were expected to bargain for what they wanted.

Another book designed for teaching French, *The French Garden*, gives a dialogue in a draper's shop where a lady is buying linen. The bargaining sounds remarkably modern:

Lady: I will give you fifteene shillings, If you will take my money make it shorte, for I have other business than to tarye heere.

Shopkeeper: Truely Madame I would be verye sorie to denie you if I could give it at that price, but in truth I cannot, unless I should lose by it.

As may be expected, the bargain is finally struck after the lady threatens to buy from the shop on the other side of the road.[22]

This lady may well have been buying linen to make into underwear for her family herself. Sabine Johnson certainly made underwear for her family.[23] On the other hand, these items could also be bought ready-made. 'Will you buye no shirts, ruffes, Falling bandes,[24] handkerchiefs, night-coyfes, Falles, sockes, edged lace Boote-hosen[25] . . . ?' asks *The French Garden's* shopkeeper after the lady has bought her linen.

The shop featured in the dialogue is in the Royal Exchange which was opened in 1566 by no lesser person than the Queen herself.[26] It was built by the famous London mercer, Thomas Gresham, as a place where merchants could meet to discuss business and make deals. It was also where the fashionable Elizabethan went to shop as the best shops in the country were to be found there.

Gresham evidently deserved his reputation as a clever businessman. Chronicler John Stow reports how he managed to make the place so successful. In order to make sure that all the shops were full and bustling with business before the great royal opening, he went to the few shopkeepers that already rented premises in the building and told them that they could take over as many empty shops as they wanted rent-free for a year. This they did, but as the Exchange established itself the rents went ever higher until Stow records them as being £4 10s a year.[27]

Stow proudly tells how the various shops in the Exchange sold everything from armour to books, and from jewellery to mousetraps. The lady in *The French Garden* buys not only fine linen but cloth of gold and gold and silver lace. She also visits a goldsmith and is shown a wide selection of stones. The shopkeepers obviously kept goods fine enough for even the most wealthy and discerning customer. The Exchange's popularity proved to be enduring as it was still the place to be seen shopping in Samuel Pepys' time a century later.

The linen draper in the Exchange was obviously serving the well-to-do if she was offering luxuries such as ruffs. They are the item of dress that most people associate with the sixteenth century but in fact they only came into fashion in the 1550s and were only worn by a small section of the population. Ruffs were expensive for several reasons. First of all, they took a great deal of fine linen to make. Lady Francis Cobham recommended Lady St Loe (who later became Bess of Hardwick) to buy 10 yards of linen for a set of neck and wrist ruffs, which probably meant 6 yards for the neck ruff and 2 each for the wrist ruffs.[28]

Another thing which made ruffs a luxury was the effort involved in laundering them. First of all they were washed in a tub to remove the dirt. Soap would usually be used on fine linen rather than the harsher lye made by pouring water though wood ash.[29] Starch would be applied, and the frills of the ruff set. At first ruffs were left to dry over wooden sticks but later steel rods were developed which could be used hot. The starching process was quite a new one at the time. John Stow attributes its arrival in England to a Mistress Dinghen van den Plasse who came from Flanders.[30] It was a difficult skill. Stow talks of Mistress Dinghen being able to charge four or five pounds for teaching how to starch and 20*s* to show how to make the starch itself.

Once the fashion had taken root, ruffs grew to an alarming size. Queen Elizabeth did try to limit their size, but to no avail. Philip Stubbes took great delight in criticising ruffs, just as he criticises everything, in his book *The Anatomie of Abuses* which was published in 1583. 'The devil, as he in the fulnesse of his malice, first invented these greate ruffes . . .' he declared.[31] He not only complained about the ruffs but also about the wire underproppers which were needed to hold them in place.

A ruff was certainly not a practical item. Anyone doing manual work, as most people did in those days, would have got a ruff dirty almost immediately. The very large and elaborate ones would simply have got in the way. This, of course, was the charm. The people who wore them were making the point that they didn't need to think of practicalities. It is not surprising that in a set of wills made in Essex in the late sixteenth century only one person mentions a ruff.[32]

Most people could only dream of owning the kind of ruffs

Philip Stubbes complains of. The cost of clothing was so high that many people bought their clothes second hand. Stow, in his famous *Survey of London*, comments that these could be bought in Birchin Lane, where you could find the 'Fripperers or Upholders, that sold old apparel and household stuff'. He then goes on to recount a story about the place which was probably the sixteenth-century equivalent of a modern urban myth:

> I have read of a countryman that having lost his hood in Westminster Hall found the same in Cornehill hanged out to be sold, which he challenged, but was forced to buy, or go without it, for their stall, they said, was their market.[33]

Clothing, as Stow's countryman knew, was something to be looked after carefully and treasured. Items which would seem quite insignificant today were carefully willed to specific people. Here are the items of clothing mentioned in the will of John Warden, a yeoman of Romford in Essex who died in 1600. He was a fairly well-to-do man.

> To my fellow Thomas Wallesse my best shirt and best band, William Betts my best doublet and second best band, my fellow Edward Tearne my frize jerkin,[34] my fellow Thomas Tanner my green breeches, John Bannister my canvas breeches, Samuel Howell a cambric ruff band and a new pair of shoes, Bridget Cocke my best pair of stockings, Anne Wells a cambric band. Lucy Copland one pair of worsted stockings and my greenish cloak laid with lace,[35] John Coplande my greenish cloak laid with lace and Jane Coplande his wife my two small gold rings. . . . to Thomas Norras tailor my hat faced with velvet, Richard Debnam my best falling band and my godson at Brentwood the child of William Flower there, my second best falling band and a green feather. Thomas Legatt esquire a gold and silver purse.[36]

This will gives a good indication of the kind of clothes worn by a well-to-do yeoman. Although some luxuries like the ruff and the hat faced with velvet do appear, they must have been for best. John Warden's wardrobe is a world away from the fashionable excess of the court. Unlike courtiers, men like John Warden took an active part in farming their lands so they needed practical clothes and only indulged in touches of luxury on holy days.

John Warden does not describe the 'new shoes' that he leaves to his friend Samuel Howell but they could have been of various different types. Shoes in the earlier sixteenth century were generally of very light construction compared with modern shoes. The soles were made of leather rather than being built up with wood so that these shoes look rather like slippers to the modern eye.

In about the late 1540s and the early 1550s shoes did start to be made with a low cork wedge, which ran the whole length of the shoe. The wedge was then soled with leather. In 1595 the first warrant for making shoes with high heels and arches for Queen Elizabeth appears.

As shoes were generally lightweight they were relatively cheap and several pairs could be worn through in a year. The shoemaker who made the shoes of the Petre family charged 10*d* a pair for Lady Petre's shoes, 7*d* a pair for those for her children and 9*d* for a pair for the kitchen boy. The kitchen boy's shoes were presumably more expensive because they were of stouter construction than those of his employer, since they had to stand up to more wear.[37]

Ordinary English leather shoes sufficed for most people, but the rich wanted something finer. For them, shoes were made up to go with their elaborate court outfits, in fine silks and velvets, sometimes richly embroidered. In the *Dynasty* portrait both Henry VIII and Edward are wearing velvet shoes, and it seems that Henry's daughter Elizabeth had the same tastes. In the 1560s a few pairs of leather shoes were made for her every year but she was also getting through about forty pairs made of velvet annually. Later Elizabeth's tastes seem to have changed and from 1575 onwards more fine Spanish leather pairs were made for her than velvet, but Spanish leather was also very expensive.[38]

Elizabeth kept her shoemakers busy not only making new shoes, but also repairing old ones. There are numerous references to 'translating' shoes, that is, taking the shoes to pieces and remaking them, cutting away worn sections where necessary. For example in 1576 Gerrett Johnson, Elizabeth's shoemaker, translated twenty-three pairs of Spanish leather shoes and pantobles.[39] Pantofles, also known as pantables, were worn to keep shoes up out of the mud. They consisted of a built-up sole with a strap to fasten them to the feet. Some of Queen Elizabeth's were even made up to match particular pairs of shoes.

Above their shoes, both sexes wore hose to keep their legs warm. Hose were made of cloth which was especially woven for the purpose. Judging from the portraits, hose makers were able to make these items fit very well. Hose made of both wool and linen are recorded, but towards the end of the century silk hose also became fashionable in wealthy circles. Knitted hose also became more common.

In 1577 Queen Elizabeth began to wear worsted knitted stockings which were made by Alice Montague, a silkwoman, and from then on she wore only knitted hose. This fashion evidently caught on as knitting hose became a good source of employment. In Norwich in 1570 one fourteen-year-old girl was even providing the main income for her family by knitting 'great hose'.[40] Knitted silk hose were a great luxury and even the Queen did not wear them all the time. Presumably the woollen ones were warmer and more comfortable for winter and for activities like riding. Some of Elizabeth's silk stockings were finely embroidered with gold and silver thread. It could well be that linen hose were worn under these both to protect the stockings against sweat and to protect the wearer from the gold and silver thread which would have been rather uncomfortable against the skin.[41]

The royal hose, whether of wool or silk, were very carefully looked after. It was certainly not a case of discarding them when they began to wear out. Instead they were returned to the hosier to be fitted with new feet. They also seem to have been sent back to the hosier to be washed, perhaps because most laundresses were not used to laundering such items and might have spoilt them.[42]

Another vital item in the sixteenth century was some type of headgear. Historical dramas love to show ladies of the time with their hair streaming loose down their backs but the Tudors themselves had a rather different view. For one thing, wearing long hair loose just wasn't practical. Even grand ladies had work to do when they were in their own homes and anyone with long hair knows how much it can get in your way. Also wearing hair loose on most occasions was not considered respectable. There were specific times when ladies did wear their hair in such a fashion, for example, it was usual for a bride on her wedding day, as shown by the bride in Brueghel's *Peasant Wedding Feast*. All the other ladies wear their hair tied up and covered by various sorts of headgear. Queens also wore their hair down for very grand occasions, like their coronation. Elizabeth I's coronation portrait shows her with her hair loose and Jane Seymour also wore her fair hair down when displaying her son Edward to the world for the first time in 1537.[43] Generally, though, people of both sexes covered their heads.

The usual headgear for a man in the sixteenth century was a cap along the lines of that Jean de Dinteville is wearing in Holbein's *The Ambassadors*. His cap is a particularly fine example, made of silk velvet and decorated with gold ornaments. Most men's were made of wool.

The usual headgear for ladies was made of linen, as shown in both the *Peasant Wedding Feast* and the detail from *The Field of Cloth of Gold*. The ladies in the foreground of the latter detail are copying a fashion of the 1530s and '40s, where a coif was worn under a cap similar to the ones worn by the men. A coif was made of linen and was rather like a modern baby's bonnet. Grander ladies also wore them, although, of course, their bonnets were of silk velvet and richly decorated with jewels. Bonnets were one option for well-to-do ladies but for the greater part of the century the most usual headdress was a hood of very elaborate construction. The back was soft, usually black silk, hanging down or pinned up on the head. The stiffened front framed the face, often with jewels and gold. The gable shape worn by Jane Seymour in the *Dynasty* portrait is typical of English ladies in the early part of the century, but this was later displaced by the French hood, worn most famously by Anne Boleyn.

In the 1570s tall black hats became very fashionable, like the one worn by Sir Thomas Fleming in his portrait. Ladies also liked them and Thomas Platter commented on having seen such hats in London in 1599. 'English burgher women usually wear high hats covered with velvet or silk for headgear,' he wrote, having already commented that many such women also wore velvet 'for the street . . . who cannot afford a crust of bread at home I have been told'.[44]

Fashions in headgear seem to have become quite chaotic in Elizabeth's time. Philip Gawdy wrote home in 1589, describing the court fashion in headgear to his sister:

> For the manner of their hoodes at the courte, some weare crespins[45] some weare none. Some weare sattin of all collars with their upper border and some wear none. Some of them weare this daye all these fashions, and the next without. So that I fynd nothing more certayne than their uncertayntie, which makes me forbeare to sende you anything further of myne owne devise.[46]

Queen Elizabeth herself had a wide variety of headgear, some of which was made by her own ladies. In her portraits she is often shown bare-headed, but this was for symbolic reasons. Very young girls were allowed to go bare-headed, although with their hair neatly put up, as in the portrait of Lord Cobham's family dining. Going bare-headed was thus seen as a symbol of virginity, and the part of the Virgin Queen was one Elizabeth loved to play. Elizabeth's hair is not shown undecorated, though. Her accounts indicate that she had several cauls which were made of knotted human hair and set with jewels, often pearls. The net would have been invisible when worn, giving the effect of jewels set in the hair.[47]

Jewels for the hair were only some of the ornaments worn at court. Wealthy Tudors adored jewellery, seeing it as a very visible symbol of their wealth and power. It was also used to convey political messages, to display religious beliefs and to remind people of their friends and relatives who had died. The sumptuous quality of sixteenth-century jewellery is such a vivid symbol that it is easy to forget that ownership of jewellery was far less widespread than today. It is not necessary to be rich today to own at least some jewellery made of precious metal, but very little of it appears in wills of Tudor time. The most usual items to be mentioned are gold rings, as in John Warden's will above. These are often mourning rings, intended as a reminder of the departed.

Mourning jewellery and *memento mori* pieces deserve a mention here as they were very popular. Mourning jewellery was not like eighteenth- and nineteenth-century pieces which often contained locks of hair or little portraits of the person who had died. Instead a mourning ring might simply be engraved with the words 'Remember Me'. *Memento mori* pieces might also be specific reminders of someone who had died, but they were further intended to be constant reminders that death was not far away. The whole idea may seem morbid today but the Tudors looked at the matter differently. After all, death was not far away and you never quite knew when it would strike. There was far less chance of living to a ripe old age than today. It was best to be prepared. Jewellery set with death's heads, skeletons and the like was a good way of reminding you that you needed to keep on good terms with God. Henry VIII had a gold ring set with a death's head.[48]

The whole idea was also much used in portraiture. People are sometimes painted with little skulls in the corner of their portrait. You may notice something on the floor in front of the ambassadors in Holbein's painting of that name. If you stand on the far right in front of the painting and look at the correct angle, the object reveals itself to be a large skull.

The design of jewellery changed over the sixteenth century as skills in gem cutting developed. In the early sixteenth century jewels tended to be simply polished. It is the light catching on the faces of a cut gem which make it glitter, so in this state they did not particularly catch attention. The goldwork around the gems was therefore as important as the gems themselves. It was only later in the century that the gems became the centre-piece and the goldwork less important.

It would be a mistake to assume that all jewellery, even in the grandest circles, was made of precious metals and gemstones. Some of Elizabeth I's pearls may have been fake ones made of glass.[49] Glass with coloured foil set behind it in imitation of precious stones was often used, sometimes set in with real gems in contravention of the Goldsmiths' Company regulations. The parish of St Martin le Grand in the city of London had ancient rights of sanctuary so it was there that the fake jewel makers could work safely. Fake gold chain was known as 'St Martin's chain' for this reason.[50]

The overall feel of Renaissance jewellery is one of opulence, whether the gems are real or not. Understated elegance was definitely not the aim. This effect is best demonstrated by the use of gold chains. Gold chains were worn by both men and women, but for men they were a particularly important status symbol. Both Henry VIII and his son Edward wear huge gold chains in the *Dynasty* portrait. Henry owned one chain that weighed 88 oz or 3 kg, which was studded with sixteen huge spinels and a number of diamonds, including one huge diamond known as the Great Mirror.[51] The truly wealthy also supplied the gentlemen who attended them with gold chains. George Cavendish describes how Cardinal Wolsey's master cook wore one.[52] At the tournament held on 7 July 1516 to commemorate the translation of the relics of St Thomas of Canterbury, Sir Edward Guildford not only wore a magnificent gold chain himself, but all his forty gentlemen also wore such chains of five fingers' breadth, made of links shaped in the shape of the letters H and K in honour of the king and queen.[53] Women were often given gold chains as wedding presents. Thomasine Petre was given one which cost 6s to make.[54] Sir Humphrey Baumaster left money for his widow to buy their daughter a gold chain on her marriage, so it seems to have been something of a traditional gift.[55]

The general aim seems to have been to wear as much jewellery as possible on grand occasions and even practical items like buttons and aglets could be made of precious metal. Aglets were pointed pieces of metal which were fastened at the ends of laces to stop them fraying and to make it easier to pull the laces through the eyelets on clothing. Men's clothing in particular was often held together with laces which were made of leather, or else of braided linen or silk. For example, the codpiece would fasten to the breeches with two laces at the top of the flap. In most cases aglets were simply practical items, made of base metal, but a wealthy man might have them made of gold and even decorated with enamel. Buttons could be equally lavish. Queen Elizabeth had buttons showing lover's knots, twinned hearts, roses and acorns, not to mention some set with ruby and pearl star.[56] Aglets were also used purely for decorative purposes. The mother in the picture of Lord Cobham and his family can be seen wearing aglets sewn in pairs all over her gown, while aglets also decorate Bess of Hardwick's loose-bodied gown in her portrait.

There were a large number of other accessories which could also be made of precious metal and set with jewels. The favourite accessory for a lady was a girdle, which hung around her waist and then down the skirt of her dress. Girdles were often made of silk but again the sky was the limit for the very wealthy. Jane Seymour's girdle in the *Dynasty* portrait is made of pearls. All manner of things could decorate the end of a girdle too. A tiny prayer book was a favourite. The cover of one said to have belonged to Queen Elizabeth is in the British Museum. It is made of richly enamelled gold. In the *Dynasty* portrait Jane Seymour has a great golden medallion set with a large jewel hanging from hers.

Jewels were not necessarily just for display. They were also a way of showing certain things about yourself, such as your religious convictions or your family connections. Initials were frequently used in this way. Anne Boleyn is famous for wearing her 'B' pendant in honour of her family. The letters IHS, the abbreviated form of the name of Christ, in Greek, was another favourite option.

If you needed to keep your views secret then your jewellery could be designed to assist. In 1571 Queen Elizabeth banned rosary beads and after that many recusants adopted the rosary ring, which had ten studs for prayer projecting from it. This was far more discreet than beads but could be used in the same way.[57]

Certain stones were also believed to have useful properties. The goldsmith in the Royal Exchange in *The French Garden* explains some of these. Agates were believed to stir up storms, to give the interpretation of dreams and to make the wearer agreeable. The sapphire was good for the eyes and cured melancholy. The most marvellous power all precious stones had, according to *The French Garden's* goldsmith, is a power that precious stones still have, that is 'the force they have to transporte the money from your pursse into ours'.[58]

This was certainly the case in Tudor England. There was really no end to the items which could be turned into jewellery. A lady might have a jewelled pomander hanging from her girdle, containing a solid lump of perfume that could be held to the nose. A jewelled fan handle was another option. The fan itself would be made of exotic feathers attached to the handle. Items such as toothpicks might also be made of precious metal.

One of the most curious to modern eyes is the jewelled fur. This would consist of a single pelt of a small animal such as a sable which would be virtually made into a piece of jewellery. Henry VIII had two of these, both made of sable. One had a clock set in its head with diamonds and rubies, and had paws of gold set with sapphire claws. The other was set with turquoise, rubies, diamonds and pearls and had a ruby for a tongue. These items would be carried, as living pets often were, or might be worn slung over the shoulder.[59] The fashion for these items was probably linked to the decline in the wearing of fur linings in clothes and the preference for wearing richly jewelled fabrics. This decline was relative, though, and certainly didn't mean that the Tudors stopped using fur. They seem to have had a great love for it. Fur was of course favoured for warmth, but like so many other things it was also a badge of rank. Henry VIII's sumptuary laws forbade certain furs to certain people. Libbard (leopard) fur was only for those above the rank of knight or baron's son, or for those with £200 a year net income.

Black budge (good-quality imported lambskin) and black coney (rabbit) were forbidden to those with incomes of less than £20 per annum. A husbandman was not supposed to wear any fur at all.[60]

A favourite fur item in the first half of the century was the 'lettice bonnet' made from the white winter fur of a weasel and much loved by ladies at the time. There are several references to such items in the letters of the family of Lord Lisle, who was Henry VIII's governor of Calais. In November 1533, for example, Frances Plantagenet, Lord Lisle's daughter, was bought a lettice cap which cost 13s 4d.[61] Lettice bonnets were designed to entirely enclose the back of the head and the ears so they must have been wonderfully warm to wear.

Queen Elizabeth's wardrobe included various types of squirrel, jennet (civet cat), foines (stone marten) and varieties of coney. Czar Ivan the Terrible also sent a most impressive gift of four timbers (a timber contained forty skins) of rich black sables, six well-grown lynx and two gowns of ermine in 1587.[62]

The royal skinners were busy men as they not only supplied, treated and made up furs, but also lined and decorated the Queen's clothes with them. In addition they also had the job of keeping them in good repair which was no small task. *The Goodman of Paris*, a housewifery manual written at the end of the fourteenth century, describes how to look after furs. They were obviously hard work. For example, the author suggests treating furs which had grown hard by sprinkling wine over them by spurting it from the mouth, then throwing flour over this. The fur was left to dry for a day and then rubbed hard.[63]

Queen Elizabeth's furs were treated very carefully. Peter Jurden, the Queen's skinner, and five other men worked for four solid days in the winter of 1598 just on airing and beating them to keep them in good order.[64] The Queen's furs were stored in bags with sweet powder, which would have helped deter the moths and fleas which were a constant problem with fur. Some of the grander furs were also stored in great style. There was a velvet and shot taffeta bag embroidered with gold and pearls for keeping sables in.

Many modern readers may disapprove of this liberal use of fur, but one thing they could only approve of was the amount of recycling that went on in a Tudor wardrobe. The reason why almost nothing survives from the period is not only because fabrics are delicate and not many have survived four or five hundred years but also clothing in real terms was far more expensive than it is today and worn out clothes were recycled even in the grandest circles. Some mention has been made above of the recycling of Elizabeth's fine embroidered items, but many other things were also re-used. From Henry VIII's wardrobe the King's velvet gowns might end up as cushions in the royal apartments. Elizabeth's gowns were sometimes completely remodelled to bring them up to date, or were given away as gifts. The gowns were sometimes given away just as they were but sometimes large amounts of time and effort were put into remodelling them beforehand. One example is the gown given to the Queen by the Earl of Warwick in 1578. At that time it was of the style known as a 'round gown'. In 1602 this same gown was given to the Countess of Kildare, but before it was presented to her it was made up into a different style of gown, a high-bodied gown, and the embroidery had also been enlarged.[65] These alterations cannot have been cheap but it was still thought worthwhile to recycle an old gown rather than make a completely new one.

To finish this brief overview of Tudor fashions it is worth considering the difficulties of dressing at the time. Ordinary people's clothes, like the ones shown in the Brueghel painting, were designed to give plenty of freedom of movement for people who had to do manual work of various kinds for a living. They were easy to get in and out of. Wealthy people's clothes were a different matter.

One of the dialogues recorded in *The French Garden* concerns the dressing of Lady Ri-Melaine. Three servants are involved in the procedure: the page, who does odd jobs like building up the fire and cleaning the lady's combs, the chamber maid and Lady Ri-Melaine's gentlewoman. The lady could easily have dressed with just one assistant, but this was an important part of the day and Lady Ri-Melaine obviously enjoyed every minute of it. She is dressing to go to church in the dialogue and so wears her French hood decorated with rubies and carries with her a silver box filled with comfits, probably in anticipation of a long sermon. She even has a new gown, as the tailor comes to put it on for her.[66]

The first stage of preparing Lady Ri-Melaine for the day was to warm her smock by the fire. After putting on her smock, the lady puts on her damask bodies which are stiffened with whalebone. There is then a great fuss while she chooses one garment and then changes her mind and chooses another, until finally she is ready for her neckwear:

Gentlewoman

What dooth it please you to have Madame, a ruffe band or a Rebato?

Lady

Let me see that ruffe. How is it that the supporter is so soyled? I knowe not for what you are fit, that you cannot so much as to keep my cloathes cleane: I beleeve that the meanest woman in this towne, hath her apparel in better order than I have: take it away give me my Rebato of cut-worke edged . . . Is there no small pinnes for my Cuffes? Looke in the pinne-cushen. Pinne that with a black pinne . . .

A rebato was a type of collar which had a wire support at the back so that it stood up behind the head. Like a ruff, it was a tricky thing to fix in place. A wealthy person's cuffs would also require pinning so that pins and pincushion were vital accessories.

This section also illustrates the job of a gentlewoman. A grand lady's personal attendant would be a well-bred lady as most of her time she would be a kind of companion to her mistress. She also had the job of keeping her mistress's wardrobe in order, which was no mean feat considering the size and complexity of some. The gentlewoman was not expected to do the laundry herself but she was expected to see that everything was kept in good order. It would indeed be her fault if the ruff and its supporter were not in a clean enough state for Lady Ri-Melaine to wear. It would also have been the gentlewoman's job to see that everything was stored away properly. The Tudors did not have wardrobes and clothes were stored in a variety of ways. A good idea of these can be found in Henry VIII's 1547 inventory.[67]

The main items used for storage in the sixteenth century were chests. These came in all shapes and sizes and were sometimes plain and sometimes richly decorated. All of Henry's chests had a wooden shell but some were covered with leather, black Naples fustian or even velvet. The more finely decorated ones had leather covers which protected them when they were moved from palace to palace.

Chests for storing valuable items such as money or jewels were bound in iron and had several locks. The rule usually was the more valuable the contents, the more locks the chest had. A wax seal might also be placed over the lock when the chest was closed for additional security. A chest belonging to Katherine Parr was sealed in this way after her death, once an inventory of its contents had been made.

Some smaller boxes were also used for personal items which might be very valuable in themselves. Henry VIII had small boxes decorated with real or fake jewels, cameos, decorative metalwork, ivory, elaborate paintwork and gilding. The 'long box' in which Lady Ri-Melaine keeps her jewels in *The French Garden* might well have been such a box. Some of these boxes came with a variety of drawers like Henry's writing desk which still survives in the Victoria and Albert Museum.

Leather cases were another option for keeping delicate objects in. Henry VIII had leather cases for knives, surgical and mathematical instruments, combs and spectacles. Perhaps the ivory comb that Lady Ri-Melaine uses was kept in such a case.

John Malt, Henry VIII's tailor, was paid a shilling a case to make twenty-four satin cases of various colour, all of which were lined with buckram which would make the cases firmer and thus better protect the contents. This may have been a special measure needed to ensure that the clothes were protected as they were moved, but it is possible that other wealthy people protected their finer clothes with similar cases before packing them away in chests. The king also had four cotton cases for keeping his hose in. Doubtless odd hose had the same ability to disappear as modern socks, so these must have been very useful.

Henry's coffer-maker, William Green, was also paid to make round cases for caps and hats, the forerunner of modern hatboxes. These must have been a necessity for all wealthy people to preserve the jewels sewn on to their hats when they were travelling and to prevent them from being crushed.

Being fashionable in Tudor England was certainly hard work, what with buying the wardrobe in the first place, seeing that it was properly cared for and then working hard to keep it up to date. Perhaps the best advice was give by that arbiter of good taste, Baldesar Castiglione. After noting the vulgarity of extremes of fashion he says, 'So my advice to the courtier is to shun this kind of dress; and I would add that he should decide for himself what appearance he wants to have and what sort of man he wants to seem, and then dress accordingly, so that his clothes should help him to be taken for such, even by those who do not hear him speak or see him perform anything at all.'[68] Surely good advice for successful dress in any age.

THREE

Tournaments and Pageantry

Court entertainments were not just for enjoyment but also for what we would now call public relations purposes. Their primary function was to display the wealth and power of the monarch while at the same time aiming to project political messages to certain people.

Lavish display was particularly important to the Tudors. Henry VII used it to remind everyone that he was King and there to stay. Henry VIII used it to demonstrate that England was a European power, not just a backwater nation on the fringes of events. Edward and Mary were not on the throne long enough to make use of it, but Elizabeth used it to try to unite a very divided nation.

It is easy to dismiss the lavish court entertainments as simply monarchs indulging themselves, but they were a very useful political tool. The letters sent by ambassadors to their masters show an incredible eye for detail as they looked for signs of the state of the king's political intentions, and the state of his finances. For example, the Milanese ambassador to the Holy Roman Emperor, Paulo de Laude, wrote a letter to the Duke of Milan describing the tournament Henry held in 1513 to celebrate the capture of Tournai. He noted that 'the King wore a vest over his armour which he had worn before, though it is of great beauty, of velvet of divers colours with embroidered stripes of gold, really exquisite'.[1] However wonderful the vest, it had been worn before.

The ambassadors were generally impressed by Henry's court. In 1515 Henry held an impressive joust at his favourite palace, Greenwich. The papal nuncio wrote to Isabelle D'Este, Marchioness of Mantua, 'In short, the wealth and civilisation of the world are here; and those who call the English barbarians appear to me to render themselves such. I here perceive very elegant manner, extreme decorum, and very great politeness; and amongst other things there is this most invincible King.'[2] Henry's policies were working. England, after being something of a backwater under Henry VII, was beginning to be seen as a sophisticated nation worthy of note.

A full-scale court entertainment would have been impressive even by modern standards. Exactly what form the entertainments took varied according to fashion and the tastes of the reigning monarch, but the tournament remained a favourite throughout the century.

The original tournaments of the twelfth and thirteenth centuries had been more or less full-scale practice battles, organised between teams of knights. In theory, nobody was supposed to be killed in them but deaths certainly did occur. They were considered a good training ground for young knights, and success in tournaments could lead to great things. William Marshal, the great friend of Henry III, rose from relative obscurity to the very highest offices through his skill in tournaments.

By the late fifteenth and sixteenth centuries tournaments had changed completely. They were far more strictly controlled than their medieval counterparts. Various different forms of combat were involved but only small numbers of people fought at one time. Sometimes small teams of horsemen fought with swords, sometimes combat with two-edged swords took place on foot. The centre-piece of the tournament was always the joust, which involved just two people taking part at one time, creating an emphasis on individual display. Tournaments were still seen in theory as good training for battle, though this wasn't the case in fact by the sixteenth century. Training for tournaments must have been a good way of keeping fit and the basic skills of horsemanship, etc. needed must have been useful. They must also have been good tests of courage but in general warfare had moved on and the skills used in the tournament and those needed on the battlefield were rather different. The most famous part of the tournament, the joust, was certainly not a skill needed in battle by the sixteenth century. The important thing about a tournament was that it set the right tone of high chivalry and romance.

Tournaments also provided good opportunities for display. The contestants arrived in fabulous costumes, riding in elaborate pageant cars. These would often be designed around a central theme. At the entertainments held in November 1501 to celebrate the marriage of Henry VIII's older brother Arthur to Katherine of Aragon, William Courtenay arrived riding in a pageant car shaped like a red dragon, pulled by a giant, while the Earl of Essex's pageant car was in turn pulled by a red dragon.

The red dragon was an important symbol to the Tudors. Tradition saw it as the banner of Uther Pendragon, the father of King Arthur.[3] Henry VII, when returning from exile in Brittany, had adopted the red dragon as his banner, playing on his Welsh blood as he landed in Wales. Genealogists later 'discovered' the Tudors to be descended from King Arthur. This would seem much less a wild claim to people of the period than it seems to us, as in those days people believed that King Arthur had existed in exactly the way he appears in Medieval romances. Even so, few people can have been fooled, but they would still have taken the point. The new dynasty was reminding everyone that they were the rightful kings of England, whatever the opposition thought.

Tournaments also provided an excellent opportunity for individual courtiers to show off their skills, particularly the young Henry VIII, who excelled at jousting. It was certainly not true that people let the King win, as Henry evidently got very frustrated when he won too easily. The tournament cheque (score-card) for 20 May 1516 records the King's anger that this had happened.[4]

The lavish cost of these entertainments was, of course, another display of power. Henry VIII spent £4,000 on the tournament to celebrate the birth of his first son Prince Henry in 1511, which was almost twice the cost of building one of his warships, the *Great Elizabeth*.[5]

The tournament was useful too in that it would be watched by a wider audience than indoor entertainments. Dignitaries such as the mayor and aldermen of London would be invited as well as members of the court. There was always some space for members of the general population too, although they had to be able to pay for their seats. A tournament could therefore impress both foreign ambassadors and the king's subjects at the same time.

A large-scale court celebration would include indoor entertainments as well as a tournament. In the early sixteenth century great use was made of pageantry, with elaborate scenery being used. Perhaps the best way of showing just how elaborate these entertainments could be is to describe one of them.

The marriage of Prince Arthur, as heir to Henry VII, was a great state occasion. It was particularly important as this young upstart dynasty had managed to persuade the King and Queen of Spain, Ferdinand and Isabella, to allow their daughter to marry into the family. Spain was very much the great power of Europe at the time, so 'official recognition' for the Tudors by Ferdinand and Isabella was particularly important. The marriage was celebrated with a tournament and four great banquets held between 18 and 28 November 1501 at Westminster. The initial banquet was held on 19 November and the entertainments included no less than three pageants, all of which centred on a theme of courtly love.

The first pageant consisted of a castle drawn into the great hall by four great heraldic beasts. It must have been a hard job to pull the pageant cart as the castle was quite large, having eight ladies standing at its windows and children dressed as 'maidens singing' standing on its four turrets.

The second consisted of a large ship on wheels which was 'anchored' near the castle. The ship contained a lady dressed like the Spanish princess and also two gentlemen dressed as Hope and Despair, the ambassadors of the knights of love. These gentlemen got out of the ship and tried to talk to the ladies in the castle but they refused to listen to them. The ambassadors then warned that the ladies would be attacked by the knights of love.

The third pageant duly contained the promised knights. The pageant cart on which they stood was in the form of a mountain, the 'Mountain of Love'. The knights then got down from their pageant and attacked the ladies' castle. In true courtly style the ladies gave in and came out of the castle to perform dances with the knights. The pageant carts were then removed from the hall to allow room for the audience to join in the dancing.[6]

This description gives some idea of the size and complexity of the scenery. The sheer cost of these entertainments was quite staggering, particularly as the costumes and decorations were made of fabulously expensive materials such as cloth of silver or gold. This was partly for practical reasons. Those taking part in the entertainments would have been very close to those watching and of course there was none of the strong lighting that can be found in modern theatres. The materials needed to be of the finest quality to look good. The use of fabulous materials was also necessary to show off the royal generosity. The people who had taken part in the entertainment were usually allowed to keep their costumes, while the distribution of parts of scenery and costumes often formed part of the entertainments.

The costumes described by George Cavendish give an idea of the splendour of a court masque. He describes Henry VIII appearing with a dozen other men, 'all in garments like shepherds, made of fine cloth of gold and fine crimson satin paned, and caps of the same, with visors of good proportion, their hairs and beards either of fine gold wire or else of silver, and some being black silk . . .'[7]

It was important that men of high rank should show their generosity. The giving of extravagant gifts was a sign of wealth and power, and high-ranking courtiers and ambassadors expected to receive them. Thomas Elyot commented in the *Book Named the Governor* that liberality well and duly employed 'acquireth perpetual honour to the giver, and much fruit and singular commodity thereby increaseth'.[8] A monarch who didn't give generous gifts made himself look mean and selfish. The theory behind such liberality may have been very high-flown but in practice plain greed often led to some rather undignified scenes. Disorder evidently broke out at the 1511 entertainments as Richard Gibson notes in his accounts that he had intended to keep the pageant, but that it had been attacked and broken up by members of the King's Guard. The people who were defending it had been beaten up.[9]

Even the king himself was stripped of his costume at the same event. The various challengers at the tournament had allegorical names, such as 'Cœur Loyal' (Henry himself) and 'Vaillant Desyr' (Sir Thomas Knyvet). Their costumes were covered in gold ornaments, Henry's with 887 pieces of gold in the shape of the letters H and K, hearts, and the name LOYAL repeated several times. Knyvet's had 893 gold decorations, including his name VAILLANT DESYR. He had, incidentally, added an extra DESYR set over his codpiece; even courtly entertainments were not necessarily subtle. Edward Hall records that the Spanish ambassadors refused to believe that Henry's ornaments were indeed real gold. In order to prove them wrong, Henry had arranged that at an agreed place and time during the entertainments they should be allowed to pluck some of the ornaments from his costume. Seeing this happen, there seems to have been a general stampede to snatch the gold from the men's costumes and both Henry and Knyvet ended up being stripped not only of their ornaments but also of their doublet and hose.[10]

The entertainments provided at court very much set the tone that the monarch wished to establish. Henry VII spent lavishly on entertainments, as is shown above, but his heart does not seem to have been in such things. Certainly he never took part in any of the entertainments himself and as a result the tone of his court was dignified but dull.[11]

His son Henry VIII was very different and took part in all types of entertainment with enormous energy and obviously took great delight in them. Tournaments were a gift for the young Henry as they were the perfect setting for him to show off his good looks and his very impressive sporting abilities. The Venetian ambassadors were certainly impressed by such display. After watching Henry joust on one occasion they wrote home declaring that he was not only an expert in arms but also so gifted with every mental accomplishment that he could have few equals in the world.[12] In the first tournaments of his reign Henry appeared in a number of allegorical disguises but he soon decided that disguise was superfluous. The costumes and settings remained as luxurious as ever, it was just that the King saw no need to appear as anyone but himself. At the most elaborate entertainment of his life, the Field of Cloth of Gold, he did not bother with disguise.

The Field was a meeting between Henry VIII and Francis I, the King of France, which took place in 1520. They were in theory meeting to discuss further a treaty of 'Perpetual Friendship' which they had signed in 1518, but essentially the meeting was a great tournament with its attendant festivities.

Display was seen very much as a sign of wealth and political power. Francis and Henry were not just political rivals, but also personal ones. They were about the same age and both admired and envied each other at the same time. Their relationship is summed up in an incident which took place at the May Festival in 1515, not long after some Venetian ambassadors had arrived in England. Henry was anxious to know if Francis was better looking than he was. He started by asking one of the ambassadors, Pietro Pasqualigo, if the French King was as tall and as stout (i.e. well-built) as he was and then went on to ask about Francis's legs. Pasqualigo admitted that the French King's legs were rather thin, so the delighted Henry opened the front of his doublet, placed his hand on his well-developed thigh and declared 'Look here! And I have also a good calf to my leg!'[13] In the circumstances it was not surprising that the whole event got rather out of hand as each king worked on producing a better display than the other. There were even underhand tactics being used, such as Francis trying to prepare his tents secretly at Tours rather than openly near Calais, where the event was to take place.

No effort was spared on either the English or the French side. One French official was sent to Florence no fewer than seven times in search of fleur-de-lys cloth of gold.[14] This is perhaps not surprising as one of Francis's tents was 120 feet high and was even topped with a gold statue of St Michael, the patron saint of France. Unfortunately the effect was rather spoiled as the weather was poor and the main central support of the tent snapped in the wind.

Henry went one step further and built a temporary palace. It was a magnificent structure, with proper brick foundations and glass windows. The walls rose to 30 feet high, although they were made of wood rather than brick and the roof was made of oilcloth painted to look like tiles. The ground floor of the palace even had all the usual offices expected in a great house, like pantries, wine cellars, a spicery, a scullery, etc. The palace contained rooms for not only Henry himself, but also the Queen (still Katherine of Aragon at this stage), the King's sister Mary who was the dowager French queen and, of course, Cardinal Wolsey.[15]

The English King's generosity was demonstrated not only by the constant stream of lavish gifts which were exchanged by him and the grandest French courtiers, but also by the two fountains which stood outside his temporary palace. One of these ran with white wine and the other with red. The wine was free to everyone who wanted it.

The general theme was the friendship between England and France, but there were undercurrents which showed that everything was not necessarily as friendly as it might have been. Henry would not even leave England until the English Channel had been cleared of all shipping as he was afraid of being taken hostage by the French. The messages he gave out were not always friendly ones, either. On one day of the tournament he wore a costume of cloth of silver damask with gold letters around the border. It was decorated with small mountains, with branches of basil made of gold springing from them. An Italian observer took the branches to be olive branches for peace but Edward Hall, who accompanied Henry to the event, records the wording as saying 'breake not these swete herbes for the rich mounte doute for damage'. The mountain was taken to represent England so the costume was basically a threat against anyone who threatened English security.[16]

The fabulous court entertainments of Henry's earlier years weren't continued throughout his reign. Cardinal Wolsey, who had been the main driving force behind many of the more spectacular events, fell from power in 1529. He had shared his master's taste for elaborate display and without him Henry's entertainments were not the same. The politics of the later part of Henry's reign also did not encourage a festive atmosphere at court. The break with Rome meant that the king had more weighty matters on his mind than entertainments, particularly when complicated by the dissolution of the monasteries. Henry was also no longer young by this time and did not take part in tournaments himself. Only three tournaments took place in the last fourteen years of Henry's reign. The breakdown in his health also meant that Henry no longer felt like showing himself off in the way in which he had once delighted.

There were tournaments in the short reign of Henry's son Edward. Edward is normally dismissed as being a weak child but this does not seem to have been the case, at least when he first became king. He seems to have delighted in exercise although he was too young to take part in full-scale jousts. Instead, there were contests of 'running at the ring'. This was a form of training for full-scale jousting. Instead of jousting against an opponent, boys aimed at a ring set up along the tilt barrier and tried to hit it with their lance. The one who hit it most often won.[17]

Mary also held tournaments during her reign but they were aimed at trying to establish some kind of rapport between the rival English and Spanish courts. Mary became Queen in July 1553 and married Philip of Spain, heir to the Spanish throne in the next year. The marriage was very unpopular and the intense rivalry between the Spanish and English courtiers hardly helped the atmosphere. The tournaments did little to change things.

Entertainments in Elizabeth's time centred around the Queen and were full of allusions to courtly love. The age of Elizabeth is often seen as a kind of golden age in England, but the truth was rather different. England in Elizabeth's time was a very divided nation. The gap between rich and poor was widening and more people than ever were ending up relying on public poor relief. The differences in religion which were literally pulling Europe apart at this time were very much in evidence in England. In response to this, Elizabeth set herself up as a kind of icon that the whole of the country could revere regardless of religious beliefs.[18] The court entertainments were designed to foster this image. Elizabeth's famous progresses were also part of the process. They were not simply ways of allowing her to save money by living on her courtiers, but were also ways of showing the Queen off to her people. In fact, Elizabeth did not save money by going on progress. Lord Burghley, Elizabeth's Lord Treasurer, estimated that it cost about £2,000 a year to go on progress, since the cost of transporting Elizabeth and her household was very high. In any case, the Queen did not always stay with her subjects, but often made use of various properties of her own. These were often little-used palaces which had to be opened up, put in good repair and furnished for the royal visit, which was obviously an expensive business.[19] Lord Burghley may have despaired of the cost of progresses but Elizabeth knew the value of them. In the days before newspapers and television they were a vital link between the Queen and her subjects.

The progresses were indeed a spectacle to behold. For most of the year Elizabeth hardly ventured twenty miles from London, but her summer progresses led her as far north as Chartley in Staffordshire, westwards to Bristol and as far south as Southampton. She travelled with between four and six hundred carts which must have been an impressive sight in itself. The beginning and end of a progress involved a formal leaving or entry into London, which was also a great public occasion when the Queen would be the centre-piece of a great procession involving her senior officers and ladies-in-waiting, together with the mayor and aldermen of London. One French ambassador witnessed a ceremonial entry in 1579 and his description conveys the public devotion that Elizabeth could inspire. He describes the Queen as 'more beautiful than ever, bedizened like the sun, and mounted on a fine Spanish horse; and with so many people before her it was a marvellous thing. They did not merely honour her, they worshipped her, kneeling on the ground with a thousand blessings and joyful remarks.'[20]

Elizabeth had a natural talent for dealing with the crowds. She took great care on her progresses that those who came to see her or who played some active part in entertaining her knew that she appreciated their efforts. She always travelled very slowly so that she could properly acknowledge those who stood by the road to watch her pass. She always took in two or three major towns on a progress and listened tirelessly to public addresses and appeared interested in what must have been hours of pageantry. Her care for the feelings of her subjects was shown many times. In Sandwich in 1573 she was careful to show her consideration for some local ladies who had cooked a banquet of 140 dishes. Elizabeth had a very small appetite but still tried many of the dishes and did so 'without assay', that is to say, without having any of the dishes tasted for poison, as a mark of her trust of the ladies. In 1578 she listened to a Latin discourse by a Norwich schoolmaster and proclaimed his speech the best she had ever heard, although this was hardly likely to have been the truth.[21]

Elizabeth loved these progresses as to her they were something of a holiday. Any important person was always surrounded by people asking them for all sorts of things, from help finding a job to direct requests for money. Elizabeth refused to listen to all such petitions during her progresses, unless made to her by people such as the civic dignitaries of the towns she visited. For example, in Stafford in 1575 she promised to look into the claim that the town had been deprived of some land intended by Henry VIII to endow a school, but the courtiers who were with her most of the time knew better than to put petitions to her on progress. This refusal to listen was a major problem for those who had government business that could not wait. In years of crisis Elizabeth's advisers would try to persuade her not to leave London, or at least not to go too far afield. Elizabeth would not be persuaded, however. Even in 1576–7 when the crisis in the Netherlands was particularly severe, she set off as usual, leaving her minister to cope.

Progresses may have been a holiday for Elizabeth, but they weren't so much fun for the rest of the court. Elizabeth was, of course, always given first-class accommodation. The wealthiest courtiers might even rebuild or alter their houses to cater for royal visits, just as Lord Burghley enlarged his house, Theobalds. There were not many houses that could happily accommodate the court, so progresses meant uncomfortable, cramped living for most members of Elizabeth's retinue. The further down the court pecking order you were, the more uncomfortable you were likely to be. People such as kitchen staff were likely to spend a progress camping out.

There is a general belief that entertaining Elizabeth was a dubious honour, since it cost so much money. It was indeed expensive to entertain the court and the problem was also made worse by Elizabeth's well-known inability to make up her mind. In July 1576 Gilbert Talbot wrote to his father:

> Since my coming hither to the Court, there have been sundry determinations of her Majesty's progress this summer. Yesterday it was set down that she would go to Grafton and Northampton, Leicester and to Ashby, my Lord Huntingdon's house, and there to have remained twenty-one days . . . but late yesternight this purpose altered, and now at this present her Majesty thinketh to go no further than Grafton; howbeit there is no certainty, for these two or three days it hath changed every five hours.[22]

This uncertainty explains why Elizabeth's progresses made running the country so difficult, as these last minute changes hardly helped those who had to get messages to the court. They also added considerably to the expense as food and drink often went to waste. Lord Huntingdon, for example, must have had huge amounts of food ready for the Queen's visit, food which would simply go to waste if the court did not arrive. In 1602 it cost Lord Keeper Egerton £1,260 12s 4d to entertain Elizabeth for four days at Haresfield, of which about £240 went on food so there really were huge sums of money involved.[23]

If a person really did not welcome a royal visit then your only hope of dissuading the Queen was to use the influence of friends at court. In 1570 the Earl of Bedford was forced to asked Cecil to persuade Elizabeth not to visit his house, Chenies, explaining that he had no time to put the house in suitable order.

The worst thing to do was to follow the example of the Earl of Lincoln who in 1601, hearing that the Queen intended to visit his house at Chelsea, promptly decamped to the country so that the court arrived to find the house all shut up. Elizabeth responded by declaring her intention to come back the next week and so the Earl ended up not only with a huge bill for entertaining the Queen but also with the problem of having offended her.

Those who could afford a royal visit seem to have welcomed the chance to have the Queen as a guest. Lord and Lady Norris were heartbroken when Elizabeth's planned visit to their house was called off, while Thomas Heneage wrote to Cecil urging him to persuade her to visit his house, Copthall in Essex.

The court entertainments in this period need to be seen in the context of the image that Elizabeth was building around herself. She liked to play various parts which suggested that she was ever young and beautiful, portraying characters such as the moon goddess Cynthia (also called Belphoebe) so that she is often portrayed with Cynthia's crescent moon in her hair. The famous 'Rainbow Portrait' which hangs at Hatfield House celebrates Elizabeth as the Queen of Love and Beauty. The bodice of her gown is embroidered with spring flowers, depicting her as Flora.[24] There are even allusions to political theory in the portrait. The eyes and ears which decorate her clothes represent her councillors, who watch and listen on the Queen's behalf but who do not have the final say in government.[25]

As she grew older and it became obvious that she was never going to marry and have children, Elizabeth also liked to make great play of her virgin status. She is therefore often portrayed with her hair loose, a symbol of virginity, or else holding a sieve. The sieve is a reference to a legend concerning Tuccia, a Roman Vestal virgin. She was accused of not being a virgin, so in order to prove her innocence she filled a sieve with water and carried it from the Tiber to the Temple without spilling a drop. The idea was that if she could perform a miracle like this, then she was indeed telling the truth. Vestal virgins had to remain virgin as their duty and this was the point that Elizabeth was making. The implication was that she refused to marry because in this way she could best serve her country.

Over time Accession Day, known usually as Crownation Day (the day on which Elizabeth took the crown), established itself as an important day in the English calendar. Its popularity built up slowly, but grew particularly after Pope Pius V declared that

Elizabeth's subjects were absolved of their allegiance to her in 1570 and again after the defeat of the Armada in 1588. It was another way of building Elizabeth up as a focus of loyalty for her subjects. Accession Day was celebrated at court by a tournament. This was the perfect vehicle for Elizabeth, who of course reigned as the lady of the tournament. These tournaments were also useful vehicles for the courtiers, giving them opportunities in their turn to put their messages across to the Queen.

At a tournament it was usual for a knight to use an impresa. This consisted of some kind of device together with a motto. An example was the impresa used by Sir Philip Sidney showing the tideless Caspian Sea with the motto 'Without flowing back'. [26] This presumably was to show his constancy in the face of changing fortune, but of course symbols can always be explained in different ways. This could cause confusion even at the time but it was usual by Elizabeth's time for a knight's impresa to be painted on a pasteboard shield, which would be presented to the Queen before the tournament as the knight made his ceremonial arrival. The impresa would be presented by the knight's page, who would explain the device. [27] Unfortunately these explanations have not survived, so we are often left guessing the meaning today. Impresas were very useful to the courtiers as they allowed them to get a message across to the Queen in a very public arena. This was particularly the case as the impresas seem to have been kept permanently in a gallery at Whitehall Palace, where they could continue to remind the Queen of the message. Paul Hentzner, a German visitor to Elizabeth's court, records having visited the gallery. [28]

Unfortunately little information about impresas survives. Some are recorded in a book published in 1612 by Henry Peacham called *Minerva Britannia*, although this is a book of emblems generally and not just a record of impresas. The other problem is that even when impresas are recorded, we don't always know the exact occasion on which they were used, or the exact intention that the knight in question had in mind.

Even so, appearance at a tournament and the use of a suitable impresa could be useful in winning the Queen's favour, or in regaining it. In 1580 Sir Philip Sidney enraged Elizabeth by writing to her urging her not to marry the Duc d'Alençon. He was even forced to withdraw from the court. In January 1581 he appeared at a tournament where he carried an impresa showing the word *Speravi* (I hoped) crossed through. This was particularly apt, as Sidney had carried an impresa showing the word *Spero* (I hope) on an earlier occasion. He had also just presented the Queen with a jewelled whip as her New Year's gift, a gift which was intended to show his subjection to her will. All this showmanship was successful and Sidney regained the royal favour.[29]

The entertainments provided for Elizabeth on her progresses also gave the courtiers a chance to convey messages to her. There was, of course, always the risk that the Queen would not be pleased by what was being suggested to her. It was perhaps to be expected that the Earl of Leicester would overstep the mark. At one of his lavish entertainments for the Queen at Kenilworth, the Earl portrayed Elizabeth as King Arthur returned and himself as the guardian of King Arthur's castle. The implication was that by marrying Leicester, Elizabeth could initiate a new golden age for England. The Queen was not pleased and a second show, which urged the virtues of marriage over virginity, had to be cancelled.[30]

Other entertainments were more successful. In September 1575 Elizabeth was entertained at Woodstock by a performance of *The Hermit's Tale* which was probably written by Sir Henry Lee, the man who seems to have established the Accession Day Tournament. It is a typically complicated plot but the story centres around two lovers, Gaudina and Contarenus. Gaudina is the heiress to a duke and ends up having to part from her lover due to her duty to her father and dukedom. This was obviously the kind of message that Elizabeth wanted to hear.[31]

Organising all these entertainments was a huge job so there was a full-time team who worked on devising them, preparing props and scenery, etc. This was called the Revels Office. In Henry VII's reign, when court entertainments were not quite so numerous, such events were organised on an ad hoc basis. A Master of the Revels would be appointed for a specific period to organise a set of revels and then after these were over, he would go back to his normal job. At the end of Henry VIII's reign the court entertainments had grown so elaborate that a permanent Master was necessary.[32] The Master of the Revels became a lifetime position and the holder organised all the court revels.

The job was one which called for a clear head as it involved co-ordinating large numbers of workers from different departments of the royal household. For example, most entertainments involved the use of one or more banquet houses. These were general-purpose structures for housing feasts, suppers and general entertainments. These houses varied greatly. They could be relatively simple, for example, the latticed bower beneath an oak tree in which Elizabeth was banqueted and entertained at the Woodstock entertainment of September 1575. Even this seemingly-simple structure was decorated with pictures and allegorical verses, and contained a crescent-moon shaped table as a compliment to the Queen, who liked to be compared to the chaste moon-goddess, Diana. There was also an underground chamber as the Queen was entertained with music which issued from it.[33] At the other end of the scale were huge banquet houses, such as the one built at Hyde Park in 1551. This had two storeys and even had clerestory windows. It was a timber-framed building rather than just a tent.

The complexity of the Master of the Revels' job becomes evident when you consider the number of different departments that became involved in court revels. The Office of the Works would provide the men to build foundations for the banquet houses. The Wardrobe supplied hangings, cloth, etc. The Office of the Tents constructed the roofs and interior ceilings, while the Serjeant Painter and the other King's painters worked on the decoration which would cover both the inside and the outside of the structure. On top of all this there would be writers, musicians and performers to co-ordinate, while the head cooks also needed to know what was going on as the food they produced was expected to reflect the theme chosen.

The standards expected were also very high. Artists at the time were seen largely as craftsmen, so that Henry's famous court artist Hans Holbein not only painted portraits but also designed tableware, jewellery and scenery for court entertainments. His *Siege of Therouanne* was designed to decorate the gallery of the banquet house at Greenwich in 1527.[34]

It was also important that the Master of the Revels should have creative talent. Novelty was a vital part of entertainment. It was not enough to repeat the same old thing, no matter how magnificent. This was the reason for the complexity of many court entertainments. The required element of surprise is best illustrated by one of Cardinal Wolsey's entertainments held in the King's honour. It was on this occasion that Henry and his companions wore the shepherd costumes described above.

The Cardinal was entertaining a great number of lords and ladies and had already given them a magnificent meal. (The King was not present at this stage.) They were now sitting at the banquet course which would have included a vast number of expensive sweetmeats and formed the usual ending to a feast. The unstated assumption among the company would have been that the day's entertainments were drawing to a close.

Henry, the other 'shepherds' plus torch bearers, drummers and other attendants then arrived quietly by water 'without any noise' so as to surprise the company. There was then a sudden peal of ordnance to announce the arrival of an important guest.

Lord Sandys, the King's chamberlain, and Sir Henry Guildford, comptroller to the King, were then sent to see what was going on. (Guildford was Master of the Revels so presumably he had planned it all.) They informed the Cardinal that visiting nobles had arrived, and so the Cardinal sent them to meet these nobles on the pretext that they both spoke French and so could greet them properly. A large number of drummers and fife players accompanied them.

The 'shepherds' then joined the company and danced with the ladies. The Cardinal then declared that he would give up his place of honour to someone in the company who was more worthy of it. He had to guess which one of the 'shepherds' was more worthy and, whether by accident or design is unknown, he chose Sir Edward Neville, who did look very like the King.

Henry fortunately found this very funny, and then took off his mask.

The King then went to the Cardinal's bedchamber to change and meanwhile the banquet was removed, the old tablecloths taken up and fresh ones put down. A complete new banquet was then served which Cavendish describes as 'Two hundred dishes or above of wondrous costly meats and devices, subtly devised. Thus pass they forth the whole night with banqueting, dancing and other triumphant devices, to the great comfort of the king and pleasant regard of the nobility there assembled.'[35]

The importance of novelty is shown by the way that the royal banqueting houses were used. The banquet house at Greenwich was originally built to house the 1527 celebrations which centred around the signing of various treaties with the French. The building measured 110 x 30 feet. Beyond it lay a 'disguising house' which was often used in conjunction with the banquet house. Neither building was remarkable in itself. They were not intended to be. Both buildings simply formed a stage for royal entertainments and it was the scenery put in them, rather than the buildings themselves which were designed to impress. When decorated they could be breathtaking. The 1527 decorations for the banquet house included gilded lead roses and leaves which were used to hide the exposed timbers of the newly erected ceiling. It was hung with new tapestries with flowers of satin silver on a gold ground while the 'disguising house' beyond it had a white marble fountain installed, and was decorated with a silk hawthorn tree to represent England and a silk mulberry to represent France. All these decorations, lavish though they were, were removed after the celebrations were over. Some of them, such as the tapestries, were of course kept for the King's use. Others simply disappear from the records. This is the last we hear of Holbein's paintings, for example. Maybe they were kept and treasured by someone, but equally they could just have been discarded as a used stage set would be today. However successful an entertainment was and however much the setting for it was admired, it could not be used in the same way again if the all-important element of surprise and novelty was to be maintained.[36]

The Tudors, having a somewhat questionable claim to the throne, were always very keen to remind everyone of their right to rule. It was for this reason that the ceremonies surrounding the Order of the Garter were always important to them. The Order of the Garter was founded by Edward III in 1361, as a way of uniting the knights and nobles to fight with him in France. Edward IV rebuilt the Garter's chapel (St George's Chapel at Windsor Castle) and reinstated the order. Henry VII completed the unfinished chapel and had made the Garter feasts great state occasions. It made sense. He used the Order to try to unify the nobles behind him just as Edward III had done.

The problem was that Windsor was out in the country, where the celebrations were only going to be seen by very small numbers of people. Elizabeth got around the problem by holding the feasts at either Greenwich or Whitehall, which were both close enough to London to allow crowds of people to watch. There was also a magnificent procession of garter knights to mark the event, besides the usual divine service and feast.[37] The procession was, of course, a public one and showed off the magnificence of the court to the people. This superb procession was another expression of royal wealth and power. The Garter Knights were all influential men and seeing them riding in the procession with the monarch was an expression of loyalty. The associations with Edward III were also useful, as they claimed descent from him, via Margaret Beaufort, Henry VII's mother. The fact that the Tudors were descended via John of Gaunt's then mistress, Katherine Swynford, was quietly forgotten.

The entire life of a Tudor monarch was celebrated with elaborate ceremonial. Birth, marriage and death were not just personal matters, but matters of state. A royal funeral, for example, involved not only the royal family but every senior officer of church and state in the kingdom.

Henry VII, the first of the Tudors, rather predictably had a funeral full of reminders that the Tudor family had every right to the kingship, or at least to remind those who had their doubts that they had better keep quiet. He died on 21 April 1509 at Richmond, his favourite palace. His body remained there for two weeks while masses and dirges were performed. On 9 May the body was finally embalmed, placed in a lead-lined coffin and put on a chariot covered with black cloth of gold. A life-sized effigy of the king was placed on top of the coffin. John Leland describes the effigy as 'crowned and richly appareled in his Parliament Roobe, bearing in his Right Hand a Scepter, and in his Left Hand a Ball of golde, over whom ther was hanginge a riche Cloth of golde pitched upon Foure Staves . . .'[38] Four barons walked at the corners of the King's chariot carrying the banners of his four patrons, the Holy Trinity, Our Lady, St George and Mary Magdalene. Hall also reported later that the chariot was decorated with banners showing the arms of Henry's dominions and titles and also his 'genealogies'. The genealogies were the arms of his ancestors, an important way of proclaiming his royal blood and his right to the throne.

Similar banners appeared at all royal Tudor funerals. Prince Arthur's funeral in 1502 featured not only the arms of Wales, Cornwall and Chester, all connected with titles the Prince held, but also those of Brutus and Cadwalader, ancient mythical kings of Britain, from whom the Tudors claimed descent.

The Tudors were great lovers of processions and no grand funeral was complete without one. They were ways of demonstrating the wealth and power of the deceased, but in the case of a king they were a way of expressing support for his dynasty. Henry VII's procession included large numbers of prelates singing prayers for the soul of the King, London civic dignitaries, judges, councillors, and the representatives of important European powers such as Spain, France, Venice and Florence. Virtually everyone of religious, political or juridical significance in the kingdom was there.

The coffin rested overnight in St Paul's Cathedral, and on the following day John Fisher, the Bishop of Rochester, preached a sermon which was later published by Wynkyn de Worde. The next day the coffin was moved to Westminster Abbey, where it was finally buried.[39]

This set the pattern for all royal Tudor funerals. This was to be expected for major figures such as Henry VIII, whose funeral procession was estimated at four miles long. However, even minor members of the royal family, such as babies who died young, were buried with considerable pomp. Prince Edmund, son of Henry VII who died at fifty-one days, and Henry VIII's first son Prince Henry, who died at about the same age, were both given grand funerals.[40]

Having described some of the court pageantry it is probably best to end with a word of warning. Today the media are so powerful that they can indeed sway general public opinion. This was hardly the case in Tudor times, and many people must have passed their whole lives without ever seeing the monarch for themselves. The Tudor 'propaganda campaign' was certainly not as carefully thought-out as a modern marketing campaign by a large company or a political party's election campaign. Evidence of this includes the lack of control the Tudors showed over the printing press and the little use they made of it. The French court was much better at exploiting its potential. From the late fifteenth century onwards most great court occasions in France were marked by a printed summary of the event, which would include good quality illustrations. This was very rarely the case in England and when they were produced, the quality was poor.[41]

The government was also often lax in exercising control even over important civic occasions. In August 1554 Mary and her new husband Philip of Spain made their state entry into London. This was a very unpopular marriage, but still nobody thought to check the plans for the various tableaux-vivant which would be seen by the royal couple as they travelled through the city.

The personnel involved in organising these celebrations were certainly not checked. The Court of Aldermen of London included on their planning team two men who must have been suspect to Mary. One of these was Thomas Berthelet, who had been the King's Printer in Henry VIII's time and had printed a number of anti-clerical works. The other was Richard Grafton, who had been King's Printer to Edward VI and had printed, among other things, the proclamation of Lady Jane Grey in 1553. This was despite the fact that the instigators of Wyatt's failed rebellion were still rotting publicly in London, giving clear messages about Mary's attitude to disobedient Protestants.

One scene of the pageant showed the Nine Worthies, together with Henry VIII and Edward VI. Henry VIII was even shown with a book in his hand with *Verbum Dei* (the Word of God) written on it. This was hardly the message that the very Roman Catholic Mary wanted to hear, but the Bishop of Winchester, Stephen Gardiner, only did something about the matter after Mary and Philip had seen it and then only by forcing the painter to paint the words out. This hardly suggests that royal control in these matters was very firmly exercised.[42]

Most court entertainments were, in any case, very exclusive. Even the largest-scale indoor entertainments were only open to a small circle of very wealthy and powerful people. The general public never got to see them at all. The very elaborate symbolism surrounding these events was also probably lost on many people, even courtiers. The message behind the red dragons used to celebrate Prince Arthur's marriage seems clear, but there were indications even at the time that some people didn't understand what they had seen. Edward Hall's long description of King Francis's jousting costumes at the Field of Cloth of Gold and his interpretation of them is followed by the comment that this was *his* interpretation of them, and that he couldn't be certain.[43]

In Elizabeth's reign matters must have become even more complicated. Without the explanation of the knights' impresas which was given as they were presented at tournaments, there might well be confusion as to their meaning. The finer points of meaning in the elaborately symbolic portraits of Elizabeth, like the one at Hatfield, must have been lost even on some of the courtiers.

The elaborate game of paying court to Elizabeth as the Queen of Love and Beauty must have become ever more hollow as Elizabeth aged. Artists had the sense to paint Elizabeth as a young, or at least youngish woman even into her old age but this could hardly have hidden the truth. On the other hand, Elizabeth wasn't stupid and she must have known flattery when she saw it. The intention wasn't really that anyone should believe this ritual flattery. The important point was that it reminded everyone that Elizabeth was the Queen and that the courtiers needed to keep on the right side of her. The clever use of symbols, the imaginative poetry and all the other trappings just made the game more interesting for everyone involved. In any case, it wasn't necessary for most people to understand the symbolism involved in court entertainments. Power was held in very few hands in the sixteenth century. As long as the particular people or person you were aiming at understood, then nobody else really mattered. It was only necessary to impress the general public to a certain extent, as they really didn't have any political power.

The most basic aim of any great court entertainment, of any of Elizabeth's progresses or of any great state occasion like a coronation or a royal funeral was to remind everyone that the Tudors were the rightful monarchs and here to stay. The symbolism, the allusions to classical mythology and theories of government were for the select few. The populace at large saw the glamour of fabulous wealth on display and maybe a few of them thought of the power that went with it and thought twice about questioning it.

FOUR

Religion and the Ritual Year

The celebrations which marked the passing of the seasons were almost all linked with the Christian liturgical year. Under the circumstances, it was inevitable that the religious changes of the sixteenth century should alter the way that the ritual year was celebrated.

The ritual year was by no means standard throughout England at this time. Some festivals were only found in certain parts of the country and were never celebrated nationally. An example of this was rushbearing, or the blessing of the rush harvest. Rushes were used either loose or made into matting as a floor covering, while dried rushes soaked in tallow were a popular form of lighting. They were therefore an important resource, so holding a thanksgiving service for them was quite natural. Rushes were used throughout the country but for some reason rushbearing only took place in the north-west, in Cheshire, Derbyshire, Lancashire and Westmorland.[1]

Even generally-kept festivals such as Easter were not celebrated in exactly the same way all over the country. For example, by the time the rite was suppressed, the Easter Sepulchre had become usual in urban parishes but wasn't found in all rural churches.[2] It cannot be assumed that just because something was being celebrated in one parish it was being celebrated everywhere.

There was, though, a whole range of festivals that were celebrated nationally. Before looking at the celebrations themselves, it is necessary to consider the changes in religion that took place at the time, since their effect on these festivals was so great. The subject is extremely complicated and has generated a great deal of literature, so no more than a brief outline will be given here.

The Reformation is often presented very simply, as if all the monarchs involved had clear, well-defined goals that they were trying to achieve in religious affairs. In general terms they may have known what they were aiming at, but no monarch of the time had the luxury of taking religious matters in isolation. They had to consider the political implications of the changes they made or wanted to make. Changes were sometimes impossible to enforce or concessions might have to be made to keep the peace. The Reformation in England was therefore a mixture of political necessity and the religious feelings of the people in power at any one time.

Henry VIII is often assumed to have been a Protestant, since he set himself up as head of the Church in place of the Pope. This was far from the case. It was high treason to call the king a 'heretic, schismatic, tyrant, infidel or usurper of the crown'.[3] In other words, Henry saw himself as upholder of the True Faith, rather than as wanting extensive reform. He was also interested in far more than merely granting himself the divorce that the Pope denied him. He wanted to make the Church subject to the Crown, without any troublesome foreign powers interfering.[4] Henry was basically happy with church worship the way it always had been, but he had a problem. There was considerable opposition to the idea of the king being the head of the Church, and to achieve his ends Henry needed the support of ministers like Thomas Cromwell who were interested in Church reform. Henry was therefore pushed into allowing more reform than he really intended, although at the time he died the Church of England was still essentially a Catholic Church.

It was under Henry's son Edward and Lord Protector Somerset, the regent, that the English Church became Protestant. However, Edward's reign lasted only six and a half years, so his sister Mary was able to reverse his reforms and to re-establish the old customs in church worship.

Mary herself reigned for only five and a half years. Her successor, Elizabeth, was hardly likely to allow the Church to remain Catholic. Her parents' marriage would never have been seen as valid by the Pope, so that she would have been viewed as illegitimate, owing her throne not to birthright but to papal authority alone.[5] Elizabeth had also been given the kind of education that was likely to make her a Protestant. She did not enjoy religious debate in the way Henry VIII had done, but she had read the works of Calvin and other Protestant authors as a child and was sympathetic towards Protestantism.[6] She was therefore interested in making the English Church Protestant, but she was no zealot. She wanted a lasting religious settlement and knew that could only be based on some kind of consensus. She was prepared to take a flexible view of matters if necessary.

Practical considerations were also brought into the reforms. The number of holy days observed was greatly reduced partly because they were holidays, or days off for workers. After the break with Rome the Crown abolished most of the holidays occurring during the Westminster Law Terms and during the summer months which were the busiest time of the agricultural year. It was a matter of great dispute in the late fifteenth and early sixteenth centuries as to whether the workers or the employers should meet the cost of holidays and simply cutting the number was an easy way around the problem.[7] The whole situation was complicated further by the feelings of local communities and even of individual priests. Some communities clung to old ways as long as possible while others were fairly happy to embrace the new ones. Trouble might also develop between a priest who felt one way and someone in the congregation who took the opposite view. An example of this occurred when a reforming ex-friar by the name of Robert Ward moved into Barking in Suffolk, an area which favoured religious conservatism in 1535. Ward and his supporters disagreed so violently with John Adryan, the parish priest, that at one stage Ward was nearly stabbed.[8] With feelings running so high it was understandable that the authorities were very careful about what seasonable celebrations were and weren't allowed.

The viewpoints of those for and against reform are not easy to summarise. Of course not all Protestants and Catholics felt the same way about all things. The main Protestant or reformist viewpoint was basically that the study of the Bible was central to Christian belief and that saints or customs not mentioned in it should be discarded. The Protestants also believed that the bread and wine used at mass were no more than bread and wine, while to the Catholics, once it was consecrated, they were literally the body and blood of Christ and had to be treated with enormous respect as a result. Another big difference was the belief in purgatory. This was the place that was believed to be in store for the dead, where they would be purged of their sins before entering heaven. Prayers for the dead were thought to speed the soul's progress through purgatory. Protestants saw no biblical basis for the existence of purgatory at all and believed that the souls of Christian believers went straight to heaven.

All this sounds like so much dry theology to people with no Christian belief or background, but the resulting change to the Church and therefore to everyday life was enormous. First of all, the physical appearance of the church building changed. Many of the old, comforting objects disappeared, being seen as mere objects which encouraged superstition under the new order. The statues of saints and the lights that burnt before them went. The chantries, special chapels set up by wealthy families where priests could pray for the souls of their dead, were destroyed. The rich wall-paintings which decorated so many churches were whitewashed over.

The church services changed too. Catholic mass was far more elaborate than the ceremonies approved by the Protestants. An example was the start of the high mass on Sundays, which involved a procession around the church in which salt and water were exorcised, blessed and mixed. The altars and the congregation were sprinkled with it and the holy water could be taken home to ensure a blessing there. To the Protestants, holy water was just water and to endow it with special powers was nonsense. The ceremony had to go.[9]

The religious changes were the most obvious force at work in altering the ritual year but they were not the only ones. Traditions are not as timeless as we like to think. They change as society changes. A good example is the modern Christmas. It does have some roots in the past but not as many as we often imagine. The Christmas tree itself was an old Rhineland tradition, but one that is not recorded even in Germany before 1520. Father Christmas may have associations with older figures such as St Nicholas but nobody seems to have thought of a personification of Christmas at all until the seventeenth century. Christmas now is seen as a time for families, whereas in the Middle Ages it was a time when communities celebrated together. Modern Christmas is not very like medieval Christmas at all.[10]

A sixteenth-century Christmas too was very different from the modern version. The season of advent was a time of fasting. Christmas Eve was particularly strictly kept, with no meat, cheese or eggs being eaten. The celebrations only began on Christmas Day when three masses were said, the first one starting before dawn. The genealogy of Christ was sung and everyone in the church would hold lighted tapers which must have given a sense of drama to the occasion. After the service they could go home and enjoy their first unrestricted meal since Advent Sunday, which was four weeks earlier.

Tudor Christmas is often represented as twelve days of ceaseless enjoyment when wealthy people kept open house. This wasn't quite the truth. A great deal of entertaining did go on, but it tended to be between social equals. The Earl of Northumberland and the Duke of Somerset entertained the local gentry and a variety of important clergy in the 1510s. A wealthy man might also entertain his various tenants, as Sir Henry Willoughby did in the 1520s.[11] All twelve days were also not celebrated equally. Most of the twelve days of Christmas were saint's days, but the main three days for celebration were Christmas Day, New Year's Day and Epiphany, or Twelfth Night.

New Year's Day was an odd celebration for the Tudors, because they saw the new year as beginning on 25 March. On this day was held the Feast of Annunciation, celebrating the time when Mary was first told of the forthcoming birth of Jesus. It was therefore deemed a logical date on which to begin the Christian year. (The celebration of 1 January was a remainder of

the old Roman habit of celebrating the new year on that date.)
The main feature of the day was the giving and receiving of gifts.
It is difficult to know how far down society gift-giving went. It is
frequently recorded by the upper classes, but there are no records
as to whether or not ordinary people did the same. Thomas
Tusser mentions Christmas gifts in his usual bad poetry, so maybe
the habit was general:

> At Christmas of Christ many Carols we sing,
> and give many gifts in the joy of that King.[12]

If gifts were given lower down the social scale, they would have
been purely a personal matter. At the top of society they were of
political significance and were treated with great ceremony.

The instructions for the reception of the royal gifts at Henry
VII's court still survive.[13] The King would finish dressing on New
Year's morning, and just as he put his shoes on a fanfare would be
sounded and one of the Queen's servants would come in carrying
a gift from her, followed by the servants of other important
courtiers bearing their master's gifts. The Queen, meanwhile, also
received gifts in her own chamber.

The acceptance or rejection of a gift was vital. In 1532 Henry
VIII accepted the gift of Anne Boleyn (whom he was to marry
in 1533) but pointedly rejected the gift of Katherine of Aragon.
In 1571 Elizabeth refused the gift of the Duke of Norfolk despite
the fact that she was obviously impressed by it, a very lavish jewel,
and would have loved to have kept it. The Duke had become
involved in the revolt of the Northern Earls and was in prison in
the Tower at the time. He was executed on 2 June 1572.[14]

The gifts sent to royalty varied considerably. It was quite
common for the upper classes to send money but from subjects
lower down the social scale even quite humble gifts were
considered acceptable. Queen Mary's Serjeant of the Pastry sent
her a quince pie while her hosier sent three pairs of hose.[15]

The gift-giving was not all one way. Those who presented the
monarch with a gift expected something in return and monarchs
had to show their generosity by making sure that the gifts they

gave exceeded in value the gifts they had received. In 1534, for example, Lord Lisle gave Henry VIII £20 but received a gilt cup with a cover which weighed 28¼ ounces. Lord Lisle's servant who presented the gift was rewarded with 20s. Ordinary knights' servants were rewarded with a mere 13s 4d. The regulations of Henry VIII's household also describe a sliding scale for rewarding such messengers. The Queen's messenger received 10 marks 'if hee bee a knight' but only 8 marks if he were merely an esquire. The reward was less for other messengers but even earls' and countesses' messengers, the lowliest ones mentioned, received 40s.[16] The grander nobles also received and gave gifts in similar style. The Earl of Northumberland was awakened by minstrels playing outside his door on New Year's Day. A fanfare then heralded his gifts just as it did for his royal master.[17]

The most sumptuous feast of the year was 6 January, Twelfth Night, which was also the feast of the Epiphany and so the day started with a church service, but it would end with some form of feasting and entertainment. At the court the King wore his full royal robes and crown, and often an elaborate masque or similar entertainment would take place.

One popular tradition in ecclesiastical communities around Christmas was that of the Boy Bishop. This sometimes took place on 6 December, the feast of St Nicholas, the patron saint of children, but it could also take place on Holy Innocents' Day, 28 December. There were a great number of local variations on the theme, but a boy from the choir would be chosen in some way to lead the community for a short period and would do everything apart from celebrating mass. At St Paul's Cathedral the Boy Bishop even led a procession through London to bless the city while many other Boy Bishops also processed around their communities, usually collecting money for the parish funds as they went. This custom, which started in the tenth century, became so popular that many parish churches took it up. At least seven London parishes appointed Boy Bishops by the 1520s and many had elaborate vestments for their use. St Mary at Hill paid for a mitre in 1485–6 which was fit for a real bishop, being garnished with silver, enamel, pearls and fake jewels.[18] The Boy

Bishops went on being a popular institution until Henry VIII banned them in 1541. He seems to have done so because they mocked the Church authorities and by implication, the head of the Church. They did reappear briefly under Mary but the custom had lost its old vigour. Outside London the Boy Bishops only appeared in cathedrals, and then disappeared again under Elizabeth.

Another famous Christmas institution was the Lord of Misrule who supervised entertainments and generally caused chaos. They were known by a wide variety of names, such as 'Prester John' who held court at Canterbury College between 1414 and 1430 or 'King of Christmas' who paraded through Norwich in 1443.[19] In fact, they were not confined to Christmas, and were often appointed to supervise various parish festivities in the summer. It is one of these summer Lords of Misrule who is so famously described by Philip Stubbes in his *Anatomie of Abuses*:

> First of all the wilde-heds of the Parish, conventing together, chuse them a Ground-Captain (of all mischiefe) whome they innoble with the title of 'my Lord of Mis-rule', and him they crowne with great solemnity and adopt for their king. the king annoited chuseth forth twentie, fortie, threescore or a hundred lustie Guttes, like to him self, to weighte uppon his lordly Majestie, and to guard his noble person . . .'[20]

Philip Stubbes goes on to complain bitterly about the Lord of Misrule disrupting church services, something which was a feature of the summer lord rather than the Christmas one. In some places there was the custom that the summer Lord and Lady (if there was one) attended a church service in their full robes before taking up office over the summer games. The process does seem to have been rather rowdy as in 1583 the youth of Wootton, near Oxford, got into trouble with the archdeacon for letting these festivities get out of hand.[21] On the other hand, the disruption of a church service can hardly have been a great problem.

The earlier royal Tudors were very keen on the idea. Henry VII had not only a Lord of Misrule but also an Abbot of Unreason, and in 1525 Henry VIII not only had one of his own but also appointed another for the household of the young Princess Mary. They reached the peak of their popularity under Edward VI, when the Duke of Northumberland was keen to keep his master entertained and lavished great sums of money on the idea. Edward's Lord of Misrule, George Ferrers, had an entire retinue which consisted of everything from an astronomer to a Master of Requests.[22] The institution was strongest and lasted longest in educational establishments like the Inns of Court. Some of the Lord of Misrule's exploits in these places would certainly be condemned today. At the Inner Temple a fox and a cat were let loose in the hall on St Stephen's Day (Boxing Day) and hunted with a pack of hounds until the two were torn to pieces.[23]

Queen Mary did not continue the institution, perhaps because it was so closely associated with Northumberland, whom she had executed. It was generally discouraged under Elizabeth who was nervous of the public disorder the exploits could lead to. Even without royal discouragement, the fashion was soon to wane. The disorder of the 1640s hardly made anyone feel like encouraging more chaos.

Another popular part of the Christmas season was wassailing. 'Wassail' was taken from the Anglo-Saxon meaning 'your good health' and the centre-piece of the occasion was the wassail bowl.

Surviving wassail songs date mostly from the eighteenth century and descriptions of how wassailing was performed in specific places date from the seventeenth century onwards. There is a description of how Henry VII's wassail was to take place, and it was all very stiff and formal. The steward and the treasurer had to be present with their staves of office, together with the court in full splendour:

Item the chappell to stand on the one side of the hall and when the Steward cometh in at the hall doore with the wassell, he must crie three tymes, wassell, wassell, wassell, and then the chappell to answere with a good songe . . .[24]

Judging from the surviving evidence, most wassails were far more fun, if considerably less grand. It was common for people drinking together at this time to share communal vessels even at the top of society. At that most elaborate of occasions, the Field of Cloth of Gold, an Italian observer was horrified to see the ladies of the English court passing a wine flask and large cups 'which circulated more than twenty times' between themselves and the French lords until they were drunk. The communal wassail bowl was just part of normal drinking practice.[25]

The wassail had elements of a fertility rite about it as, at least in areas where orchards were important, participants often went out and drank to the health of the orchard, or to the biggest tree in it. John Aubrey describes this in the late seventeenth century and also describes West Country ploughmen drinking to the 'ox with the crumpled horn'. Whatever the finer details of the wassail in different areas, the most important part of the ceremony was the communal drinking.

The first Monday after Twelfth Night was known as Plough Monday. Before the widespread introduction of winter cereal crops in the twentieth century Plough Monday was when the ploughing would begin. A plough was an expensive item and only the wealthier villagers would have their own. Other less fortunate farmers had to wait their turn to use the communal one. The communal plough could be kept in the church and a plough light might also be kept burning before the Sacrament or the Rood. Plough Monday was celebrated by the young men of the parish who would harness themselves to a plough and drag it around the parish, ploughing up the ground before the door of anyone who refused to pay them something.[26] The Plough Monday fun must have made the dreary return to work after Christmas more bearable but even so the ceremonies did not survive the Reformation. These festivities were banned in 1548 under Edward VI. The plough lights in churches had been banned even earlier, in 1538, when Henry VIII banned most of the sacred lights in churches.

The next important feast after Christmas was Candlemas, or the feast of the Purification of the Virgin, which took place on 2 February. It supposedly marked the ritual purification of Mary after the birth of Christ, but in England it was seen more importantly as the official opening of spring. The Candlemas church service involved all the parishioners processing with candles which were blessed and lit by the priest. In theory the candles represented Christ but it was almost inevitable that they were seen as having special powers. They were thought to be particularly potent at driving away evil spirits but they could also be used for harm. There was a belief that witches dropped wax from the holy candles into the footprints of those they hated, causing their feet to rot.[27]

St Luke's Gospel describes the presentation of the baby Jesus at the Temple in Jerusalem.[28] The prophet Simeon took the baby in his arms, realising that this was the Messiah. Some towns commemorated this with one of the ever-popular processions, such as the one which took place at Beverley in Yorkshire. One of the members of the Guild of the Blessed Virgin dressed as Mary, followed by two men dressed as Simeon and Joseph and two men dressed as angels. The 'angels' carried a frame which held twenty-four candles, while the remaining members of the guild walked behind, also carrying candles. Musicians followed the procession. Once the procession reached the church 'Mary' presented a doll to 'Simeon' at the altar while the rest of the procession had their candles blessed.[29]

There were so many superstitions surrounding Candlemas that it was an obvious target for the reformers, who also disliked the close association of the festival with the Virgin Mary. Henry VIII obviously enjoyed Candlemas as he protected it by proclamation in 1539, although he was careful to stress that the blessed candles should not be seen as being magical in any way. This made no difference. Candlemas candles were still lit in times of storm or sickness and placed in the hands of the dying. The Protestant Duke of Somerset would not stand for it and after 1548 it was abolished. Like so many other things, it was revived by Mary but was finally banned by Elizabeth in 1559.

Not long after Candlemas came St Valentine's Day. It was evidently celebrated in some way in the late fifteenth century as it is mentioned in the Paston letters three times in the 1470s.[30] It seems that valentines were chosen by lot from among a group of friends, who then had to buy their valentine a gift. In the household of William Petre, the steward's accounts show gold trinkets and lengths of cloth being given to valentines chosen by lot. One of the maids was even fortunate enough to draw Sir William himself one year, and was given a whole quarter's extra wages as her valentine. There is no way of knowing if this was a general custom throughout the country or if it was simply a pastime for the wealthy. In any case the whole festival was low key, seen mainly as just a bit of fun. In the days when marriages were arranged for most people it could scarcely be anything more.

The next important celebrations were the most elaborate and dramatic church services of the year, being those which surrounded Lent and Holy Week. Holy Week marked the end of the long Lent fast, which lasted six and a half weeks. The beginning of Lent was marked by Shrovetide, which started on Shrove Sunday, the seventh Sunday before Easter. It was the last opportunity for fun before the Lent fast began when meat, eggs and cheese were forbidden. Stocks of these forbidden foods which couldn't be kept had to be used up. That was why the Monday after Shrove Sunday was known as 'Collup Monday', a collup being a cut of fried or roasted meat. Shrove Tuesday was also celebrated with entertainments like plays, music and masques in royal circles. The Shrovetide celebrations were quite rowdy and this is understandable. The early spring was a difficult time, with the weather still being cold and wet and food stocks running low. The six weeks of Lent also lay ahead. It was a time when some kind of celebration was necessary. Not all the celebrations associated with Shrovetide would be considered acceptable today. Threshing the cock was one such pastime. A cock was tethered with a string and then people tried to kill it by throwing things at it. If you killed the cock you won it as a prize. There were other variations on this process. Sometimes the cock was buried with just its head sticking out of the ground and then blindfolded people would try to kill it with a flail. Evidently hens could also be used as this is the game that Thomas Tusser describes:

At Shroftide to shroving, go thresh the fat hen,
if blindfold can kil her, then give it thy men.[31]

Once Lent started the rowdiness had to stop. Not only were
there restrictions on diet, but in theory sex was forbidden too.
Churches took on a different appearance as the altars and the
lectern would be hidden away beneath cloths. This symbolised
that the way to salvation was hidden. A Lent veil would even hide
the chancel from the nave, being lifted only during the gospel
reading during mass.[32]

Holy Week began with Palm Sunday. The story of Christ's
entry into Jerusalem was read and then branches of greenery were
blessed for use in the procession that followed. It was obviously
impossible to find palms in England so other alternatives like yew
and willow were used. During the service crosses were made,
probably from the blessed foliage, and these, like the Candlemas
candles, were seen as being useful protection against evil.[33] As
the 'palms' were being blessed a special shrine containing the
church's relics and the blessed Sacrament (to represent Christ)
was prepared. This would be processed around the outside of
the church by the clergy, while the laity walked in their own
procession. The two processions met to come into the church. As
they did so, the Lent veil was drawn up although it was lowered
again later.[34]

On the Wednesday, the passage concerning the veil in the
Temple in Jerusalem being rent was read and the Lent cloth
dropped to reveal the chancel once more, this time for good.[35] On
Maundy Thursday the altars were stripped, washed with water
and wine, and generally spring-cleaned. Most people also went to
confession.

On Good Friday the ceremony of Creeping to the Cross took
place. The clergy went on hands and knees up to a crucifix held
up before the altar. They kissed the feet of the figure of Christ
upon it and then the crucifix was carried down to the church for
the laity to do the same. Another ceremony which took place
in many churches on the same day was the preparation of the
Easter Sepulchre, where an image of Christ and the consecrated

host would be laid. The Easter Sepulchre took various forms, sometimes being a permanent stone niche, sometimes being made of wood, but the idea was that it would be covered with a cloth overnight to represent the sealed tomb of Christ. It was often watched over by members of the congregation who would tend the candles surrounding it. On a more earthly note they also made sure that nobody stole the pyx in which the Sacrament was kept, as it was often extremely valuable.

The Easter Day service began with the extinguishing of all lights, which would then be re-lighted from a fire lit by flints by the priest. The Easter Sepulchre was also opened. As soon as mass was over, Lent ended and celebrations could begin although it was no good hoping to be given a hot-cross bun. These are first recorded only in the eighteenth century.[36]

The elaborate ceremonies did not survive the Reformation. The Easter Sepulchre, Creeping to the Cross and the blessing of the greenery for the Palm Sunday procession were all banned. Easter continued to be celebrated by the Church, of course, but in a less elaborate form. Some parts of the old ceremonies still survived outside the church. During the eighteenth century it was common to go out and cut greenery to bring home on Palm Sunday, a practice which survived into the early years of the twentieth century.[37] Easter also remained a time for general celebration as it was seen as a celebration of the return of spring. Anyone who could afford it had new clothes and Easter Monday was a favourite time for sports and fairs. The weather would most likely still be too uncertain for the summer round of entertainments to begin, but it was a sign that they were not far away.

The festival of St George on 23 April fell at about the same time as Easter. In the early middle ages Edward the Confessor was usually seen as the patron saint of England but both Edward III and Henry V felt that he was not a warlike enough saint for the job. Both kings were engaged in war with France and St George seemed a more suitable saint to rally their troops in battle. He proved to be a very popular choice. By the sixteenth century a number of towns held processions in his honour on St George's Day, often including not only statues of the saint himself but also model dragons. By 1530 the day had all the makings of a national celebration, which is exactly what you would have expected the Tudors to have encouraged. Unfortunately St George fell foul of the reformers. He is not a biblical saint and so his worship was forbidden. In a few places, such as Norwich and Chester, the procession survived without St George's image, with the dragon becoming the centre-piece. The Chester procession died out in the seventeenth century, although the Norwich one survived until the nineteenth as it formed part of the celebrations around the election of the new mayor.[38]

St George's Day and Easter brought not only the promise of better weather but also of good times socially. Social life on a large scale was very difficult during the winter. It was only very wealthy people who had houses which were big enough for large-scale entertainments and these houses were hardly open to ordinary people. The largest building was the church but even before the Reformation people were not too happy about using this for purely social occasions. There was also the practical problem that it was a difficult building to heat. Communal feasts therefore had to take place either outside or in barns, something which was only practical during the warmer months. The coming of spring meant not only a return to more pleasant life generally, but also a return to communal social life.

The most famous of the spring celebrations was that of May Day. It was one of the great annual celebrations which was not a Christian festival, but simply a celebration of the return of summer warmth. It was common for young people to 'make the May' by going to woods and collecting greenery while wearing garlands of flowers. There were numerous bawdy songs associated with this and reformers endlessly criticised the celebrations. An example of this criticism can be found in Philip Stubbes' *Anatomie of Abuses*. Stubbes seems to have enjoyed criticising just about everything, so May games were hardly likely to escape. Stubbes wrote 'I have heard it credibly reported (and that viva voce) by men of great gravitie and reputation, that of fortie, threescore, or a hundred maides going to the wood over night there have scaresly the third part of them returned undefiled.'[39] Stubbes' men of 'great gravitie' evidently enjoyed a good bit of gossip as much as anyone else. The truth behind Maying seems to have been rather less scandalous than the rumours. If May Day had lived up to its reputation you would have expected a boom in births nine months later, but this was not the case. The busiest time for conceptions was late summer. After all, an English May is often a bit too damp and cold to be thinking of spending all night in the woods.[40]

Maying was a very popular tradition in which even royalty liked to get involved. Edward Hall describes a very elaborate royal May Day celebration, when Henry VIII and Katherine of Aragon and their retinue were 'surprised' by no less a person than Robin Hood himself, accompanied by his merry men. In fact, they were the royal bodyguard, the Yeomen of the Guard, dressed in green for the occasion. All 200 of the yeomen shot arrows at once to impress their royal master. Edward Hall records the noise as being 'straunge and great'. The royal retinue were then led to an 'arbour' in the woods made of green boughs. It was very large for an arbour, having a hall, a great chamber and an inner chamber. Here the royal party were entertained to an 'outlaw's breakfast' of venison and wine.[41]

The royal May was, of course, hardly a typical one but it contained elements that were part of most Tudor May celebrations. In his *Survey of London*, John Stow describes the London May of his youth as including 'divers warlike shows, with good archers . . .'.[42] The Yeomen of the Guard's display of their skills was a fitting entertainment for the day just as the royal 'arbour' was a grander version of the ordinary people's collection of green boughs to decorate their houses.

A centre-piece of the May celebrations was the maypole. Some places had large, permanent maypoles, but many were set up each year, like the large one described by John Stow which was set up in front of the church of St Andrew in Cornhill.[43] The maypole was often painted and decorated with greenery and people did dance around it, but exactly what dances they performed are unknown. The ribbons that modern maypole dancers hold were not added until the nineteenth century. Protestant reformers did object to maypoles as 'idols' but in fact they seem to have been more a simple focal point of the games than anything else. They were sometimes indirectly responsible for public disorder because stealing a neighbouring village's maypole was a favourite sport of the season. Such rivalry lead to violence on many occasions, such as in Hertfordshire in 1602.[44]

The spring was, of course, the time when everything started growing again. The new crops in the fields were watched anxiously and they were blessed by the church to ensure a good harvest on Rogation Sunday, the fifth Sunday after Easter. Processions of clergy and people walked around the fields carrying the church cross and banners. The people who carried the cross and banners were often paid with money or food and sometimes the day ended with a communal meal. The Rogation processions were another victim of reform. They were not formally banned but the general air of disapproval in the 1540s caused them to die out. It was possible that the processions could be seen as superstitious by the reformers and perhaps nobody felt like taking a chance.[45]

Whitsun fell at about the same time as Rogationtide. It was the celebration of the coming of the Holy Spirit to the first Christians but in lay terms it was a favourite time for holding games and church ales. In a few places, such as Leicester and Exeter, splendid processions were held. In the fifteenth century the Leicester procession included a statue of the Virgin, suitably robed and crowned, carried by four people together with statues of the twelve apostles, or possibly twelve people dressed to represent them. The unmarried young women of the town also followed the procession. Unfortunately lack of evidence means that nobody knows how far into the sixteenth century the tradition survived.[46]

Chester celebrated Whitsun with a play. Originally this had taken place at Corpus Christi (see next page) but for some reason it was moved in the late fifteenth century. By the early sixteenth century it had gown into a cycle of biblical pageants provided by the craft guilds and then it expanded again into a sequence of twenty-four different subjects requiring both Monday and

Tuseday for the performance. The Norwich Whitsun pageants also spread over the Monday and Tuesday. In both cases the pageants were drawn on carts around the city.[47]

Corpus Christi was a very popular festival which took place on the Thursday after Trinity Sunday, which in turn was the eighth Sunday after Easter. This made it another summer festival so it was an ideal time for yet another procession. It was particularly popular in towns, where rival parishes seemed to have enjoyed the competition of trying to outdo each other. All records surviving from early fifteenth-century town corporations or urban parishes have evidence of Corpus Christi processions.[48] The festival itself had been proclaimed in 1317 by Pope John XXII in order to remind Christians of the holy nature of the Eucharist. Unfortunately this meant that the holiday had no chance at all of surviving the Reformation, because, as described above, the Protestant reformers objected strongly to the idea of the Eucharist being anything other than simple bread and wine. The procession, while it was allowed, was indeed an excellent opportunity for the display of civic pride. The host, which was consecrated for the occasion, was carried in a shrine by the local clergy, with a canopy over it to protect it from rain and birds. The shrine could be very elaborate indeed. The one used in York was of silver and crystal. Behind the clergy would walk the town councillors and craft guilds. Elaborate crosses and banners were carried, those at Coventry being made of silk damask and velvet and embroidered with gold thread. The largest London procession was provided by the Skinners' Company and had over 200 clergy walking in it.

Corpus Christi was also celebrated with plays by the sixteenth century. The plays were on biblical themes and varied in complexity from place to place. Sometimes just a single play was held, but sometimes there were whole cycles of plays, like the ones held at Coventry. The York cycle contained no less than fifty-two plays. If all of them were performed it would have taken at least twenty-one hours. In fact, exactly how the more elaborate plays were staged is a mystery. It would have been difficult to perform them as part of the procession so they probably were performed afterwards. Perhaps only some of the plays were produced each year. On the other hand some towns, including London, did not produce any plays at all at this time, although why this was the case nobody knows. Sadly, the plays, like the festival itself, fell foul of the reformers and were abolished by the 1570s.[49]

Midsummer followed soon after Corpus Christi. It was technically the feast of St John, but the main celebrations were not connected with the religious feast. It was a favourite time for bonfires but exactly how widespread they were is impossible to say. The main way of finding evidence for local traditions is via payments for them in accounts, and the bonfire wood could be collected locally and not paid for. They were evidently part of the summer celebrations in London as John Stow records them in his *Survey of London* with evident nostalgia:

> In the months of June and July, on the vigils of festival days, and on the same festival days in the evenings after the sunsetting, there were usually made bonfires in the streets, every man bestowing wood or labour towards them; the wealthier sort also, before their doors near to the said bonfires, would set out tables on the vigils, furnished with sweet bread and good drinks and on the festival days with meats and drinks plentifulls, whereunto they would invite their neighbours and passengers also to sit and be merry with them in great familiarity . . .[50]

In some Tudor towns, though, midsummer was marked not only by bonfires but also by marching watches. The London watch was particularly spectacular, with about 4,000 people taking part. There were morris dancers, model giants and pageants. The 1521 procession even included a pageant on the theme of 'Pluto' which included a serpent which spat fireballs into the crowd.[51] The marches did sometimes include pageants on religious themes but they were not religious events in themselves. On this level there was no reason why they could not have continued unchanged throughout the sixteenth century. However, the authorities did mistrust them. Even today large-scale events of any kind taking place in a town are carefully policed. In the sixteenth century riots could break out all too easily and the tense political atmosphere did not help. In 1539 Henry VIII banned the London midsummer watch on the excuse of saving money and it was only allowed once again, in 1548, by Lord Protector Somerset. He only did so in compensation for having banned the Corpus Christi celebrations, which was a very unpopular move. The marching watches did last longer in other cities, but they gradually became less popular and stopped altogether in the mid-seventeenth century.

Another more enduring celebration of midsummer involved a fiery wheel. A cartwheel would be packed around the edge with straw, set alight and then rolled down a hill. If it rolled the whole way without going out it was said to foretell a good harvest. This is one of the few traditions which really can be traced back to pagan times, the wheel being seen as a symbol of the sun.[52]

The last good weather of the year in late summer and early autumn was marked by the wakes. These were the feast days celebrating the dedication of parish churches which would be marked with communal entertainments. It seems that people made the most of the opportunity by staggering the dates when they were celebrated so that neighbouring parishes could entertain each other. This must have been why Henry VIII decreed that all churches had to hold their dedication feast on the first Sunday in October, saying that too much time was being taken up with too frequent holidays.

Wakes were not described in detail by anyone at the time, unlike the May games, but they may possibly have got out of hand from time to time. Thomas Tusser, a man who generally approved of celebrations, did not have a high opinion of them:

> Then Everie wanton may daunce at hir will,
> both Tomkin with Tomlin, and Jankin with Gill.[53]

Very similar to the wakes were church ales. These were not held in celebration of any particular event but rather were fund-raising events that churches held from time to time. They were held throughout the summer months and included a great deal of eating and drinking. Philip Stubbes, of course, dismissed them as times of gluttony and drunkenness, and also because the money raised from them was used for the maintenance of the church. Stubbes was a puritan and objected to the money being used to buy 'cuppes for the celebration of the Sacrament, surplesses for Sir John [i.e. the priest] and other such necessaries . . .' of which he did not approve.[54] Stubbes disapproved of so much that his criticism does not mean that church ales were disapproved of in general. Even so, like so many other communal festivities of the time the church ales gradually faded in popularity and died out completely.

Another highlight of the same time of year was the harvest home. There seem to have been numerous superstitions associated with the harvest home and concerned in particular with the last sheaf of corn harvested. Paul Hentzner, a German visitor to England in 1598, witnessed one harvest home near Windsor:

As we were returning to our inn, we happened to meet some country people celebrating their Harvest-home, their last load of corn they crown with flowers, having besides an image richly dressed, by which perhaps they would signify Ceres, this they keep moving about, while men and women, men and maid servants riding through the streets in the cart shout as loud as they can till they arrive at the barn.[55]

The highlight of the harvest was the harvest home supper. Tusser talks of giving a goose to the ploughman after the harvest is complete[56] and stresses that the harvest labour force should be well fed during their hard work and feasted at the end. The very real relief at getting the harvest in must have added to the joy of the occasion. Tusser stressed that harvest was a time to be thankful to God.[57]

The biggest Christian festival of the autumn was the feast of the dead, called Hallowtide or Allantide. It was a spectacular event, designed to help the passage of the souls of the dead through purgatory. After evensong the church bells would be rung to comfort the dead in purgatory and the churches would be illuminated with candles. Sometimes quite elaborate entertainments were laid on as part of the service. St Mary Woolnoth in London paid for five garlanded maidens to play harps by lamplight as part of the service in 1539.[58] It was a very important festival emotionally as it provided a time when the dead could be remembered and even helped by the living. It was so much linked with the belief in purgatory, though, that despite its popularity it was not going to survive the Protestant Reformation. The feast of All Saints was retained but only to commemorate biblical saints as outstanding Christians. The bell-ringing was forbidden, as were prayers for the dead.

So far the impression is that the pleasant rituals which marked the seasons were all destroyed by Protestant reformers, but the picture is somewhat more complicated than that. For one thing, ritual celebrations did not just suddenly stop as the various monarchs changed. May Day celebrations, Lords of Misrule and many other traditions went on into Elizabeth's reign but gradually declined and often disappeared completely.

Elizabeth seems to have enjoyed many of the old festivities. She ordered a May to be performed before her in the very first year of her reign and even in the last two years of her life she was still visiting certain people on May Day and dancing in their houses.[59] She also tried to persuade the Lord Mayor of London to revive the marching watch at midsummer, but he and the corporation of London made excuses. Perhaps the enormous scale of the watch had made it so expensive and difficult to organise that they were happy to see it go. Elizabeth's accession to the throne did not in fact lead to a sudden end to many of the old celebrations. Church ales are recorded in forty-seven parishes in the 1560s. Some parishes were still crowning various types of Lords of Misrule at different times of year and there are plenty of examples of people enjoying entertainments like morris dancing and maypoles.[60] Instead, such entertainments died away gradually.

The Elizabethan Privy Council was not opposed to old pastimes like morris dancing as long as order was maintained. This was an important point. The banning of festivals on the grounds that they caused disorder was not always an excuse. John Stow notes how a May Day riot had led to the May games in

London falling out of favour: 'These great Mayings and May-games made by the governors and masters of this city . . . by means of an insurrection of youths against aliens on May-day 1517, the 9th of Henry VIII, have not been so freely used as afore . . .'.[61] Despite the threat of disorder, though, the Privy Council stated that such pastimes were lawful. In 1589 it made this quite clear in a directive to the lord-lieutenant of Oxfordshire in response to a local attempt to ban summer festivities in the Banbury area. It only objected to such entertainments if their contents were felt to be offensive to the Protestant Church, which was why the Chester cycle of Whitsun plays was banned in the 1570s.[62]

There was a strong element in society which wanted traditional festivities banned on religious grounds but towards the end of the century there was also a very real social anxiety concerning all communal entertainments. The gap between rich and poor was widening and the number of poor and landless people was increasing. Inflation was a very real threat to incomes. This, combined with the political tensions of the time, made people nervous of large gatherings and very critical of festivities like Maying, which in theory at least led to production of bastard children to add yet another burden to the parish rates. There were, however, still those who thought nostalgically of the old ways, such as John Stow who provided such loving descriptions of them in his *Survey of London*. The popularity of pastoral themes in Elizabethan literature was also to lead to a renewed interest in them in the seventeenth century.

There were also some new Protestant feast days added to the calendar. One of these was Crownation Day, the celebration of Elizabeth's accession to the throne which was celebrated on 17 November. The feast had originally been St Hugh's Day, so those who preferred the old ways could also feel quite free to celebrate. For example, at Bishop's Stortford in Hertforshire 2*s* 8*d* was spent on bread, drink and cheese for those ringing on St Hugh's Day in rejoicing of the Queen's prosperous reign.[63] The great ceremonial tournament held at court on that day is described in Chapter 3, but the celebration was also observed country wide. The usual response was to ring the church bells but more elaborate entertainments could also take place. In 1576, for example, the mayor of Liverpool ordered a great bonfire to be lit in the market square and gave instructions that all householders should light fires throughout the town. He held a banquet and also distributed sack outside the door of his house.[64] At Norwich it was celebrated by the firing of the city ordnance, and a torch-lit procession accompanied by the playing of the city waits.[65] The festival became more generally observed as time went on. It became particularly popular after the Pope excommunicated Elizabeth in 1570 and after the defeat of the Spanish Armada in 1588. However, it was never a holiday in the sense of being an automatic rest from work and it was never universally celebrated, as even some London churches did not bother to ring for it. St George, Botolph Lane, and Holy Trinity Minories both never did, for example.[66]

It might have been expected that Elizabeth's Accession Day would not go on being celebrated for long after her death, but as a celebration of the defeat of the Armada it might have lasted. However, it died away perhaps because of the celebration of the defeat of Guy Fawkes on 5 November 1605 which proved to be a more lasting Protestant festival.

The radical changes that were made to the ritual year in the sixteenth century were a very good reflection of the changes that society itself underwent at the time. It demonstrates very vividly how the changes brought about by the Reformation affected the lives of even the most ordinary Tudors. It must have been bewildering for most people to see radical changes not only in the weekly church service but also in the annual festivals. It also demonstrates how powerful the monarchy became in the sixteenth century in being able to alter the ritual year so comprehensively.

FIVE

Christenings, Weddings and Funerals

Life was not private in the sixteenth century. The main events of life were considered public events to be shared with friends and family, so that most Tudors came into the world surrounded by their mother's female friends and left it surrounded by all the friends and family who could reach them in time.

Rites of passage were public too. Christenings were the public acceptance of the child into the family of the Christian Church. At a time when marriage was as much a business arrangement as a matter of the heart, marriage was the public joining of two families as well as two people. Death was a time not only for private mourning, but also for a demonstration of the social network to which the family of the deceased belonged.

The actual religious ceremony surrounding christening was a matter of hot debate, as was to be expected at a time when all religious matters were strongly contended. Before the Reformation, the christening ceremony centred around driving the devil out of the child by the use of holy water, salt and the sign of the cross. To neglect to christen your child was to imperil its spiritual health, as the unbaptised child could not enter heaven. The reformed Church of England still insisted that christening was necessary, but the meaning of the ceremony was seriously debated. The Puritan element of the Church felt that the ceremony was completely unnecessary, and objected violently to the whole idea. In the sixteenth century there were not many people who refused to comply altogether, but this response was not unknown. Elizabeth and William Whiting of Cirencester in Gloucestershire refused to have their child baptised in 1574 and in the end the ecclesiastical commission baptised the child by force. This led to such a violent outburst from the father that he ended up spending a year in prison.[1]

Most Elizabethan children were christened within two or three days of birth. Baptisms were supposed to take place on the first Sunday or holy day after the birth, in the presence of the full congregation. This was not always the case, though. Weak children who were likely to die were christened at birth, although the fact that female midwives were allowed to perform the ceremony was another bone of contention.[2] Grander families often went to the other extreme, if the baby seemed healthy, and delayed the ceremony because of the time needed to organise what was for them an important social event. Mothers did not go to the ceremony. It was not considered good for their health to get up so soon after the birth and usually they did not go back to church until it was time for their 'churching', or ritual purification, which usually happened about a month after the birth.[3] The father often did not attend either, although he could go if he wanted to. If he did go he was expected to remain silent, and it was the godparents who spoke for the child.

The tradition was that a boy should have two godfathers and a godmother, with the opposite being true for a girl. As with many other matters surrounding baptism, the existence of godparents was a matter of contention. The godparents promised, on behalf of the child, to renounce evil and follow Christ. The Puritan element felt that no one could reasonably make this promise on behalf of someone else. This problem did not lead to too many practical difficulties as it was fairly easy to get around. As Archdeacon James Calfhill reminded his readers in 1565, the idea of godparents was invented by Pope Hyginus and, though not necessarily a problem, was not a part of original Christian practice.[4] The Church of England did not insist on them, and godparents could be called by different names, such as 'promisers', 'witnesses', 'delegates', etc., so as to avoid offence. Exactly how much a part the godparents would play in the life of the child varied enormously, but choosing them was important in an age when a family's social network was vital to success. Godparents, like relatives, could be called upon at times of need so an influential godparent was an asset. They were also expected to provide the child with a gift, especially a silver spoon if they could afford it, but very wealthy ones might also provide silver plate such as bowls or a salt.[5] Godparents might also remember a godchild in their will, so that a fifth of Elizabethan yeomen made bequests to godchildren.[6]

Weddings were also important social events and celebrations of the grander ones could continue for days. Much is often made of the fact that some 20–30 per cent of Tudor brides gave birth less than eight months after their church wedding, suggesting that many couples only married once the bride was pregnant. In fact, the situation was rather more complicated than it first seems.

A marriage was seen as binding once the contract had been agreed between the parties involved, rather than once the church ceremony had taken place. Particularly in lower-class families, couples seem to have felt free to sleep together once the contract was agreed and often the church ceremony only took place a month, or even later, after the formal agreement of the contract. The couples concerned therefore *considered* themselves married when they slept together. The Tudors seem to have had quite a respect for marriage and did not take extra-marital sex as lightly as is often assumed. The actual illegitimate birth rate at the time was only about 2–4 per cent.[7] There were, of course, plenty of cases of adultery brought before church courts but the fact that they were punished shows that they were not taken lightly.

Of people of the period who survived to adulthood, 90 per cent married and the average age at marriage was very similar to modern times: 25 to 26 at the time of a first marriage for women and 27 to 28 for men. Only the children of the great tended to be married as teenagers, although many of them only married for the first time in their twenties.

The marriage ceremony itself changed in some details through the century. The early Tudors were mostly married at the church door, with only those of high degree being married further inside the church. A knight might be married within the door, and an earl's son or daughter inside the church at the choir door, but most people had to be married outside.

After the priest had called the banns three times to ensure there was no reason why the couple could not marry, he might then also ask about the woman's dowry, which could then be given to the man in public. After this, the priest would ask if both of the couple were willing to be married and then the groom laid the ring, together with an offering of money, on a dish or a book. The ring would be blessed by the priest and sprinkled with holy water before it was put on the bride's finger.

In the reformed Church of England, marriages were performed inside the church, whatever the social degree of the couple concerned. The ring was still used, although a certain Puritan element felt it was an unnecessary Popish symbol, but it was not sprinkled with holy water. The ring was not necessarily a plain gold band, but could take any form the couple chose.

The church ceremony was only part of the celebrations. A wedding day normally started with the bridal procession, which led the bride to church. In the late sixteenth century Thomas Deloney described such a procession in his book *The Pleasant Historie of Jack of Newbery*, about a wealthy weaver who even entertained Henry VIII himself. Jack's second wedding is lovingly described and although it is a rather sentimental work of fiction, it does portray the sort of bridal procession that was usual right into the seventeenth century.

The bride is dressed in her finest clothes, not, incidently, in a white dress with a veil: both of these items only became popular in the nineteenth century.

She was led to Church betweene two sweete boyes, with Bride-laces and Rosemary tied about their silken sleeves: the one of them was sonne to Sir Thomas Parry, the other to Sir Francis Hungerford. Then was there a fair Bride-cup of silver and gilt carried before her, wherein was a goodly bunch of Rosemary gilded very fare, hung about with silken Ribands of all colours:

next was there a noyse of Musicians that played all the way before her: after that came all the chiefest maydens of the Country, some bearing great Bride Cakes, and some Garlands of wheate finely gilded, and so she passed into the Church.[8]

The fact that the parents of the two boys are named is an important point. Thomas Deloney was stressing to his largely middle-class readers how the virtues ascribed to Jack could lead you to the very highest social circles, and marriages gave a good opportunity to renew and demonstrate social links. Deloney also noted that 'most of the Lords, Knights, and Gentlemen thereabout were invited thereunto'. An elaborate wedding was a crown to social success.

The accompanying feast and celebrations could last some time. Jack's are recorded as lasting ten full days. It was also usual to give gifts to your guests and also to send them to connections who were unable to attend for some reason. Gloves were favourite items, but ribbons were also common. The local poor were not forgotten, and providing them with some kind of gift of food or money, or even both, was not unusual.

Wedding presents were common. At a grand wedding these might take the form of plate or jewellery, although food for the feast was also acceptable.[9] At poor people's weddings it was usual to give gifts of some kind to help the couple set up house. One writer described how 'invited guests do assemble together, and at the very instant of the marriage, doe cast their presents (which they bestow upon the new married folkes) into a bason, dish or cup, which standeth upon the Table in the Church, ready prepared for that purpose. But this custom is onely put in use amongst them, which stand in need.'[10] Bride ales, at which money was raised by selling food and drink, were also traditional ways of supplying the needs of poorer people's weddings. This custom, however, was dying out by the end of the century.

A marriage was truly finalised not by the church ceremony, but by consummation. The formal bedding of the bride and groom was therefore a lively event, surrounded by games, flirtation and much bawdy talk. Part of the ceremony involved the bride's garters being removed by the groom's men and the wedding party throwing their stockings at the bride and groom as symbols of fertility. It would be some time before the party could be finally driven from the bridal chamber to give the couple some peace.

A more sombre part of the ritual of Tudor life was the funeral. The ceremonies began as the dying person neared the end. The church bell would be rung to summon people to the bedside, to remind those around to pray, and to comfort living and dying alike. Prayers for the dead were, of course, discouraged by the reformed Church of England but ringing the passing bell for the dying, and ringing again for the funeral, was still quite acceptable.

The dead were usually buried very quickly, as corpses in crowded houses were obvious health hazards. In wealthy households, where the funeral might be an enormous affair which took a while to organise, the body was often embalmed or sealed in a lead coffin.[11] Most bodies would have been washed and laid out by family and friends but wealthier people often paid poor women to do this service. Sir Nicholas Bacon, who died in 1579, was laid out by two women who were paid 13*s* 4*d*.[12]

Coffins were an expensive luxury but it was considered vital that even the poorest should be covered in something when they were buried. It was only animals that were buried uncovered. Many parishes owned a reusable wooden coffin that the body lay in during the funeral service, and then the body would be buried in just the winding-sheet that covered it.[13]

It was usual to 'watch' a corpse by sitting with it all night. This was the last real chance for friends and family to say goodbye, but even so the duty was again sometimes left to poor women who were paid to do it, as was the case at Nicholas Bacon's death. The corpse of Queen Elizabeth even did not receive the reverence due to royalty. After the Queen had died, at Richmond, John Clapham, a contemporary observer, recorded that the body had been left unattended for a day or two and that 'mean people' had had access to it.[14] The body was later taken to Whitehall Palace where it was duly watched by her ladies and later buried in suitable royal style.

For ordinary people, wearing black to the funeral was not usual as black was an expensive dye and most could not afford a special new set of clothes. However, wealthy people might go to their graves surrounded by black. Black cloth might also be hung in their house and in the church, and the entire household might indeed have had black outfits made for them. Thomas Meade, an Essex Justice of the Peace who died in 1585, was determined to be buried in style. He stipulated that at least £100 was to be spent on black cloth and other items and that black clothes should be made for everyone from his serving men to various named members of his friends and family.[15]

The body would be moved from home as simply or elaborately as the family deemed fit and could afford. Most bodies were carried on wooden biers, usually by friends or family. Middle- or upper-class Tudor corpses might be carried by poor people, again paid for the purpose, but the pallbearers would be the principal mourners. Pallbearers tended to be men at male funerals, and women for females.

It was usual for funerals to be accompanied by some kind of provision of food, again depending on the status of the dead. As was the case with weddings, largesse was also usually shown to the local poor. Nicholas Bacon left no less than £193 6s 8 d for the purpose but this was unusually generous.[16]

It has sometimes been said that people in the past were somehow used to death, particularly the death of children which was so very common. This was definitely not the case as a great deal of evidence shows. For example, Thomas Elyot, in his medical manual *The Castel of Helth*, talks of how matters of the mind can affect your health, and includes not only loss of goods, lack of promotion and general bad luck as leading to problems, but also the death of children.[17]

The strength of feelings surrounding death was not in doubt, but indulging these feelings was seen as unhealthy. The Christian religion is quite certain of the fact that those who die in faith go to heaven. 'Deth is the discharger of al griefes and mysteries, and to them that dye well, the fyrst entrie is to lyfe everlastynge' was how Sir Thomas Elyot put it.[18]

The Tudors had no long and elaborate system of mourning as the Victorians had and given the high death rate at the time this would not have been practical. Most Tudors also did not have the leisure or the money to indulge in such things. It was enough to see that the dead were properly buried according to their social rank, but then it was time to return to the concerns of everyday life.

SIX
Dancing and Music

Dancing and music were important in the social lives of the sixteenth-century English. A knowledge of dancing in particular was essential. It didn't matter whether you were poor or rich, male or female; if you were going to have a good social life, you needed to be able to dance. Most social occasions included dancing. Great court entertainments could be followed by literally hours of it. George Cavendish describes an occasion in the reign of Henry VIII when the dancing went on 'from five of the clock until two or three after midnight'.[1] Much smaller private celebrations so frequently included music and dancing that the high chamber, the most important room in the house, was often decorated with themes appropriate to both.[2]

Dance manuals of the time emphasise the social role of dance. Thoinot Arbeau, a Canon of Langres in France, wrote such a manual. It is called *Orchesography* and was first published in 1589. It takes the form of a dialogue between Arbeau and a young person called Capriol who wishes to learn to dance. The reason Capriol has come to Arbeau is because he has found his social life to be lacking. 'I much enjoyed fencing and tennis and this placed me upon friendly terms with young men. But, without a knowledge of dancing, I could not please the damsels upon whom, it seems to me, the entire reputation of an eligible young man depends.'[3]

This explains the great popularity of dancing, as it was the way that the sexes were allowed to meet one another. People in the sixteenth century were certainly not coy about sex and even Puritan writers of the time, like the Elizabethan Thomas

Becon, openly mentioned the subject in the books they printed. Young unmarried girls, especially better-off ones, were expected to have no experience of it and they were usually kept away from temptation. There were, of course, illegitimate births in the Tudor period, as at all times in history, but the sexual behaviour of Tudors was not quite as free as modern people often think. Young men wishing to socialise with prospective wives could only easily do so through dancing. Dancing not only allowed them to show off their grace and good health, but it also allowed them to get physically close to someone of the opposite sex in a way that good manners simply did not permit otherwise. Arbeau puts it this way:

> Dancing is practised to reveal whether lovers are in good health and sound of limb, after which they are permitted to kiss their mistresses in order that they may touch and savour one another, thus to ascertain if they are shapely or emit an unpleasant odour as of bad meat.[4]

The courting aspect of dance is very clear in the sixteenth century. Arbeau himself describes a dance called the gavotte, which is basically a kissing game. Fabritio Caroso, a well-known Italian dancing master who wrote two books on dancing, *Il Ballerino* and *Nobilita di Dame*, gives several of his dances names associated with love, such as *Specchio d'Amore* (*The Mirror of Love*) or *Forza d'Amore* (*The Power of Love*). The link between dancing and love meant that dancing was condemned in certain circles as encouraging immorality. In the mid-sixteenth century this attitude caused dance schools, particularly those in London, to come under attack. An ordinance of 1553 suppressed them altogether, although it was evidently unsuccessful as in 1574 the system was changed and schools were allowed to function provided that they were authorised.[5]

It was because of these claims that those who defended dancing looked to the greatest authorities of the time, the Bible and the classics, for precedents that proved dancing to be perfectly acceptable. Sir Thomas Elyot in his *Book Named the Governor* strenuously defends the teaching of dance to young aristocrats. He upholds the impressively intellectual neo-Platonic theory that the harmonious movements of the dance echo the movements of the stars. Likewise men and women dancing together symbolised perfect harmony, the man's fiercer 'male' attributes being counterbalanced by a woman's 'gentler' virtues. He also includes a number of classical precedents for dancing, and the Biblical precedent of King David dancing before the Ark.[6] Arbeau also strenuously defended dancing, using many of the same arguments as Elyot. However, Arbeau was not an intellectual passing comment on dance like Elyot, but a man who had a great love of dancing and who realised its practical benefits. 'Dancing, or saltation, is both a pleasant and a profitable art which confers and preserves health, proper to youth, agreeable to the old and suitable to all provided fitness of time and place are observed and it is not abused.'[7]

The aspect of 'preserving health' was particularly important where women were concerned. As Arbeau pointed out, women were not allowed the same freedom as men so their opportunities for exercise were limited. Dancing was the perfect choice of exercise for them. This was particularly true as it was perfectly acceptable for women to dance with each other as well as with male partners. Queen Catherine Howard danced with Anne of Cleeves at the Christmas celebrations of 1540, as Henry had gone to bed early, leaving her without a partner.[8]

The point of 'fitness of time and place' that Arbeau makes was a very important one, at least to the upper classes. Skill at both dancing and music was considered good in a courtier, but he had to be careful how he used them. This was also the case when displaying skills in sports such as wrestling and tennis. Castiglione describes the correct attitude in the *Book of the Courtier*. A well-bred person takes part in such things 'as an amateur, making it clear that he neither seeks nor expects any applause. Nor, even though his performance is outstanding, should he let it be thought that he has spent on it much time or trouble.'[9]

Castiglione makes it very clear that it is ill-bred to draw attention to your skills, such as by starting to sing *sotto voce* when there is a lull in the conversation or dancing as you walk through the streets. Of course, performing for money was out of the question for a courtier, which was why it was perfectly permissible to take part in elaborate court masques, but socially unacceptable to be a professional actor. Dance *was* an essential skill for a courtier but you aimed to make it look as though your skill was a natural talent rather than the result of hours of practice.

However, anyone with any experience of performance knows that it is only rehearsal that makes a performance appear natural. A dance master was a necessity for those who wished to shine at court. Since dancing was so closely bound up with the idea of courtship and of showing off your breeding, dancing masters taught not only dancing but also general deportment and etiquette. According to Cesare Negri, another Italian dancing master of the sixteenth century, dancing masters also taught riding and fencing, besides choreographing court dance performances and displays of military arts.[10] This may or may not have been the case. Negri's nickname was 'il Trombone' suggesting quite literally that he knew how to blow his own trumpet and so he may be exaggerating.

Whether Negri is exaggerating or not, dancing masters did evidently teach etiquette as Caroso's *Nobilita di Dame*, which was first published in 1600, contains a section on how to behave at balls. It isn't exactly clear when Caroso was born but he could have been seventy-four when the book was published, suggesting that the etiquette described would have been suitable for the ballroom in the second half of the sixteenth century. He is, of course, writing for an Italian audience but as Italy was very much seen as the leader of cultured society at the time, it is not unreasonable to assume that similar rules would have been acceptable in England.[11] A ball was the ideal chance to show off good breeding, but of course it was easy to show yourself up if you got things wrong. Even small details were important. Caroso explains how both a lady and a gentleman should sit on these occasions, remembering that they looked so much more elegant if they held something like a handkerchief in one hand. Ladies had to be particularly careful when wearing farthingales, as it was easy to reveal rather more than intended as they sat down. Ladies also had particular problems while dancing if trains were in fashion. Caroso thought it very bad manners for a lady to lift her train with her hands when she needed to dance backwards. Instead she was to sway in such a way as to lift the train out of her way before she stepped back. It was important too that all her dress was properly fastened in place before starting or else all manner of clothing could drop onto the floor during dancing, to everyone's embarrassment. It was particularly vulgar for a lady to drop a glove while dancing, as it 'causes many gentlemen to bestir themselves, running like a flock of starlings' to pick it up. This was an unladylike way of drawing attention to yourself – but no doubt a ruse that many young girls found useful all the same.

Arbeau also explains the polite way for a gentleman to ask a lady to dance. He should remove his hat with his left hand and then offer her his right hand to lead her out to dance. The right side was the side of honour in the sixteenth century so it was important to offer the right, and not the left hand. The gentleman didn't just walk away from his partner after the dance was over, either. Arbeau describes how a gentleman should thank his partner, bow to her and then escort her back to the place where she was when he asked her to dance.[12]

It was bad manners to take your partner's hand while wearing gloves, as this suggested that you did not want to touch them. As it was usual to wear gloves at the time, this meant that it was necessary to be able to take them off quickly and easily. Caroso warned gentlemen not to be swayed by vanity into wearing their gloves so tight that 'they must take more time than an *Ave Maria* to remove [them]: and if they do not succeed with their hands, they even use their teeth', quite destroying the desired image of effortless grace.

Ladies were also allowed to ask men to dance. A lady had to go over and ask a gentleman quietly, making it clear just which gentleman she was inviting to avoid embarrassment. It was important that the lady should not beckon the gentleman with her hands or call his name. Asking someone to dance was not as terrifying as it might sound given the public nature of a formal ball. It was bad manners for both men and women to refuse an invitation, so if someone had the courage to ask they knew that their potential partner was bound to accept.

There was a great deal to remember in order to be an ideal guest at a ball. Superfluous formalities were considered to be affected, but rigorous attention to etiquette was still required. Caroso's instructions range from 'the manner in which a lady should greet a princess and other ladies at a party' to etiquette 'for a new bride when a princess chooses to depart before the ball is over'. There is also a strong warning for 'Ladies who are not invited to dance'. It was the height of bad manners to sulk. Instead the lady had to pretend to be as happy as possible and to spend her time conversing with the ladies sitting nearby.

Many of the rules given by dancing masters were simply reminders of polite behaviour. Despite the formality of some dances, the basic aim of dance at the time was enjoyment, so it was important that everyone felt included and that people treated each other with consideration. It was rude to steal someone else's seat while they were dancing so good manners dictated that it should be given up to them again when they wanted it back. It was also bad manners to spend all the time dancing with the same person. A considerate guest danced with as many different partners as possible.

Having established some idea of how to behave while dancing, what sort of dances were likely to be performed? The answer depended on where and who you were, but whatever your circumstances the choice seems to have been a wide one.

As most dance was social, not all dances were designed to be danced by individual couples. Arbeau comments that pavans and basse dances can be danced in threes (one man and two ladies). Caroso too includes a dance called the *Fedelta* which is for at least three couples and is better with more. The dancers work their way around the circles, dancing with all the members of the opposite sex. Even where dances were designed for couples, the couples often danced together in sets rather than as individual couples. Renaissance dance was a world away from the ballroom dances of the nineteenth and twentieth centuries.

At this stage it should be said that knowledge of Renaissance dance is far from being complete. The dance manuals surviving from the time are nearly all Italian. Italy was setting the fashion in so many ways at the time that it is reasonable to assume that they were also leading the fashions in dance, and Italian dance masters were known to have served at courts throughout Europe.[13] It is reasonable to assume that they give an idea of what was fashionable in England at the time, but this is not certain.

There is also the problem that most of the surviving evidence concerns wealthier people. Arbeau's manual is different, as it describes dances like branles which were danced by all classes, but even so there is the usual difficulty of a great deal less evidence surviving about ordinary people's lives than about wealthier people. This does not mean that we know nothing of ordinary people's dances. It is not known how much folk dance and court dance influenced each other in the sixteenth century, but it is not unreasonable to assume that dances performed in both circles were not dissimilar. Dance in western Europe has always tended to move both up and down the social scale. Dances described by John Playford in *The English Dancing Master*, a dance manual aimed at the middle classes and published in 1651, are described in literary sources in the sixteenth century as folk dances.[14] Lower-class dances were therefore probably very like those enjoyed by the wealthy, but less complex. There would have been differences, though. Lower-class people would have had neither the time to practise nor the level of instruction that wealthy people had, so doubtless their dancing would not have been as elegant. The more complicated display dances for couples described by Caroso would have required a great deal of practice and so would not have been danced by ordinary people.

It was not only the dancing that changed according to the wealth of the dancers, but also the music. The tunes may have been the same, but the instruments used would have been different. Arbeau talks of workmen employing hautboys and sackbuts[15] to play for dancing at their weddings.[16] Bagpipes and hurdy-gurdies were other lower-class options or a pipe and tabor. The musician would play the pipe with one hand while using his other hand to play the rhythm on the tabor, or small drum. Upper-class dancers, on the other hand, were more likely to dance to the sound of violins, the lute or the guitar in private rooms and to the sound of louder instruments like shawms[17] and sackbuts in larger, more public areas.

Reconstructing Renaissance dance today can be difficult as not all the manuscripts provide a detailed explanation of both the dances and the music that went with them. One example is the instructions which survive for dances performed at the Inns of Court, the law schools where wealthy young men learnt not only the law but also social graces such as music and dance. These give the steps, but do not provide the music that went with them.[18] Another problem is that dance steps are very difficult to write down. The descriptions can be interpreted in different ways, so that even the experts argue over exactly what different types of step should look like.[19] Despite the problems enough evidence does survive to have a good general idea of the type of dances performed at the time. There really were dances to suit all tastes and all occasions.

In the formal atmosphere of the times there was a need for stately processional dance. This was the pavan or its close relative, the basse dance. The steps were simple. Arbeau maintains that 'when one knows the step and movements of one pavan and one common basse dance one can dance all the others'.[20] The aim of these dances was not only to demonstrate your dancing skills but also to show off your finest clothes to greatest advantage. They were dances performed by all social classes but Arbeau describes how they were used on solemn feast days 'by kings, princes and great noblemen to display themselves in their fine mantles and ceremonial robes. They are accompanied by queens, princesses and great ladies, the long trains of their dresses loosened and sweeping behind them, sometimes borne by damsels.'[21] Pavans and basse dances were also useful for court masques as they provided a good form of entry for important characters such as gods and goddesses or kings in full majesty.

A livelier and less formal form of the pavan was the Spanish pavan which Arbeau describes as being similar to the canary. This dance was an excellent opportunity to show off dancing skills. Arbeau describes how a couple would dance together to the far end of the room, and then the man would withdraw to where he started from, leaving the couple facing each other at opposite ends of the room. After this the dance would continue with first the man and then the lady performing solo variations on the steps, first dancing towards their partner and then retreating again. The variations used could be ones that you had learnt, or ones you made up for yourself, the more ingenious the better.

The best opportunity of all to show off your skills was presented by the galliard. This was a very lively dance which involved, for the men at least, a great deal of strenuous leaping. Arbeau describes what he feels is the best way of performing a galliard. It is very much a display dance. The couple danced around the room together a couple of times and then split, one to each end of the hall. They then took turns performing variations until the music stopped. Both men and women could show off their skills at the galliard but the ladies were hampered both by their skirts and their need to behave in what was then seen as a feminine way. High leaps and displays of strength were considered more suitable for men. The men's steps for the galliard could be very strenuous indeed. Caroso describes one variation in which a tassel would be held at about the same height as a man. The gentleman performing would then jump and twist so high that he could kick the tassel with his toe – definitely no mean feat. Anyone who could perform this gracefully would have to be a very fine dancer indeed.

Some dances were designed to marry contrasting styles of dance, such as the galliard and the more stately pavan. The dance would start with the pavan, so that the dancers could make their entry on to the dance floor in suitable magnificent style and then break into the more energetic galliard.

Arbeau also describes how the galliard could be danced to include as many people as possible. The gentleman would retire, leaving the lady performing a solo passage. She would dance alone for a while, then she would choose a new partner. Later on she would drop out, leaving the gentleman to choose a new partner and so the dance went on. The idea was that the new partner should always be someone who hadn't yet danced, so that gradually everyone got their chance.[22] Another variation on the galliard was la Volta. This dance was described by Arbeau but he did not approve of it. It was a very energetic dance indeed in which the gentleman would pick the lady up by putting one arm around her waist and by using his other arm to grab hold of her busk, the stiffened front of her bodice. She would leap into the air as he did this, so that they whirled around so violently that the lady had to use her left hand to hold down her gown for decency's sake. The busks on ladies' gowns were also quite long at some stages of fashion so that having the gentleman grab hold of it might well have added to the attractions of the dance. Arbeau was quite shocked by it. 'I leave it to you to judge whether it is a becoming thing for a young girl to take long strides and separations of the legs and whether in this lavolta both honour and health are not involved and at stake'.[23] It was a very popular dance, though, and no doubt one which Arbeau himself would have enjoyed if it had been the fashion in his youth.

Arbeau is much more approving of branles, simple dances which were very popular throughout society and were performed in a number of ways such as in couples, as round dances, or for groups of people holding hands in lines. They were lively dances which everyone could join in. Some of these are still danced in Brittany.

Arbeau describes a number of them, some of which are mime dances. One involves the dancers imitating washerwomen arguing with their clients; another, the hermit's branle, mocks hermits greeting each other. Considering that Arbeau was a canon, it is surprising that he records this one, although he does include a warning. The dance should not be done in religious dress and the dancers should not mimic the behaviour of the clergy 'because one should respect both their cloth and their persons'.[24] Presumably the warning is tongue-in-cheek, as anyone performing the dance was hardly showing respect for the clergy in the first place.

Branles were the perfect social dance as not only were the steps easy, but some were actively designed to involve as many people as possible. Most could be danced by as many people as felt like joining in. An example given by Arbeau is the candlestick branle, in which the dancers passed lighted candles between them. People would join in and drop out as the dance progressed so that in this way everyone attending the dance could be included.[25]

At the other end of the dance spectrum were the dances described by Caroso in his books. Many of these are designed to be performed by a single couple, perhaps as a solo or maybe with several couples dancing at once. They mix a variety of steps and are usually based on the ever-present theme of love, with all the inevitable ups and downs of a courtly love affair represented by the movements. There are solo sections for both the man and the woman and complicated floor patterns to remember. If you were called upon to perform them in the presence of aristocratic company every penny you had ever spent on dancing lessons would have been well spent. A successful performance would demonstrate your skills as a courtier and failure would be very embarrassing indeed.

Love was only one theme that ran through Renaissance dance. Another popular theme was that of war. There are several dances with a military theme, such as Caroso's *Barriera* and *Barriera Nuova* which both play on the idea of a courtly tournament.[26] Arbeau also describes a dance called the *Buffens* in which the dancers imitate a battle with much clashing of swords.[27] He also includes a section on drum rhythms for marching and for the performance of martial dances.[28]

The link between dancing and war was quite a strong one at the time. Despite the fact that education was becoming increasingly important in court circles, men of the aristocracy were still trained for war. In fact warfare was becoming more a matter for professional soldiers than well-bred amateurs but even men like Roger Ascham, Nicholas Bacon and Thomas Elyot who encouraged academic education make it quite clear that training in martial skills was still a vital part of a wealthy boy's education. Thomas Elyot includes a whole section in the *Book Named the Governor* on exercises which adapt a boy's body to 'hardness, strength, and agility and to help therewith himself in peril, which may happen in wars or other necessity'. He starts off with sports such as wrestling and running, works his way through hunting and ends with dancing.[29] The other important factor was that dancing was very much about showing yourself off to your peers. Ladies showed off the essential sixteenth-century feminine attributes of gentleness and grace, while men showed off how fit and strong they were and implied that they were fine soldiers too.

Music was another way of showing off your abilities, but attitudes to music were rather mixed. Castiglione is at pains to stress that a gentleman should have musical skills, but that 'the courtier should turn to music as if it were merely a pastime of his and he is yielding to persuasion, and not in the presence of common people or a large crowd. And although he may know and understand what he is doing, in this also I wish him to dissimulate the care and effort that are necessary for any competent performance and he should let it seem as if he himself thinks nothing of his accomplishment which, because of its excellence, he makes others think very highly of.'[30]

Sir Thomas Elyot praised music as a form of relaxation from the hard work of academic study but stressed that a gentleman should not spend too much time practising. He warns his readers against following the example of the Roman Emperor Nero, who devoted all his time to music and so turned his back on his greater responsibilities in government. A nobleman was to use music 'for the refreshing of his wit, when he hath time of solace' or else was to display his knowledge of the subject in conversation. In other words, the well-bred were to have a knowledge of music, but it was ungentlemanly to be too good a performer.[31]

Despite these warnings, there was a definite increase in interest in music in the late sixteenth century for a number of reasons. One was the lead given by the court. The Tudor monarchs were keen musicians and did a great deal to improve the music at court and to make the study of music fashionable. Foreign travel was also becoming an accepted part of a wealthy young man's education, so that more people had direct experience of foreign

The Boarhunt cottage at the Weald and Downland Museum. This fifteenth-century cottage was built with a hall and open hearth. (Weald and Downland Museum Open Air Museum/ Alison Sim)

Pendean farmhouse at the Weald and Downland Museum. This yeoman farmer's house was built with several smaller rooms downstairs rather than a hall, and with a chimney and wall-mounted fireplaces rather than the old central open hearth. (Weald and Downland Museum Open Air Museum/ Alison Sim)

The 'Rainbow Portrait' of Elizabeth I, stunningly magnificent and surrounded by imagery. (By courtesy of the Marquess of Salisbury)

The Wolsey Closet, Hampton Court. The painting and panelling has been moved from elsewhere but the room gives a good impression of how a wealthy person's private rooms would have looked in the time of Henry VIII. (Historic Royal Palaces, Crown Copyright)

Queen Elizabeth receiving the Dutch emissaries in about 1585. Note the ladies sitting on the floor in the foreground. (Staatliche Museem Kassel)

Holbein's Ambassadors, *painted in 1533. The gentleman on the left, Jean de Dinteville, wears the fashionable men's dress of the time including a luxurious fur-lined gown and a black velvet jerkin. The gentleman on the right, Georges de Selve, Bishop of Lavaur, is wearing clerical dress.* (© National Gallery, London)

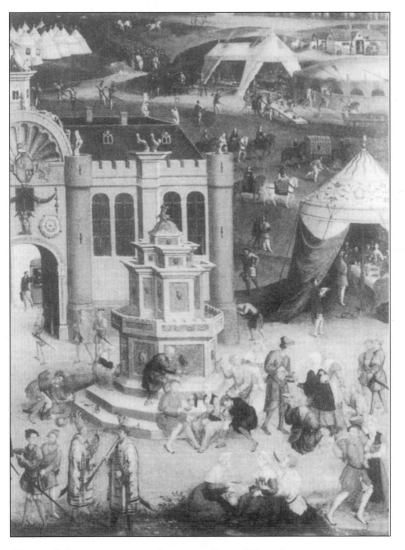

This detail shows costume worn by more ordinary Tudors. Outer garments are made of wool, whilst linen is worn next to the skin. These clothes would give far more freedom of movement than the elaborate clothes of the courtiers.
(The National Trust Photographic Library, London)

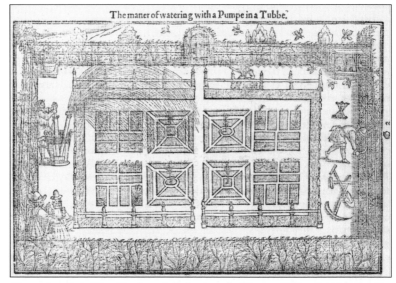

Plate taken from The Gardener's Labyrinth *by Thomas Hill, printed in London in 1608. This shows a knot garden, and gives an idea of how such gardens were laid out.* (Guildhall Library, Corporation of London)

Sir Thomas Fleming, by an unknown artist. He wears a high-crowned black hat, fashionable for both sexes. (By courtesy of the National Portrait Gallery, London)

Bess of Hardwick is wearing a 'loose-bodied gown' which was also known as an English gown. Her gown is decorated with gold aglets. She is wearing a French hood which was fashionable in slightly differing forms for most of the century. (The National Trust Photographic Library, London)

Lord Cobham and his family dining. (The Marquis of Bath, photograph Courtauld Institute of Art)

Brueghel's Peasant Wedding Feast, *showing more ordinary people's clothes. As it is a wedding feast, they are all dressed in their best. (Pieter the Elder Brueghel, c. 1515–69)* (Kunsthistorisches Museum, Vienna/Bridgeman Art Library, London)

The Tudor Dynasty portrait. Henry is reminding viewers that Edward is his true successor. (The Royal Collection © 2002 Her Majesty the Queen)

musical trends, particularly those of Italy. The printing press also helped the spread of musical education, making instructional manuals and music available to a wider audience, although the bulk of music books were imported.

It is difficult to define 'musical ability', as the only way to get an accurate idea of someone's talents is to hear them perform. The study of the spread of musical literacy, or the number of people who could read music rather than simply improvising by ear, does give a good general indication of the interest in music. It follows that someone who can read music also performs it, rather than just having a theoretical knowledge of the subject. Musical notation is something we take for granted today but it was only just becoming popular in the sixteenth century. Prior to this, people had learnt music by ear, which tended to limit their repertoire. The very fact that notation became more standardised and easier to read during the sixteenth century shows that it was being used more frequently.[32]

There is also evidence of children being taught to sing from song books, such as Sir Thomas Chaloner's daughter who was taught Italian part-singing in this way in 1552.[33] It was very common among the wealthier classes to be taught to sing and the idea was to be able to sight sing your part. This was no small skill as you would only be given the music to your part, unlike today when it is usual to work from music which shows the parts for everyone singing. There were also no bar lines, making it easy to lose your place. The result was that you really needed to get it right first time, as it was hard to sort yourself out if you went wrong.

The skill seems to have been a fairly common one, at least among those with the money and leisure to learn. Thomas Morley even brought out a 'teach yourself' manual in 1597, entitled *A Plaine and Easie Introduction to Practicall Musicke*.[34] In the introduction Morley sets out the reasons for learning to sing by giving the example of Philomathes, the 'pupil' whose efforts in learning music are followed in the book. Philomathes went to supper at a friend's house and had the following embarrassing experience:

> But supper being ended, and Musicke bookes according to the
> custome being brought to the table, the mistresse of the house
> presented mee with a part earnestly requesting mee to sing. But
> when after manie excuses I protested unfainedly that I could
> not everie one began to wonder. Yea, some whispered to other,
> demaunding how I was brought up . . .

Some allowance must be made for dramatic licence here. Morley
was, after all, writing an introduction to a singing manual, so he
was bound to make singing appear to be a vital social grace. On
the other hand, singing must have been the kind of social grace
that people were interested in acquiring if there was a market for a
'teach yourself' manual. Interest in music seems to have increased
over the century. It took time for the example set at court to filter
its way down, waiting for the generation influenced by Henry VIII
to begin educating their own children. Henry VIII transformed the
royal musical household. He was a very keen musician himself,
and was also both a wealthy man and one determined to have the
most glittering court in Europe. This meant that he wanted the
very best performers, English or foreign.

Henry did not just see his musicians as a way of increasing
his prestige. He very much appreciated their talents. He would
sometimes listen to his Venetian organist, Dionisio Memo, play
for four hours at a stretch. Henry did not just listen to music,
either, but also performed himself. The King's personal collection
of instruments was impressively large, containing, among other
things, twenty-six lutes. Henry played not only the lute but
also the virginals, and the organ to a certain extent. He enjoyed
singing, too and is recorded as having sung with courtiers like Sir
Peter Carew. If you wanted to be part of the King's social circle it
would obviously have helped to have a knowledge of music.[35]

The expansion in the number of musicians employed at the
court was impressive. In the time of Edward IV, Henry VIII's
grandfather, there were five resident musicians. Henry VII had
a larger musical household, employing a Welsh harper, four
sackbuts, some shawm players, and a dozen trumpeters among
others. The royal children were also taught music, as was the

tradition.[36] Henry VIII maintained thirty-seven musicians by 1540 and perhaps as many as fifty-eight by the time he died in 1547. Quite a few of his musicians were foreigners, including the eight Italians who made up his viol consort, three Flemish flautists and two lutanists who came from the Low Countries. Henry's courtiers could enjoy the very finest music.[37]

The royal interest in music did not die with Henry. All the Tudors were keen musicians, although neither Edward nor Mary reigned for long enough to have much influence in the field. Queen Elizabeth, who was not as well off as her father, reduced the number of royal musicians. In 1570 she had about thirty-three musicians and twenty-nine in 1590, but that did not mean that musical standards fell. Elizabeth was happy to pay a premium price to keep the services of a favoured musician. The famous Italian composer Alfonso Ferrabosco was given a pension of £100 a year.[38] Like her father, Elizabeth was a keen musician herself, having been taught to play the lute and the virginals as a girl.[39] She kept her interest in music throughout her life, spending £75 on lute strings in the first ten years of her reign. She also performed before a number of foreign dignitaries, such as the ambassadors who came to ratify the Treaty of Blois in 1572.[40]

The court therefore set the fashion for foreign music and musical literacy, although it was slow to spread among amateurs. There are not many household papers surviving from the early sixteenth century but the few that do still exist show little evidence of either musical servants or of masters being able to read or write music before the 1540s. With the exception of the very great households, like those of Cardinal Wolsey or the Howards, there were not many families in Henry VIII's time who supported resident musicians or music teachers. By the later sixteenth century, though, the fashion began to take hold and both musicians and teachers begin to appear more frequently in household accounts. The Willoughby family were obviously keen musicians as they were being taught the virginals in the 1550s. In the 1570s, the Kytson family of Hengrave Hall in Suffolk had a resident musician, a musicians' chamber and a great variety of instruments, while the children had been bought song books.[41]

The increased interest in music certainly did not mean that all households maintained music masters even in the late sixteenth century. In fact, very few did. At Longleat, the wealthy Thynne family did not employ any musicians before 1540 and it was the early seventeenth century before they employed a music teacher.[42] Even so other evidence points to an increased interest in music.

A rising quantity of published music and music manuals became available. There was very little music printed in England before the 1550s and it wasn't until psalm music became popular in the 1560s and '70s that any form of printed music began to rival sales of printed literature. There also seems to have been little, if any, demand for printed secular music at the beginning of Elizabeth's reign but this does not necessarily mean that there was no interest in it. Sales of printed music can be an unreliable guide to musical literacy and only give an idea of general trends. This was because there was a monopoly on printed music in England from 1575. It was originally operated by the musicians Thomas Tallis and William Byrd, and then by Byrd alone after Tallis died in 1585. The monopoly was very badly run and seems to have hampered the publication of music in general. It probably encouraged the long standing tradition of the private copying and exchange of music and the use of imported printed music.[43]

There is other evidence that people were actively practising their music. Both Oxford and Cambridge had granted degrees in music since the mid-fifteenth century, but the study of music centred on musical theory rather than performance. Anyone who wanted to learn the practical side of playing an instrument or singing had to employ a private music tutor. Many students did just this. The musician Thomas Whythorne, whose autobiography survives, spent some time as a private music tutor to a young gentleman at university.[44] Henry Howard, 8th Earl of Northampton, took lessons on his own lute while studying at King's College, Cambridge in 1560 as did Francis and Anthony Bacon.

The evidence suggests that music was seen as a gentlemanly pastime rather than a serious part of the students' studies. In 1576 St John's College, Cambridge, forbade the playing of instruments during the hours set aside for quiet and study. Playing instruments was obviously seen as a better alternative to study as far as the students were concerned.[45] Outside the hours of study, music was readily accepted as a suitable pursuit and even encouraged. Some colleges had their own instruments which the students could play, like Trinity College, Cambridge, which paid for a new set of viols and a sackbut in 1593. Some dons encouraged music too. Thomas Legge, fellow of St John's, Cambridge, included a three-part song, probably composed by William Byrd, in his production of *Ricardius Tertius* at the College in 1579.

Despite the general improvement in musical knowledge among the well-to-do in the sixteenth century, it was not the case that everyone born in Elizabethan England had a comprehensive musical education. Music was only a standard part of the curriculum at the larger and more expensive schools, such as Eton, Westminster and St Paul's. Most grammar schools did not show any particular enthusiasm for music although evidently some did teach it. The musician Thomas Whythorne records that he was taught to sing at school, although the school he attended was not a prestigious one.[46] The only surviving evidence of a full-time music master working at a school concerns the one employed at Christ's Hospital, London, which was a charity school opened in 1552. The children were very much being educated for service and apprenticeship and it was unusual to train such children in music.[47]

The bulk of the population had neither the time nor the money for formal musical instruction. If they learnt an instrument, they were taught on an informal basis by someone they knew and would probably restrict themselves to either playing dance tunes or accompanying the singing of folk songs. Their only regular exposure to other types of music would have been in church. Music in the pre-Reformation church could be very elaborate indeed and was often of a very high standard. There were about two dozen places where you could expect really superb music, such as at cathedrals, at the principal colleges of Oxford and Cambridge, and at a few schools, like Eton.

The cathedral choirs could produce music of the highest

standards but even some of those who were not supporters of
Martin Luther queried the use of their music. Church music of
the time was very elaborate, favouring polyphony. The effect was
wonderful, but it was impossible to hear what words the choir was
singing. In any case it was normal for them to sing in Latin, which
few people understood. In this atmosphere it was inevitable that
many reformers saw music as a hindrance rather than a help to
worship. Going to church was more like going to a concert than
taking part in a religious service. Thomas Morley, in his *A Plaine
and Easie Introduction to Practicall Musicke*, described how he felt
churchmen should sing, by pronouncing the words carefully so
that everyone could understand what they were singing. They
should also sing 'expressing their wordes with devotion and
passion, whereby to draw the hearer as it were in chaines of gold
by the eares to the consideration of holie things'.[48]

Sir Thomas More, despite his strong commitment to the
Catholic Church, criticised over-elaborate music in his book
Utopia when he describes Utopian church music: 'the sound is
so well adapted to the sense that whether the theme is prayer or
rejoicing, agitation or calm, sorrow or anger, the melodic line
exactly represents the appropriate emotion. It therefore enters
deeply into the hearer's consciousness. . . .'[49]

Despite the misgivings of many Protestant reformers about the
use of music, the 1559 Settlement still allowed for a 'hymn or
such like song' to be included in the Church of England service.
Congregational psalm-singing became very popular, leading to
publications like Sternhold and Hopkin's metrical psalters. The
first version of this psalter to contain music appeared in Geneva
in 1556 and singing 'Geneva-wise' became very fashionable in
churches. From the 1560s onwards there was a flood of Sternhold
and Hopkins publications, some of which contained good-
quality four-part settings which suggest a fair amount of musical
skill in the performers.[50] It is easy to over-simplify the situation
regarding religious music in the sixteenth century. The whole
religious debate was very complicated and it was not a simple
matter of Protestants disapproving of church music and Catholics
approving of it. Protestant noblemen like the Cecils kept choirs

which were used in their chapel services[51] and people of either side who disapproved of church music might love secular music.

The music of the Chapel Royal demonstrates just how contradictory the position could be. As Elizabeth had decided on a Protestant settlement for the Church you would have expected the Chapel Royal's music to reflect this, but this was not the case. The Chapel was under direct royal control and was seen as part of the royal household. As such, it reflected the tastes of the monarch rather than of the Church in general. Elizabeth's love of music very much showed through in her Chapel Royal, where all manner of elaborate music continued to be performed, even if it was disapproved of in other churches. She continued to employ very skilled musicians like William Byrd and John Bull (who was famous in Europe as well as in England), who were both organists in the chapel. Elizabeth might decide on one thing for the Church in general, where politics had to be considered, but she herself was going to have exactly the music she liked best.[52]

The other important point about church music was that it was only a minority of churches that could afford a full choir with its attendant song-school, etc., even when such music was encouraged. Many parish churches had been forced to hire professional musicians for special occasions even before the Reformation.[53] The composers of the day also wrote virtually nothing which would have been suitable for parish church resources. Given that the place of music in church was rather a delicate one at the time, there can't have been too many people wanting to either write or perform something that could get them into trouble with the authorities. The possible political difficulties in getting involved in church music were one factor which drove musicians into taking a more active interest in secular music. Another practical reason for this was that the dissolution of the monasteries took away much of the Church's huge wealth and along with it many of the opportunities for careers for musicians. At this stage it is worth considering the position of professional musicians in England.

Professional musicians in general did not enjoy high social status at the time. The talents of the very skilled and very fortunate musicians who gained favour at court were greatly admired but they were hardly typical musicians of their day. The successful few were keen to emphasise their social status. Thomas Morley describes himself as 'Batchelor of Musicke and one of the gent of her Majesties Royall Chapell' on the title page of *A Plaine and Easie Introduction to Practicall Musicke*. Thomas Whythorne had an impressive woodcut made to appear in his two publications, showing not only his portrait but also his family coat of arms. Both men wanted to emphasise the fact that they were gentlemen.

Lower down the scale musicians had even greater problems. Those who wandered the country looking for work were mistrusted as vagrants and possible troublemakers, and were liable to all the punishments that vagrants were likely to suffer. These varied throughout the century, but they could include whipping, branding and in theory at least, during a brief time under Protector Somerset, even death.[54] The problem was that there was not a great deal of employment for male musicians and no employment at all for female ones. Women were not yet allowed to appear on the stage so performing as an amateur was the best a woman could hope for, however skilled she was.

The Church did still provide a certain amount of work for musicians, but not only did the Reformation take a great deal of the institution's wealth away, but sixteenth-century inflation helped erode the value of the remaining endowments. The number of musicians employed had to be reduced, so that, for example, the number of choristers employed at Salisbury Cathedral was reduced from fourteen to eight in 1550.[55] The Church's decline also affected the choir schools. These schools provided a good entry into the musical world for the young boys who received their education there. The boys were, of course, taught music but they were also given a general education as well. They usually lived at the school and received board and lodging, but this was not always the case. At Salisbury Cathedral the master in charge of the boys was so incompetent that he had to be removed in 1568 after five years in office. The next master was also incompetent and looked after the boys so badly that they all went back to living at home.[56]

Salisbury was a rather extreme example but the decline in the cathedral schools and in the music in church generally was noted and lamented by Thomas Whythorne. The Church was the main training ground for musicians and Whythorne felt that not enough new musicians were being trained in the new reformed Church of England 'so that when the old store of musicians be worn out, the which were bred when the music of the church was maintained . . . ye shall have few or none remaining . . .'.

In fact Whythorne was being pessimistic. The Church did continue to produce good musicians, such as Thomas Morley who served as cathedral organist at Norwich Cathedral before entering the Chapel Royal. The choir schools also continued to provide a good start in life for many boys, albeit in reduced numbers and even if the boys did not always follow musical careers later on. Many went into the Church instead, such as Thomas Cooper who was a chorister at Magdalen College, and who went on to become Bishop of Winchester in 1584.

The best secular opportunity for employment outside the court was work as a city wait. Waits seem to have originally been watchmen who patrolled various cities and who played their instruments to assure the inhabitants that all was well. By the sixteenth century their role had changed and they had become municipal musicians. They would play at grand civic occasions, but they were also available for private hire.[57] The city which provided the best opportunities for its waits was, of course, London. There seem to have been six waits, who from 1548 onwards were allowed two apprentices each, bringing the number to eighteen. They were given summer and winter livery of blue gowns and red caps. They also wore silver chains and a silver badge showing the arms of the city. They were made freemen of the city without charge on their appointment, showing that they were considered respectable men.

The London waits had plenty of employment. They were in great demand for playing at weddings and also performed for important people like Thomas Kytson and Lord Willoughby.

They would have had no difficulty in making a reasonable living, but their position was more privileged than that of the waits of other less important cities.

Most cities employed waits. Canterbury, for example, employed three waits at the beginning of Elizabeth's reign, as did Leicester at about the same time. The number of waits employed generally was increasing, so that Oxford employed two in 1577, three before 1588 and five from 1588 onwards. Waits were always given liveries to wear and most had badges or chains as symbols of their office. They were an accepted part of civic life. The waits were not paid a living wage, but this was fairly standard for Elizabethan officials. The city that employed them usually gave them some money, but not very much. The Cambridge waits were paid £2 a year in 1567, which was not enough to live on. Instead it was usual for them to enjoy a monopoly of playing for money in the town where they worked, so that money received for their official duties was only part of their income. There were other benefits, too. Many towns provided their waits with instruments, which must have helped them considerably as instruments were expensive.

If it was not possible to get a job as a wait, another alternative was to make a living by whatever musical work came along, which usually involved teaching music. Thomas Whythorne was one such musician. He published the first set of English madrigals in 1571 and brought out a volume of duets in 1590, but he is not particularly noteworthy as a musician. If his autobiography had not survived then we would know nothing about him. Whythorne is interesting precisely because he was the type of struggling musician of whom little is usually known. He was not a musician of the first order but the fact that he was employed by the Archbishop of Canterbury, Matthew Parker, to direct the music at Lambeth Palace suggests that he was reasonably skilled. Parker had employed Tallis at one time, so he seems to have known good music when he heard it. Whythorne came from a gentry family which, although being respectable, had little money. He therefore had to earn his living and took a number of jobs working for families ranging from that of John Heywood, who had been Princess Mary's music tutor in her youth, to a wealthy widow who seems to have spent most of her time flirting with him. Like many musicians of his day, he spent some time travelling on continental Europe, so that his life was adventurous if nothing else. His autobiography certainly conveys how very difficult it was to make a living as a musician.

The best musicians could make a good living, by combining the patronage of the court, the Church and private individuals. Sales of printed music could also supplement their income. The most succesful ones, men like John Dowland and Thomas Campion, were accepted by society. However, these men were exceptional and life was much harder for most musicians showing that in some ways not much has changed.

SEVEN
Reading

The introduction of the printing press into England at the end of the fifteenth century and the expansion of education in the sixteenth century brought the pleasures of reading to a wider audience than ever before. Literacy certainly did not become universal, though, and the reading public was far more restricted than today. To understand Tudor reading habits some knowledge is needed of attitudes to education at the time.

In the Middle Ages academic education was not really necessary unless you wanted to go into the Church. Even the upper classes, who had the best opportunity to become educated, saw only a limited need for it. It was their job to be the men of action needed to lead armies. The nobility were seen as having been raised to their exalted position by kings in reward for their abilities on the battlefield. The longer the noble lineage, the more able to serve the king in battle. The aristocracy saw themselves as being those who had both the best ability and the best right to serve the king as his advisors. All the education that was felt necessary and appropriate to members of the upper classes, apart from their training in war, was a nodding acquaintance with skills such as music to give a courtly gloss to their manners. The few government posts that needed to be filled by people with education, such as that of chancellor, went to men from the Church.

The sixteenth century saw a change to this. Henry VII, having fought his way to the throne, did his best to wipe out those with royal blood since they constituted a possible threat. Henry VIII continued his father's policy. The result was a distinct lack of people with long aristocratic lineages who could claim the right to high office. The time was ripe for a change in philosophy towards the humanist idea that nobility was conferred not so much by blood as by ability and education.

Most of the men who served Henry VIII had been raised by the king from the gentry or yeomanry. Thomas Cromwell, Charles Brandon and Thomas Cranmer were just a few of the men who rose to high office in this way. At the same time the government was changing as it became far more centralised, as discussed in the introduction, so that academic education became more important for those aspiring to high office.

The humanist philosophy of the time saw education as not simply providing a child with a certain amount of knowledge, but as also moulding his or her moral character. An educated child was seen as more likely to make good moral choices in life, just as a well-educated member of the upper classes was more likely to rule for the common good than an uneducated one. This was why people with strong humanist views, like Erasmus, Thomas Elyot and Roger Ascham, produced books on the theory of education.[1] Elyot's *Book Named the Governor* was reprinted no less than eight times between its first publication in 1531 and 1580, showing what a popular subject educational theory was.

The stimulus for education at court was made all the stronger by the fact that Henry VIII himself was an educated man who enjoyed reading and intellectual debate throughout his life. He was the first English king to write a book. It was called *Assertio septem sacramentorum* (In Defence of the Seven Sacraments) and was a work of theology, a subject which always interested the King even before his need for a divorce gave him a particular reason to study the subject.

The King had not one library, but at least three. The main one was at Whitehall Palace, but evidence suggests that there were other libraries at Hampton Court and Greenwich. The Whitehall library contained 329 books at the time of the King's death in 1547 and was furnished with seven desks and a table. These desks would have been a kind of lectern and bookshelf in one. These desks were the normal way of storing books until bookshelves came into use later in the century.[2]

Henry was a very keen reader and made constant use of his books. Many of them are annotated in the margins, showing that the King not only read them but also noted their contents with interest. He also saw that his children were all well educated and his daughter Elizabeth kept her love of reading throughout her life. Even after becoming Queen she liked to use the period after dinner for reading her favourite passages from the classics and seems to have turned to reading as consolation in moments of crisis. In 1593 she turned to translating Boethius' *De Consolatione Philosophiae* as a distraction after having had bad news from France.[3] As success at court depended on making yourself an agreeable companion to the monarch, this example must have helped popularise education at court.

The rising middle classes were also deeply affected by the humanist view of education. They owed their own improved social and financial situation to hard work and thrift, and the idea of education as improving not only their material prospects but also their moral and spiritual health was very encouraging. There was therefore enormous demand for books which they felt to be 'improving' in some way. Some were very practical, teaching languages or navigation or some other skill which would help them in their work. Others were aimed at improving the soul, another important aim of literature at the time.

The changes in religious views also put a new emphasis on education. The ideals of the new learning, which basically became what would now be called Protestant views, placed enormous emphasis on the ability to read and study the Bible. It was not enough to listen to a priest expounding the Bible, you had to study for yourself. Encouraging education was seen as bringing about the spread of true religion.

The introduction of the printing press not only made the rapid spread of these ideas possible, but also brought down the price of books to such an extent that a far wider range of reading was available than ever before. However, before looking at the range of books available, it is worth adding a cautionary note. The expansion in literacy was by and large limited to the wealthier section of society. During the sixteenth century it became more usual for the middle classes and the yeomanry (usually seen as the independent, land-owning farmers) to be able to read and possibly also to write, but the people at the bottom of society remained pretty much illiterate. In fact until the great expansion of education in the nineteenth century, about 80 per cent of husbandmen (basically farm labourers) remained illiterate.[4]

It is difficult to judge people's standards of literacy as no official records of literacy rates were kept at the time. One thing that gives a general idea is how many people were able sign their names on official documents. Wills do not give a good indication, because people made wills when they were dying, so they often were not physically capable of signing even if they knew how to write. In any case, only a small percentage of the population made wills as most people didn't own enough to make one worthwhile.[5] A better indication comes from the people who were able to sign depositions, or statements which were made by witnesses before various courts. You didn't necessarily have to be a person of social standing to be called as a witness in a court case so these cover all social classes. The evidence from these depositions shows that literacy rates varied considerably, not just between the different social classes but also in different geographical areas. The literacy rate for all classes was higher in London than elsewhere in the country, while in the further north of England it tended to be lower.

It was certainly not the case that the literacy rate improved steadily throughout the century, as sometimes it seems to have fallen rather than improved. At the time of the Reformation in the 1530s and 1540s the literacy rate generally was improving, but during the reign of Edward, despite the foundation of many grammar schools, basic education seems to have declined. This decline went on through the reign of Mary, so that yeomen in the diocese of Norwich who had been educated between about 1548 and 1558 were less likely to be able to write than those of the previous generation. The same seems to have been true in the diocese of Exeter. The period from about 1560 to 1580 did see quite an expansion of education, so that matriculations at Cambridge rose from approximately 160 a year in the 1550s to more than 340 a year in the 1570s and 1580s, although after that there seems to have been something of a decline until about 1610. This could well be due to the difficult economic conditions of the time, which made education a luxury that many people could not afford.[6]

To give a general feel for literacy rates, between 1560 and 1580, when literacy seems to have been at its height, in East Anglia about 30 per cent of husbandmen were literate, as were 75 per cent of yeomen, while 60 per cent of the tradesmen who lived in Norwich could read and write.[7]

The differing literacy rates between social groups and geographical areas was due to a number of reasons. One was that career opportunities were reasonably wide in the city, giving an incentive to learn. In less well-favoured areas, not everyone felt that the ability to read and write was worth the effort. Today people learn to read and write so young that most cannot remember being unable to do either and we also live in a society where the inability to do either is a great barrier, giving us a great incentive to learn. The result is that most people tend to underestimate the effort needed by both the pupil and the teacher in the process.

The people at the bottom of society would not necessarily have seen literacy as an asset. They certainly did not need to be literate to live and the ability to read and write did not necessarily improve a child's material prospects. The career opportunities open to the lowest rungs of society were very limited whether they could read and write or not. Apprenticeship to a profession with prospects cost money which they simply didn't have. Unless they had a particular reason for wanting to read and write, such as wanting to read the Bible, then even those who had the opportunity might not have considered worthwhile the sacrifices it entailed.

Access to education was another factor which could help or hinder literacy. There were very limited facilities in the country villages where most people lived at the time. Education also had to be paid for and even the so-called 'free schools' were not really free. Parents did not pay for the actual education their children were given but there were endless charges for everything from fuel to heat the building and candles to light it to charges for writing materials.[8] There was also the problem that if a child was in school he couldn't be helping out at home at the same time and the loss of a child's labour could be a real difficulty.

Such education as existed was generally open only to boys. This is not to say that all women in the sixteenth century were illiterate, but their education usually took place at home.[9] Even if a child did attend school he didn't necessarily learn much. Many of the teachers who were supposed to provide basic education were hardly educated themselves. There was also no training for teachers in those days and education was generally not very inspiring, particularly as teaching was not a highly regarded profession. Roger Ascham comments that 'it is a pity that commonly more care is had, yea, and that among very wise men, to find out rather a cunning man for their horse than a cunning man for their children'. He goes on to complain that although such men may claim this is not the case, they pay far more to those who train their horses than to those who teach their children.[10] Roger Ascham was, of course, a tutor himself, teaching both at Cambridge and in the royal household, as tutor to Princess Elizabeth. His complaints are certainly not without an element of bias, but even allowing for this it remains true that teachers were not well paid and teaching in general was uninspired. For example, reading was taught by sounding letters rather than whole words which must have made the process harder for children.

Teachers were not necessarily kind to their pupils either. Excess of discipline in the classroom was common and must have discouraged a great number of children. This was why Roger Ascham talks at great length of the need to encourage children as 'learning is robbed of her best wits . . . by the great beating . . .'.[11] A boy who was sent to school did not necessarily emerge an educated man.

A great number of the books on educational theory were really concerned with the teaching of upper-class children, being those who would go on to hold high office. It was only towards the end of the century that books were produced which were aimed at the improvement of education at the most basic levels. Edmund Cook, one of the most celebrated schoolmasters of his age, produced a book which went through no fewer than forty-eight editions between 1596 and 1696. It was a particularly encouraging book as Cook felt strongly that you didn't have to be a teacher in order to teach reading, so that, for example, a mother could teach her children to read herself.[12] Unfortunately, a great deal of basic education remained lacking even so.

Education for women was a different matter altogether. School was for boys, rather than girls. There were some very well-educated sixteenth-century women, such as Thomas More's daughter Margaret and the celebrated Lady Jane Grey, who so impressed Roger Ascham.[13] These ladies were very much the exception to the norm. For most women, education was a very practical matter of learning the numerous skills needed to run a house, and academic education was not generally seen as a necessity.[14]

The literacy figures do not tell the whole story, however. The number of people who could read was almost certainly higher than the number of people who could write. Reading is a much easier skill to acquire than writing and in the sixteenth century the two skills were taught separately. Children were only taught to write after they had acquired the ability to read, so there were perhaps those who never got beyond the reading stage. As reading was simpler, there might have been those who never went to school but who were taught to read at home. The problem is that there is really no way of judging the number of people who could read but not write.

One piece of evidence that suggests that more people could read than could write is the amount of literature printed that was aimed at women. The literacy rate was much lower among women than men. In the seventeenth century more than two-thirds of men could not sign their name, while four-fifths of women could not do so.[15] Even so a wide range of books, from household manuals to herbals, was produced mainly for the female market. The herbals were, of course, of general interest, but, as it was the women of the house who looked after the family's health, herbals were of more use to them than to men. The 1542 Act limiting the use of the Bible mentioned women specifically so the female reading public must have been reasonably wide.

Another factor which limited the enjoyment of reading for men and women alike was the cost of books. The printing press did make books a great deal cheaper than they had been, but they were still hardly throw-away items. One reason was the cost of paper. About 75 per cent of the cost of producing a book in the sixteenth century was the cost of the paper.[16] Until 1670 nearly all the white paper used by English printers was imported, coming mostly from France. By the late sixteenth century there were a number of English paper mills but they suffered from a shortage of skilled labour and also from a lack of the linen rags which were used in the making of paper at the time.[17] The fact that paper had to be imported made it more expensive still. In the early sixteenth century books sold at about $0.5d$ a sheet although by 1598 production costs had fallen to between $0.15d$ and $0.25d$ a sheet including the paper. In this year the Stationers' Company laid down that the maximum retail prices, depending on the type used, ranged from $0.5d$ a sheet to $0.67d$ a sheet. In practical terms a complete book was a luxury for many people.

The market for books did widen even so. This was because between about 1560 and 1635 book prices remained quite stable, while the price of other commodities doubled and wages rose by between a half and two-thirds. A building craftsman in the 1560s was making about $8–10d$ a day, but by 1600 he was making a shilling a day. A lesser yeoman with £40–£50 a year could easily have bought shorter books and pamphlets.[18]

Some printers also realised that there was a market for cheaper items, particularly the one-page broadside ballads. These cost a penny or even less and were very widely read. As early as 1520 the Oxford bookseller John Dorne sold 170 ballads at a halfpenny each, with discounts for those buying several copies, such as seven for 3*d* or twelve for 5*d*. They were intended to be sung to popular tunes and covered every conceivable topic. Huge numbers were in circulation. The Stationers' Register for the second half of the sixteenth century lists about 3,000 of them. The smallest practical print run would have been about 200, so at least 600,000 of them must have been circulating at the time.[19]

The ballads were in some ways the tabloid newspapers of their day. Sensational crime was a popular topic. *The wofull lamentacon of mrs Anne Saunders, which she wrote with her own hand, being a prisoner in newgate, Justly condemned to death* was one such ballad, which appeared in 1573.[20] It described how George Saunders, a London merchant, had been murdered by his wife's lover, with her connivance. Others told of strange wonders or of oddly deformed animals or children. Some were aimed at the improvement of their readers, such as William Feelwood's *A New Ballad against unthrifts*, written in 1562, which tried to discourage drunkenness. On the other hand, some were simply stories of love, some ribald, some merely sentimental.

The popularity of the ballads was understandable as they served a wide variety of purposes. At one level, they could be pure entertainment. At another, they provided a way of passing on news or disseminating religious or political views. The ballads were printed with cheap woodcut illustrations, and so they were even stuck up on walls as decoration. Although they were cheap, wealthier people were as keen to buy them as poorer ones. A gentry lady in the early seventeenth century collected them, looked after them carefully and even left them in her will to her clergyman son.[21] The ballads were so popular that the Tudor monarchs tried to control them. Henry VIII issued the first proclamations against them, banning offensive ballads in 1533 and again in 1542. Edward VI and Mary also took similar measures. The growing market for ballads evidently required more careful control by Elizabeth I's time, as a licensing system was set up. In 1557 the Stationers' Company was granted its charter. All printers, except the crown printers and the university presses, had to be members of the London companies and copies of all printed matter were supposed to be entered on the company's register.

Entry on the register was both a record that the item was licensed and also proof of the publisher's copyright.

The laws surrounding licensing were quite complicated but basically the job of licensing the ballads, among other items, fell to the Archbishop of London, although Archbishop Whitgift delegated this to a panel of twelve 'preachers and others' around 1588. Evidently the licensing procedure must have been creating a great deal of work. The fact that the whole system was thought necessary is an indication of how important a method of communication the ballad was seen to be.

A very wide range of reading matter was also available in book form. One very important area of interest at the time was matters spiritual. This was understandable given the huge changes that were taking place as the Church was reformed. Religion, politics and everyday life were all bound together and so interest in such matters was very strong. The Tudors were also very aware that death was never very far away and that you needed to be prepared. How better to do that than by reading spiritual books? The most important of these books was the Bible itself. By the end of the period, a copy would have cost around 3s 4d in octavo, which was a great deal of money to some people. If you couldn't afford your own Bible, you could look at the church copy, as by the reign of Elizabeth a copy of the Bible in English was supposed to be kept in all churches.[22] The provision of the Bible in English had been a matter of enormous controversy at the beginning of the century. For one thing, it had hardly been common reading. A medieval theologian might know his Bible well, but ordinary parish priests rarely did and, as books were scarce and rare, ordinary people certainly did not read it for themselves.

The Bible used by the Church in the Middle Ages was the Latin version generally known today as the Vulgate. It was not until 1526 that a complete English translation of the New Testament was available and the complete Bible was not available until 1535. The first entire version published in English was the Coverdale Bible which was originally published abroad, although two English editions were produced in 1537.

An English Bible today hardly seems a controversial object

but at the time it certainly was. General access to the Bible opened up the religious debate to everyone capable of reading it, which was an enormous change from the days when they simply believed what the parish priest told them. A strong body of educated opinion, including men such as Thomas More, felt that allowing ordinary people to read the Bible was wrong. Ordinary people didn't have the education to interpret it correctly and might therefore be led into error by not understanding what they read. This seems unbelievably patronising today, but these men were right in fearing the spread of the English Bible to some extent. The differing opinions which resulted due to the general availability of the Bible did indeed cause the Church to fragment.

Reformist opinion, of course, welcomed the spread of the English Bible. Cromwell ordered the clergy to see that every parish owned a copy. The version used was the so-called Great Bible (its name came from its large size) which was published in 1539. The Bible was, in theory at least, only supposed to be read by men of the middle and upper classes. A statue of 1542–3 forbade servants, labourers and women from reading it, even in private. Henry VIII was only prepared to allow religious reform to go so far.

It was under Edward VI, who became King in 1547, that England first became a Protestant nation. English Bibles were allowed to be circulated freely, although during Mary's reign (1553–8) the printing of the English Bible stopped, at least in England.

Under Elizabeth English Bibles were again allowed to circulate freely, but the Bible was only the tip of the iceberg as far as religious literature was concerned.[23] Readers concerned with the state of their soul could choose from a great variety of works, from collections of sermons to cheap broadside ballads aimed at reminding people of their religious duties. Some books were very serious reading indeed, such as William Perkins' *A Direction for the Government of the Tongue according to God's Word*, which appeared in 1593. It advocated that conversation should be serious. Laughter was allowed, but only sparingly. The book was quite popular, going through eight editions by 1634. Collections of sermons were favourite reading too. Going to listen to sermons was almost a form of entertainment at the time and there was considerable interest in the collected printed sermons of the more popular preachers, such as Henry Smith. Sermons were such a favourite form of communication at the time that the government kept a close eye on them. Lord Burghley, Elizabeth I's right-hand man, worked very hard to ensure that preachers did not incite their congregations to extremes, either Catholic or Protestant, which might damage Elizabeth's delicate religious settlement.

Henoch Clapham's *A brief of The Bible, Drawn First into English Poesy and then illustrated by apte Annotations*, which was published in 1596, took a different approach to furthering the cause of true religion. It took the form of a versified scripture-history, followed by explanations, doctrinal and otherwise, concerning matters in the Bible. Writing instructional books in verse was quite common at this time, as it helped to make the contents of the book easier to remember. Thomas Tusser even chose to write his book on farm management called *Five Hundred Points of Good Husbandry* in rhyme.

Religious books were not only concerned with Bible study in various forms, but very much with how religious belief should affect everyday life. In a changing society attitudes to all manner of subjects were open for discussion. An example was the rash of books concerning behaviour within marriage. In the Middle Ages, when society was very much dominated by a celibate clergy, virginity was seen as the highest calling, marriage being seen as a lesser option for those too weak-willed to be celibate. As married clergy gradually became accepted, a more positive view of marriage became the norm. Marriages were still largely business deals rather than matters of the heart at the time, but parents were warned not to force their children into unsuitable marriages merely for material or social gain. George Whetstone in his *An Heptameron of Civil Discourses* warned against the forced marriage of unequal partners, whether the inequality was in age or in social degree. Differences in religious views were also dangerous 'for if theyre love be not grafted in theyr souls, it is like theyre marriage will be insymed with defects of the body'.[24] Such marriages were bound to be disastrous and unhappy marriages merely brought the whole institution of marriage into disrepute.

Women were still seen as the inferior sex, but some writers at least became more positive in their attitudes. *Tell-Trothes New Yeares Gift*[25] not only spoke against forced marriages, but also criticised husbands who mistreated their wives by beating them or locking them away. 'The man that will lift up his hand against his wife, is like the horse that doth fling out his heles to strike his keeper.'

The religious writers in general seem to have been keen to corner the market for literature, as Puritan opinion discouraged any but serious reading. Romances, books of jests and suchlike were seen by them as being not only a frivolous waste of time but also encouraging sin. One writer even felt that light reading which was based on Italian tales, as many were, was likely to lead to popery: 'More Papists be made by your merry bookes of Italie, than by your earnest books of Lovaine. This complaint ought wise men to consider well of, for that the world was never more full of Italian conceits, nor men more in danger for the long contempt of Gods trueth to be Italianted.'[26] (Louvain, in what is now Belgium, was home to an important religious seminary.)

These dreadful warnings fortunately did not discourage most readers, although middle-class readers preferred to feel that even their recreational reading had some improving quality to it. Even stories which were really just for entertainment were often given a varnish of usefulness by being presented as providing good moral instruction. An example is Thomas East, who assured his readers in the preface to *The Third part of the first booke, Of The Mirrour of Knighthood*, published in 1586, that this work 'may serve to the exalting of vertue and weldoing, and to the repressing of vice'.[27]

Tastes in recreational reading did change in the sixteenth century. The tales of chivalry which had originally been devised for aristocratic audiences in the Middle Ages, like *Le Morte D'Arthur* and *Bevis of Hampton*, were still being printed even at the end of the century. However, they were definitely on their way down socially, being produced in cheaper editions to appeal to people with less money. Wealthier readers regarded them as old-fashioned. Their place was taken by a variety of literature. Short stories taken from the Italian 'novelles' were very popular, although they were often given a heavy moral gloss for English audiences which they lacked in the original. George Pettie's *A Petite Pallace of pettie his Pleasure*, which was first published in 1576, followed this format and was popular enough to go through five editions by 1613.

The very latest in literature was not limited to court circles. Sir Philip Sidney's *Arcadia* was frequently reprinted and so must have been bought by people outside the court. It was so popular that a cheap edition was produced in Edinburgh in 1599 which was aimed at under-selling the more expensive folio version produced in London.[28] Other writers even deliberately used the word 'Arcadia' in the titles of their books in order to attract attention. Gervais Markham, a writer well known in his day for writing anything he thought would sell, recognised the trend. In 1607 he brought out *The English Arcadia, Alluding his beginning from Sir Philip Sidneys ending*.

Tales glorifying the attributes which made a businessman successful, like hard work and thrift, were naturally popular at a time when the business world was expanding. Thomas Deloney's *The Pleasant Historie of Jacke of Newbery* (1596–7) told of the famous Jack of Newbery, weaver, who made his fortune and rose to the dizzy heights of entertaining the king and even provided a hundred men at his own expense to fight at Flodden.

Another very popular subject at the time was history. This was because history was seen as being absolutely vital in teaching good moral behaviour, encouraging citizens to follow the good example set by the great figures of the past. The way people looked at history at the time was thus very different from the modern view.[29]

Modern historical teaching centres around how to use the evidence which survives from the past to work out what was happening. Today great emphasis is placed on stressing relative values, as events can be viewed very differently according to the perspective of the viewer. People of the Renaissance, on the other hand, looked to history for moral and political advice, reading into the past things which a modern historian might dispute ever existed. For example, Sir Thomas Elyot in the *Book Named the Governor* makes great play on the finer details of the life of Alexander the Great, although a modern historian would find no evidence at all that Alexander ever held some of the views attributed to him. To Renaissance eyes the important issue was the moral of the story.

History was thus the perfect literature for the sixteenth-century middle classes. The strictest of Puritans, who would have forbidden his family to read much recreational literature, could hardly deny them the moral benefits of a good history book. On the other hand, many histories contained thrilling stories of battles, and the mighty deed of heroes and heroines, so they were very entertaining reading. Histories could also remind the patriotic English that their nation had a great and noble past. A great number of history books were printed and many enjoyed considerable success. Edward Hall, a barrister at Gray's Inn, published *The Union of the Two Noble and Illustrious Families York and Lancaster* in 1542 which went through five editions in the next ten years.

Richard Grafton was another producer of histories. He was both a printer and a prosperous member of the Grocers' Company, and certainly had an eye for business. He started out in publishing by distributing the edition of the Bible printed in Antwerp known as 'Matthew's' Bible, which he did in partnership with another grocer called Edward Whitchurch. They were good businessmen, as they had this licensed under the privy seal, which stopped other people underselling them. He then turned to history and published the *Chronicle* of John Hardyng, which was a history written in verse. Grafton even brought the work up to date by adding the history of the kings from Edward IV to Henry VIII.[30] The large chronicles, like Hall's, were expensive but plenty of much smaller and cheaper editions of histories were produced. One was even produced in broadside ballad form. It was called *The Cronycle of all the Kynges: that have Reygned in Englande: Sythe the Conquest of Willyam the Conqueroure.*[31] Unfortunately not all writers even of a popular subject like history had Grafton's commercial sense.

John Stow, whose famous *Survey of London* has enjoyed many reprints right into the twentieth century, died in poverty.

The changing social conditions of the time required not only moral advice but also much more practical instruction. The middle-class merchant and yeoman might well find that his increased wealth opened his social horizons, so that he and his children could mix in circles hitherto closed to them. Books about polite behaviour were much in demand as a result. One example of such a book was Robert Peterson's English translation of the Italian *Il Galateo* by Giovanni della Casa, which gave practical instructions on how to behave in all circumstances.

There was also the tricky problem of conversation to be dealt with. Learning was in vogue and it was fashionable to slip suitable quotations from various learned sources into both your correspondence and your conversation. This was all very well if you had enjoyed the benefits of a university education but that was hardly true of most people. Books full of suitable quotations, proverbs, etc., were therefore a useful addition to your library, as were books on letter writing. Letters were not intended to be brief and to the point, but to demonstrate the sender's writing skills. Books such as *The Enimie of Idlenesse*, published in 1568, provided instruction, while *The English Secretary* (1586) even gave form letters which could be copied. It went through eight editions by 1626.[32]

One of the most basic changes that the printing press and the spread of education brought about was the acceptance of English as a language of instruction. In the days before the printing press, when books were very expensive to produce, it followed that it was best to produce them in a language that could be read by as many people as possible. The learned community in Europe was quite small and so the use of Latin as a common language was very sensible. All educated individuals could talk to each other, regardless of where they came from. The problem was that before people could even start their education they had to become fluent in Latin. The time and trouble this took closed education to many. Producing books in English, on the other hand, widened the market for them, an important point when the printing press was introduced and printers had their profit margins to think of.

Setting up a press was quite an expensive and time-consuming business. It could take as long as two years to print even a small edition of a large book and if only a few copies were produced the cost per copy would be high. In the sixteenth century printers normally produced around 1,000 to 1,500 copies of each book. If they produced more than this the overheads became uneconomic. Printers usually allowed several months' credit to their customers after the book was delivered and if they had paid for the paper as well they would have to wait until the books sold to get their money back. They wanted to produce works that would sell and books in English, reaching a wider audience, would sell faster than books in Latin.[33]

In the early days of English printing, translated works had to be published as there was nothing else. Educated people wrote in Latin, not in English, and it took time for a suitable body of work in English to be written. The middle-class audience was also hungry for books translated, not only from Latin, but also from other languages. Italy was definitely the centre of all things fashionable in the sixteenth century, so there was a desire to read translations of Italian books. Works were also translated from other languages, particularly if the translator felt that he could widen the spread of useful knowledge in this way. John Frampton, a retired merchant, translated *Joyfull News Out of The Newe Founde Worlde*, from the original Spanish as the book described drugs newly discovered in America.[34]

Translating spiritual works also provided an outlet for the skills of the few highly educated women of the day. Provided the work was produced with suitable protestations of feminine modesty it was considered appropriate that women should help the spread of true religion in this way. Margaret More-Roper, Thomas More's daughter, published a translation of Erasmus' *Devout Treatise upon the Paternoster* while the five Cooke sisters produced a number of translations of other religious works.[35] Despite the obvious market for translated works, translators still felt the need to justify their actions. Thomas Wilson, a translator of the time, commented:

But such as are grieved with translated bokes, are lyke to them that eating fine Manchet, are angry with other that feede on Cheate breade. And yet God knoweth men would as glady eat Manchet as they, if they had it. But all can not wear Velvet or feed with the best, and therefore such are contented for necessities sake to weare out Countrie cloth, and to take themselves to harde fare, that can have no better . . .'[36]

Manchet was best-quality white bread and definitely a luxury item, while cheat bread was coarser, cheaper and therefore more common. Wilson was therefore making his point that, while reading something in the original was the ideal, it wasn't an option open to many people.

Those who wrote works in English also often apologised for doing so. Sir Thomas Elyot, when writing his *Castel of Helth*, felt he had to justify writing in English by saying that he wanted as many people as possible to benefit from being able to read his book.[37] This feeling gradually lessened as time went on and more writers began to write in English rather than Latin. Sir Philip Sidney, for example, was happy to produce works in English.

This did not mean that learning Latin fell out of favour. The grammar schools continued to place a great deal of emphasis on Latin and even merchants, who hardly had much time for study for its own sake, realised that there was a benefit to having a knowledge of the language. As it was so widely used, it was likely that they would be able to talk to educated people at least in Latin, even if they didn't have any other language in common.

Latin was not the only language that merchants found useful. French was commonly learnt and a number of French-English dialogues were produced to help to teach the language. Hollybrand's dialogues, some of which are reproduced in Chapter 2, were produced for this reason. Hollybrand also kept a school for teaching children French, so books were not the only way to learn a language. A merchant with contacts in several countries might need a knowledge of several languages, so polyglot dictionaries were produced. These would contain vocabulary in a variety of languages, such as Spanish, Italian, Latin, English, French and Dutch.[38]

The range of reading materials available in the sixteenth century was therefore remarkably wide, although the market for longer books remained restricted to the middle and upper classes. Some readers at least read a remarkable variety of subjects. Robert Laneham, a London mercer, wrote to his friend Humphrey Martin about the contents of the library of Captain Cox, a prosperous Coventry mason. Captain Cox had all the old favourites, like stories of chivalry and tales of Robin Hood, that had been enjoyed since the Middle Ages. He also had books of jests and riddles, Spencer's Shepherd's Calendar, *Stans puer ad mensam* (a book of etiquette) and books on scientific subjects like astronomy and health, plus the inevitable few volumes on religious subjects. Captain Cox's library was not typical, or else Robert Laneham would hardly have thought to write about it in such detail to his friend. Even so it does give an indication of just how wide a person's reading could be in the sixteenth century.[39]

EIGHT
The Theatre

The history of drama in the sixteenth century is so over-shadowed by Shakespeare that it is easy to forget that English drama has a history that stretches back long before his time. Plays had taken place in the open air, in wealthy people's houses and in schools and universities for centuries before the purpose-built theatres opened at the end of the sixteenth century.

In the Middle Ages one of the main forms of public entertainment was religious drama of various kinds, often associated with public holidays like Corpus Christi. These plays were written in English and were designed to instruct the audience in religious doctrine. The problem is that little is known about them as not many texts survive and those that do are not always complete. The texts, in any case, were not designed as reading material but as working scripts for the actors and may only give a general idea of what was said.[1]

Individual plays were performed, especially by small touring troupes of actors, but the big public entertainments were on a rather grander scale. Cycles of plays were performed, the idea being that there would be a general theme which would include many smaller, individual plays. A favourite theme in England was the story of life from Creation to Doomsday. The whole cycle was known as a play, while the individual short plays which made up the whole were known as pageants.

There were a number of different ways of staging the plays although the details of any forms of staging are not known for certain. Some, such as the York cycle, seem to have been performed on pageant wagons. The wagons followed a well-defined route, and made a certain number of stops around the city. The York route contained between twelve and sixteen stops. It was an early start for the actors in the first plays as, according to the city ordinances, they had to be ready to begin at 4.30 in the morning. The first of the pageants, telling the story of the Creation, would set off, then stop at the first stop. The actors would perform their piece and move on to the second stop, while the second pageant left the starting point, proceeding to the first stop, and so the play continued.

The result would not have been as seamless as the description suggests. It would not have been a case of the plays following one another without a break. The pageants were of different lengths, the shortest being ten minutes and the longest forty, so inevitably there were gaps between some of them. This would not necessarily have been a problem. The audience was not a captive one, as they simply lined the York streets, so when there was nothing happening where you were standing you could wander off and do something else or watch a pageant being performed somewhere else along the route. The mayor and aldermen, who conversely were a captive audience watching from their chamber, were probably very glad of the breaks. If the whole cycle was performed at once, then it would have taken about twenty-two hours. Even if only some of the plays were produced each year, as was probably the case, the total performance time would still have been several hours. The breaks would have been necessary.[2]

The actors would all have been amateurs recruited locally, but this does not mean that such events were not impressive. The individual pageants were all sponsored by a particular craft guild and there was intense rivalry between them. A great deal of money and effort went into creating the pageants, so that the Noah's Ark pageant at Hull cost £8 8s to produce in 1494, a time when a labourer could be earning about £3 a year.[3]

The York pageants carts were specially built for their purpose. Some were even double deckers with lifts to allow characters to ascend into 'heaven'. When not in use they were stripped of their scenery and stored in special pageant houses. They were quite literally stages on wheels, not converted carts.[4]

Quite a few dramatic effects were included, such as 'setting the world on fire' as part of the Coventry Doomsday pageant, while the Holy Spirit falling upon the disciples seems to have been portrayed with real fire at Chester. The plays were far from being crude or childlike.[5]

Not all such drama was produced on pageant carts. It seems that other plays were produced on stages erected around an open space in which the audience stood. In the case of much smaller productions, like the ones performed by the companies of travelling players, a booth stage might be set up.

Dramatic productions were not always intended for public viewing. The spectacular court entertainments described in Chapter 3 were of course only for the select few. Equally, a great many plays were produced in educational establishments like the Inns of Court, the universities and various schools. The plays produced tended to be classical dramas, as part of the reason for producing them was to help the students with their studies. The Lord of Misrule's pastimes in Christ Church College in 1554 were limited to four productions, which was to be a comedy and a tragedy in Greek and the same in Latin. Modern plays in classical languages were also produced, such as Nicholas Grimald's *Christus Reclivivus* which was performed at Brasenose College in 1540.[6] When Queen Elizabeth and her court visited Cambridge in August 1564 the entertainments included some quite elaborate dramatic productions.

The Oxford and Cambridge colleges also employed travelling players in their Christmas entertainments in the early sixteenth century but as time went on the university authorities began to see the professional actors as a source of trouble. In October 1575 the vice-chancellor of Cambridge wrote to the Privy Council complaining about the 'misdemeanour of divers badd persons which wanderinge aboute the Countrye under the colour of licenses for the makeinge of shewes, and playeigne of Enterludes and settinge furth of other vaine games and pastimes . . . thereby allure manie of our Scholers from the good course of theire studies and usual exercises for the increase of learninge'.[7] These complaints sound very similar to the ones being made in London by the city authorities at around the same time, but whether they were justified or not, performances were prohibited in Cambridge within the university or town, or within five miles of it.

The Inns of Court, the law schools of the time, also showed a lively interest in drama. Like the universities, the students both performed plays themselves and employed professional troupes to perform. There seems to have been less emphasis on classical drama at the Inns of Court, where Italian comedy seems to have been popular. Gascoignes' *Supposes* (Arioto's *I Suppositi*), Jeffere's *Buglears* (Grazzini's *La Spiritata*) and *Two Italian Gentlemen* by an unknown writer (Pasqualigo's *Il Fedele*) were all produced at Gray's Inn.[8]

Drama was also included in the education of younger boys. The grander public schools produced plays and the tradition of drama at the choir schools of the Chapel Royal and St Paul's was so strong that it led to the development of the professional boy troupes which were popular in the late sixteenth century.

It would be easy to over-emphasise the part drama played in education as the universities, Inns of Court and grander public schools only educated the wealthy. Drama did not play a part in the formal education of those lower down the social scale. Even so it does give an indication of how strong the interest in drama was at the time. However it was produced, the power of drama was certainly realised. The religious plays of the Middle Ages all centred around the fight between good and evil, so people were used to seeing the abstract ideas of vices and virtues personified as people. In other words, they were used to interpreting what they saw on the stage just as in court circles people were used to interpreting the political messages behind the pageants.

The power drama could have is demonstrated by an incident described by Edward Hall. A play was performed before Cardinal Wolsey at Gray's Inn during the Christmas festivities of 1526:

This Christmas was a goodly disgiusyng plaied at Greis inne whiche was compiled for the moste part, by master Jhon Roo, seriant at the law xx yere past, and long before the Cardinall had any authoritie, the effecte of the plaie was that lord governance was ruled by dissipacion and negligence by whose misgovernance and evill order, lady Publicke wele was put from governance: which caused Rumor Populi, Inward grudge, and disdain of wanton sovereignetie to rise with a greate multitude, to expell negligence and dissipacion and to restore Plubik welth again to her estate, which was so done.

Hall describes the play as being enjoyed by most people, except Cardinal Wolsey who 'imagined that the plaie had been divised of hym, and in a greate time sent for the said master Roo, and set hym to the Flete, and after he sent for the yong gentlemen that plaied in the plaie, and them highly rebuked and thretened, and sent one of them called Thomas Moyle of Kent to the Flete . . .'.[9]

In fact Hall's comment that Wolsey 'imagined' the play to be about him is tongue in cheek. There were many who felt that Wolsey encouraged Henry VIII's love of extravagance to an unhealthy degree. Another writer, Henry's ex-tutor and poet laureate John Skelton, wrote a play called *Magnificence* on the same theme at around the same time, which was also performed before the court. Wolsey knew quite well that the play was aimed at him. The power of the play was an accepted thing. It was this very power that made the Tudor monarchs determined to control drama. The sixteenth century was an age when the power of the central government increased considerably and this, coupled with the religious changes of the age, could hardly leave drama unaffected.

The first moves to control it came as religious drama associated with the great annual festivals was gradually suppressed, as is discussed in Chapter 4. At first sight it might have seemed logical to replace the drama connected with the Roman Catholic Church with Protestant themes but this would have been difficult. Religious feelings were running so high that it was felt best to leave the subject alone altogether for fear of provoking riots.

This was particularly the case after Kett's Rebellion of 1549. This was a turbulent year, with unrest in the West Country having to be suppressed. Shortly after there was further trouble in East Anglia, which started as a protest against the enclosure of some common land but which snowballed into more serious trouble. Kett led 16,000 men to blockade Norwich, apparently in the knowledge that a public play produced at Wimondham, not far from Norwich, would have attracted a useful crowd of people 'to enter further unto their wicked enterprise'.[10] The heady mixture of large crowds and religious plays was dangerous. It was no coincidence that the Archbishop of York, Edmund Grindal, confiscated the texts of the York Corpus Christi play in 1570 after the revolt of the Northern Earls in 1569.

Queen Elizabeth was perfectly aware that her religious settlement was fragile and so she felt it best to steer entertainments at court away from religious themes. She did allow some anti-Catholic drama at the beginning of her reign. In 1558 she saw an entertainment which showed crows in the habits of cardinals, asses dressed as bishops and wolves dressed as abbots,[11] but this type of entertainment wasn't something she encouraged. She certainly did not want any of her subjects stirring up religious tension either, so she tightened up the procedure for licensing drama by a proclamation of 16 May 1559:

The Quenes Maiestie doth straightly forbyd al maner Interluded to be playde, eyther openly or privately, except that the same be noticed before hande, and licenced within any Citie or towne corporate by the Maior or other cheife officers of the same and within any shyre, by suche as shelbe Lieuetenauntes for the Queenes maiestie in the same shyre, or by two of the Justices of the pax inhabyting within that part of the shire where any shalbe played.[12]

The control of drama was strengthened yet again in 1572 when the Act for the Punishment of Vagabonds was made law. Under this act every company of actors had to be authorised by a noble or by two judicial dignitaries of the realm. In 1598 the licensing power was taken away from the magistrates, leaving only great nobles with the ability to license a company. If any company bearing its name was to perform work which offended the monarch, the noble patron could expect trouble, so this was quite an effective way of making sure that no offensive material was produced. It was not only the players who needed a licence to perform; plays also had to be given official consent. The Lord Chamberlain had to license the plays with the Master of the Revels acting as his executive. In 1581 the Master of the Revels was given the power to censor plays so control was quite strict.[13]

The Tudors may have wanted to control drama, but they definitely did not want it destroyed. It was too useful a tool for that and in any case court life would have been dull without pageants and plays. It was often cheaper to summon an existing company of actors to perform a play at Christmas before the court than it was to put on some kind of court disguising, so actors were frequently summoned to court. Nobles and gentlemen also liked to entertain their friends in the same way, so there was plenty of support for good professional troupes among the ruling classes.

This was a very important point as there were many among the ruling élite, particularly in London, who disliked actors and plays. There was, of course, the usual fear of the possibility of disorder when large numbers of people came together in one place, but the distrust went deeper than that. There was a puritan element that felt that plays led to all kinds of vice and that the acting itself was simply a dangerous form of pretence and illusion. This is how the city authorities described their objections in 1574. The section is quite long but it is worth quoting in full as it does explain their objections in detail:

Whereas heartofore sondrye greate disorders and inconvenyences have benne found to ensewe to this Cittie by the inordynate hauntyinge of greate multitudes of people, speicallye youthe, to plays, enterludes and shewes, namelye occasyon of ffrayes and quarrelles, eavell practizes and incontinenge in greate Innes havinge chambers and secrete places adjoyninge to their open stagies and gallyries inveglynge and allurynge of maides, speciallye orphanes and good Cityzens Children under Age, to previe and unmete Contractes, the publishinge of unchaste uncomelye and unshamefaste speeches and doynges, withdrawinge of the Queens Majesties Subjects from dyvne service of Sonndaies and hollydayes, at which tymes suche playes weare chefelye used, unthriftye waste of the moneye of the poore and fond persons, sondrye robberies by pychinge and cuttinge of purses, utteringe of popular busye and desycisous matters, and manie other Corruptions of youthe and other enormyties, besydes that allso soundrye slaughters and mayheminges of the Quene Subjectes have happened by ruines of Skaffoldes, fframes and Stagies, and by engynes, weapons and powder used in plaies. And whear(as) in tyme of goddes visitacion of the plague suche assemblies of the people in thronge and presse have benne verye daungerous for the spreadinge of Infection. . . .[14]

In other words both plays and players were considered highly disreputable and undesirable.

This might have been the opinion of the city élite but judging by the popularity of the theatre in London most people would not have agreed. English drama was so popular that by the late sixteenth century it was being played not only in England and Scotland but also in mainland Europe. English drama, in English, could be seen in Germany, Holland, Belgium, Denmark, Poland and France.[15]

The opposition of the city authorities coupled with the Londoners' enthusiasm for plays led to the development of purpose-built theatres. The 1572 Act for the Punishment of Vagabonds, which led to troupes of players being sponsored by great nobles, gave the players a measure of protection. The time seemed right to venture into building purpose-built theatres. The idea of constructing special buildings in which to stage dramatic performances was further prompted by the fact that, in the mid-sixteenth century, galleried inns like the George Inn, shown above, had become favourite places for holding such events; the city authorities were not very happy about this and, at some point in the late sixteenth century (the exact date being unclear), they did manage to have inns banned from being used as theatres. It was perhaps in anticipation of this ban that the development of purpose-built theatres began.

There were two basic types of purpose-built theatre at the time. One was the amphitheatre, which is of the same type as the rebuilt Globe Theatre. The more expensive seats and the stage were both roofed over, but the body of the theatre was open to the sky. The other type was the hall, which was based on the great halls of wealthy people's houses in which drama had been performed for centuries. This type of theatre was smaller than the amphitheatres, but was completely roofed over and therefore more comfortable. Due to their smaller capacity, the tickets cost more in a hall theatre, so that poorer people could not afford to go to them. The cheapest seats at the Globe in 1600, standing in the open air in the yard, cost $1d$, which was cheap entertainment. The cheapest seats in the hall houses were $6d$, which was half a London artisan's weekly wage.[16]

The transition to purpose-built theatres was by no means a simple one. The story of the famous Globe Theatre gives a good indication of the problems involved. The Globe had its origins in a building known as The Theatre. The problem was that The Theatre stood in Shoreditch, to the north of the city, in the Liberty of Holywell, which was conveniently outside the city jurisdiction. It was built on leased land, and building on leased land without the owner's permission was illegal. The owner of the land did not like theatres and made it clear that he would not allow it to continue once the lease was up. On top of that, the city authorities were gradually winning their battle to keep playing out of inns. The Theatre was an amphitheatre-style building, which meant that it was not very practical for use during the winter. The galleried inns were a logical place to retreat to during the winter, so this ban posed a serious problem.

The Theatre's owner, James Burbage, decided that it was time to move upmarket. He decided to transfer his company, which, incidentally, was the one Shakespeare worked for, to a hall playhouse. This also had the advantage of being usable all year round.

In 1595 Burbage spent £600 on buying an impressive building in Blackfriars and converting it to a theatre. It had originally been the upper frater of the Blackfriars' priory and the site was again conveniently outside the city jurisdiction. It was also on the fashionable western side of the city, close to where the wealthier theatre-goers lived. Unfortunately the residents of Blackfriars were not quite ready for such a theatre. The only theatre they had tolerated before had been one used by the Chapel Children, a boys' company. The boys' companies were somehow seen as being more respectable than the adults, possibly because children could hardly be accused of all the crimes associated with actors at the time. The boy players also only played once a week while the adults performed daily, so the adult company brought more problems in the way of traffic congestion etc. with them.

The result was that the residents felt that the tone of the area was being lowered by the presence of an adult company and petitioned the privy council. It must have been particularly galling to Burbage that the company's patron, Lord Hunsdon, the Lord Chamberlain, also signed the petition. This left James Burbage with a theatre he couldn't use and nowhere for the company to perform. He never had time to resolve the problem himself as he died in 1597, leaving his sons Cuthbert and Richard to sort out the problem. The solution to the problem was to finance a new theatre by offering shares in the building to the five leading players in the company (including Shakespeare) and then taking down The Theatre building in Shoreditch and rebuilding it on a new site under a new name, the Globe.

The gamble paid off. The Globe was, of course, a successful venture and to add to the success, in 1608 the King's Men, the Globe theatre company, was also allowed to use the Blackfriars' theatre, where they performed in winter. The financial arrangements also helped tie the leading players to the company which gave it a rare degree of stability in an age when theatre company personnel in general changed rapidly.[17]

The opposition to the theatre that existed in the sixteenth century does give the impression that playgoing was a disreputable pastime. In fact many of the Blackfriars' residents who so violently opposed a theatre on their own doorstep would have been regular theatre-goers themselves. Despite the city authorities' dislike of it, the theatre was patronised by all social classes and by both men and women.

London at the end of the sixteenth century was a growing city. Despite the many outbreaks of plague and the general cramped conditions for many people who lived there the population had increased about four times between 1500 and 1600 to about 200,000 people. The size of the population at this time is only an estimate due to the lack of reliable figures but, given that by 1600 there were probably about four million people living in England,[18] London was a very large city.

The Londoners wanted entertainment, the poorer people wanted something cheap – and the theatre fitted the bill nicely. A penny only bought you a place standing in the yard, the section open to the sky, but it was a cheap afternoon out. Wealthier Londoners wanted to show off their fine clothes, something they could do by sitting in a box, particularly one of the expensive 'lord's rooms'. The theatre had something for everyone.

The London audience was not only large but relatively well educated. There were, of course, no detailed figures concerning literacy kept at the time but it seems that in London only 18 per cent of apprentices and 3 per cent of servants could not sign their names, whereas in the provinces in the same social class of people 73 per cent or even 100 per cent may not have been literate. These figures are only a rough and ready estimate but it does give an indication that the London audience was liable to appreciate writers like Shakespeare and Marlowe.[19] Theatre audiences were large, even considering London's growing population. The amphitheatres held about 2,500 people and the halls about 1,000 and estimates for 1595 suggest that about 15,000 people visited the theatre weekly.[20] The programme changed very frequently, so that the same play was rarely performed on consecutive nights. You could go to the theatre every week and see a different play each time.

The number of plays being staged in London certainly seems to have impressed visitors. Thomas Platter notes that 'daily at two in the afternoon, London has two, sometimes three plays running in different places, competing with each other, and those which play best obtain most spectators.'[21] The players certainly had to work for their money as a result. They often performed a different play every day and had to produce new plays frequently. In the 1594/5 season the Admiral's Men performed six days a week and offered no fewer than thirty-eight plays that season, of which twenty-one were new. Two of the new plays were only given one performance and only eight of the new plays were performed in the next season. Even the really popular plays were only performed about once a month.[22]

As the amphitheatre playhouses were so much cheaper to go to than the halls it is easy to assume that the wealthy went to the halls and the poorer people to the amphitheatres, but the division was not as simple as that. Certainly the halls were too expensive for many people but the wealthy went to the amphitheatres and the halls alike. This fact was highlighted in 1602 when a rather odd incident took place. At this time soldiers were being impressed for the war in the Low Countries and the city authorities, always on the lookout for a chance to discourage theatre-going, used it as a chance to raid the amphitheatres. Philip Gawdy, a London lawyer, wrote to a friend that as a result 'they did not only presse gentlemen and sarvingmen but Lawyers, Clarkes, country men that had lawe causes, aye the Quenes men, knights and as it was credibly reported one Earle . . .'.[23]

It could have been that Gawdy exaggerated the numbers of gentry but the numbers given by him, about 4,000 people from three large amphitheatres and a few bowling alleys, seem reasonable. Certainly the well-to-do German visitor Thomas Platter went to an amphitheatre in 1599 as did Prince Lewis of Anhalt-Cothen, who visited England at about the same time. The amphitheatres were obviously seen as respectable enough in the sixteenth century.

It was one thing for a man to visit the playhouse but another for a woman. Right up until the time when the playhouses were closed in 1642 there was a popular prejudice that all female playgoers were looking for sex, either for profit or pleasure. Southwark theatres were surrounded by brothels, so it was a difficult image to shake off. This prejudice did fade a little after

1600 but it still existed. This did not mean that women could not go to the theatre and still be seen as respectable, but it did mean that they had to go with a male escort. It was also more acceptable for a woman to visit the more expensive hall playhouses than the amphitheatres. Anne, Lady Halkett's autobiography does suggest that playgoing became easier for women in the 1630s as she says that she was the first to start the habit of unmarried women going to the theatre together in groups. She describes 'three or four of us going together without any man, and every one paying for themselves by giving the money to the footman who waited on us, and he gave itt to the play-howse. And this I did first upon hearing some gentelmen telling what ladys they had waited on to plays, and how much itt cost them; upon which I resolve none should say the same of mee . . .'.[24]

Theatre-going seems to have changed by Anne Halkett's time. By the 1630s it does seem that the amphitheatres in the northern suburbs were catering to a less gentlemanly audience than the city hall playhouses. Perhaps in consequence the hall playhouses were considered more socially acceptable so that Anne Halkett and her friends felt free to go without men.[25]

A respectable woman would have sat in a box, and would not have drawn attention to herself by sitting up on the stage. In the amphitheatre playhouses the people standing in the yard had to look up at the raised stage, so people could not be allowed to obscure the view further by sitting up there. The hall playhouses, however, were constructed very like a modern theatre, so that the audience looked down on the stage. People could be allowed to sit on stools around the stage, right next to the actors. This was where the 'gulls' chose to sit. 'Gulls' were the young men who wanted to draw attention to themselves. Thomas Dekker, the playwright, wrote *The Gull's Hornbook*, a tongue-in-cheek guide telling these young men how to behave. To gain maximum effect, Dekker suggests that the gull should arrive late. 'Present not yourself on the stage, especially at a new play, until the quaking Prologue hath by rubbing got colour into his cheeks, and is ready to give the trumpets their cue that he's upon point to enter. . . . '[26] The gull having made a suitably dramatic entry, Dekker then suggests that the best way to continue to attract attention was to laugh loudly in the serious part of the tragedy, to give the audience the benefit of your 'wit' by talking loudly during the performance and generally to annoy actors and audience alike.

Dekker's gull's behaviour does beg the question as to how theatre audiences in general behaved at the time. The impression is that sixteenth-century audiences tended to be more lively than modern ones. In March 1632 the court visited Cambridge and a play was put on for their majesties' entertainment. Students in any age have always been liable to cause trouble so the university published strict rules of conduct for the performance:

> Item: that no tabacco be taken into the Hall nor anywyere else publicly, and that neither at their standing in the streets, or before the comedy begin, nor all the time there, any rude or immodest exclamation to be made, nor any humming, hawking, whistling, hissing or laughing be used, or any stamping or knocking nor any such other uncivil or unscholarlike or boyish demeanor, upon any occasion; nor that any clapping of hands be had until the Plaudite at the end of the comedy, except his Majesty, the Queen or others of the best quality here do apparently begin the same.[27]

These regulations, of course, show audience behaviour at its worst, but it does indicate what might have gone on.

Audiences did react strongly to what they saw. Comments by playwrights of the time suggest that hissing, clapping and shouts in response to the action were the norm but at least these were in response to the play, which suggests that people were following with interest. This is of note in itself as there were a number of distractions for the audience, especially at the amphitheatre playhouses.

The performance would have taken place in full daylight, unlike today when audiences sit in the dark so that all your attention is naturally focused on the stage. There was also no interval and the performance lasted about three hours. This was an age when people could listen to sermons which lasted for hours, so presumably they must have had more staying power than a modern audience. However, concentrating for the whole time would have been hard work given the distractions, particularly the hawkers who were walking around selling food and drink. Thomas Platter commented that 'during the performance food and drink are carried round the audience, so that for what one cares to pay one may also have refreshment.'[28] The favourite foods seem to have been apples and nuts. For example, in his play *Wit Without Money* Fletcher talks of people who 'crack Nuts with the Scholars in penny Rooms again, and fight for Apples'.[29] Cracking nuts seems to have caused the same annoyance that people rustling sweet-papers does today.

Another annoyance was the smoking of tobacco. Pipe-smoking was a common habit in England by the end of the sixteenth century, a habit which did not go unnoticed by Thomas Platter:

> In the ale-houses tabacco or a species of wound-wort are also obtainable for one's money, and the powder is lit in a small pipe, the smoke sucked into the mouth, and the saliva is allowed to run freely, after which a good draught of Spanish wine follows. This they regard as a curious medicine for defluctions, and as a pleasure, and the habit is so common with them, that they always carry the instrument with them, and light up on all occasions, at the play, in the taverns or elsewhere . . .[30]

The instructions for behaviour at the royal play in Cambridge include the banning of tobacco and Dekker's gull smoked a pipe. The annoyance of tobacco at the theatre was evidently understood. Sitting next to someone smoking a pipe for three hours in a theatre must have been very unpleasant.

The conditions in the theatre were not very comfortable by modern standards but ordinary people of the time can hardly have thought them that bad. Thomas Platter comments that it was possible to pay for cushioned seats at the theatre, but that such seats cost 3*d* as opposed to the 2*d* it cost for a wooden bench or the 1*d* it cost to stand in the yard. Most people were used to hard wooden benches though, as upholstery was a luxury for the wealthy.

Another hazard of sixteenth-century theatre-going must have been headgear, as wealthy people's hats were high-crowned at the time. In the amphitheatre playhouses this must have been less of a problem, as the wealthy people sat in the more expensive seats around the edge of the theatre. In the hall houses it must have been more of a problem as the wealthier patrons there sat at the front.

Different conditions pertained in the hall houses in other ways too. They did not have the benefit of natural light and so had to be lit with candles. This meant that there had to be breaks in the performance to allow the candles to be trimmed. The audience was also smaller, and everyone sat down so that probably the audiences here were rather less lively. The criticism of those who opposed the theatre does make it sound as if audiences were virtually on the point of riot most of the time and that most of them were prostitutes or pickpockets anyway. If this had really been the case then it would have been unlikely that the aristocracy and even the Queen herself would have encouraged the theatre. There were without doubt always both prostitutes looking for trade and pickpockets around, but they were to be found anywhere where crowds of people gathered. Lively the audiences might have been, but not as dangerously so as is often maintained.

It is understandable that people did not want to live near playhouses, especially the amphitheatres. The noise from the performances carried a long way since not only was there no roof to deaden the noise but a great deal of music was a standard part of the performance. The hall playhouses provided a musical performance which preceded the play itself, while the amphitheatres offered a 'jig' after the performance. The jig was a lively combination of ribald verse, dancing and singing. William Kemp, who was for five years a member of the Lord Chamberlain's Men, was famous for performing them. After he left that Company he even performed the famous 'Nine Day's Wonder' in 1600, when he danced from London to Norwich in nine days.[31]

The noise of the music was such a standard complaint that it was one of the many reasons set forward by the inhabitants of

Blackfriars for keeping Burbage's troupe out of his new theatre. They conveniently forgot that the new playhouse was a hall, not an amphitheatre, so the noise would not carry.

The popularity of the theatre did bring another problem which particularly affected hall playhouses since they stood within the narrow streets of the city. This was the very modern-sounding problem of traffic. The amphitheatres did not cause so much nuisance as they were sited away from the city and in any case many of their audience came and went on foot. The hall playhouses attracted wealthier audiences who often travelled by coach. Once the hall theatres became established in the seventeenth century the problem became quite serious as there was nobody to police traffic in those days.[32]

Despite the popularity of plays, the professions of both actor and playwright were not highly regarded at the time. Then as now, most members of both professions were certainly not well off and there were still many actors who scraped a living by wandering about the country and who never enjoyed the relative prosperity of working with a London company. At a time when 'masterless men' were mistrusted, actors must have hardly seemed like respectable members of society. The actors working in the permanent theatres in London were far better off than those who had to tour constantly. At times of plague the theatres were closed, so the actors had to go on the road to make a living Philip Henslowe's contract with one of his hired men, William Kendal, states that he is to be paid 10s a week while working in London but only 5s on tour 'in the country'.[33] This demonstrates how much lower the troupe's profits were expected to be if they had to go on tour. Those who combined acting or playwriting ability with a good head for business could do well. Edward Alleyn was one example of such a man. He was a very famous actor, but he retired before he was forty to spend the rest of his life building and renting theatres, buying and selling costumes, play scripts, houses and land, and running the Bear Garden as master of the royal Game of Bears, Bulls and Mastiff Dogs. Eventually he bought the manor of Dulwich, established Alleyn's College of God's Gift there and died very much a gentleman.[34]

Shakespeare, of course, also made his fortune through the theatre, but like Alleyn he can hardly be considered a typical actor or playwright of his time. He had regular work with a successful theatre company, unlike most of his fellow playwrights, and also had a flair for business so that he invested his money wisely. He was also a sharer in the company he worked with, which helped greatly towards his success.

The sharers were not paid a set wage but took a percentage of the receipts from each performance. They were sometimes the leading actors but equally the arrangement could be a purely financial one with the sharer having made an investment in the company. Some never made their mark as actors, if indeed they ever went on stage at all. It was unusual for a playwright to be made a sharer. Thomas Dekker, for example, does not seem to have been one. The sharers were the élite of a company, being the people who could make important decisions such as who to hire or fire and what plays to perform. Lower down the company came the hired men, for whom the chances of financial success were fairly slim. Some of the hired men were actors and/or musicians, but they also included people such as the wardrobe staff and the prompt, who did many of the things that a modern stage manager would do, such as seeing that props were in the right place and organising the offstage noises.[35]

The boy apprentices formed the very bottom rung of the profession, although they were an important part of the company as they played the women's roles. Apprenticeship was, of course, the standard way of learning a trade at the time but apprenticeship in the theatre was never as well regulated as in other professions. The length of the apprenticeship seems to have varied, as did the age at which it started. The point at which an apprentice graduated to adult roles must have been governed by both his ability and the time when his voice broke. What all actor's apprentices had in common was that they were bound to a certain player rather than to a particular troupe. Exactly how the boys came to be recruited in the first place is not clear. There were some who started their careers working in the professional boys' companies of the time but not enough to suggest that this was a standard process. Shakespeare's younger brother Edmund is thought by some to have come to London as a boy player, through his brother's influence, but this is not certain. There was evidently no accepted path to becoming an actor. However they were recruited, life as an apprentice was not easy. Like other apprentices of the time they were not paid, but were given food, clothes and their training. The fee paid for a boy's services went to his master, not to the boy himself.

The situation was different for the boys in the boys' companies. These were based on the choir schools of the Children of the Chapel Royal and St Paul's. Playing was only part of their education, as they were also given more academic training. This was perhaps another reason why the boys' companies were always seen as more socially acceptable than the adult ones.

The fame of the London theatres of the time is such that it is easy to forget just how many provincial touring companies there were at the time. We have no exact figures but over a hundred such companies are known to have existed in the late sixteenth and early seventeenth centuries.[36] Life for a touring actor was very different to the life of the favoured few in London. The first thing a troupe had to do on arriving at a town was apply to the authorities for permission to play. If they were lucky, they would be welcomed and allowed to perform before the mayor, aldermen and other city authorities. There was sometimes a mayor's play, when the mayor paid the players himself so the audience watched free of charge. An account by R. Willis, published in 1639, describes such a play to which 'my father took me with him and made me stand between his legs as he sat upon one of the benches where we saw and heard very well . . .'.[37] At the time of the printing of this account Willis states that he was seventy-five years old and yet obviously the memory of seeing the play was still strong.

This kind of welcome was the sort that actors dreamt of, but it was by no means assured. In other places the actors were received less willingly or were even sent away without being allowed to play. This could be for a very practical reason, such as fear of the plague. Visitors were never very welcome during such times in case they brought the infection with them. Sometimes permission was refused because the authorities simply disliked plays and playing. If permission was denied the players were sometimes paid to go away. This was particularly the case if the company involved had a powerful patron, as nobody wanted to risk offending a great person. The King's Lynn Chamberlain's accounts show the following entry for 22 July 1603, a time when the plague was very bad:

> xxs allowed to Mr Mayor for ii companies of players. Paid out of the hall here to Mr Mayor that he bestowed on the Earl of Huntingdon and the Lord Evers their players to keep them from playing here this dangerous time.[38]

A powerful patron was such a useful asset to a company of players that the forging of patents was not uncommon. In theory, of course, troupes were not even supposed to exist without a patron, as discussed above. Theatre companies had a tendency to splinter, and those who left troupes to go their own way were often tempted to claim patronage they did not really have. An order sent out by the Lord Chamberlain in 1617 gives an idea of what went on:

> Whereas Thomas Swinnerton and Martin Slaughter being two of the Queen's Majesty's company of players, having separated themselves from their said company, have each of them taken forth a several exemplification or duplicate of his Majesty's letters patent granted to the whole company and by virtue thereof they severally in two companies with vagabonds and suchlike idle persons have and do use and exercise the quality of playing in diverse places of this realm to the great abuse and wrong of his Majesty's subjects . . .[39]

If the touring companies were allowed to perform, the conditions they worked in were usually very different from the luxury of the purpose-built London playhouses. One of Ben Jonson's characters in his play *Poetaster* is telling the player,

Histrio, how fine a playwright Cripsinus is: 'If he pen for thee once, thou shalt not need to travel, with thy pumps full of gravel any more, after a blind jade and a hamper; and stalk upon boards and barrel heads, to an old cracked trumpet.'

Playing on a stage supported by barrels was fortunately not the only option. If they were lucky, players might be allowed to perform in the town hall, which was why some anti-theatre city authorities passed laws forbidding playing there. The Ipswich moot hall was closed to players in this way.

Another option was to use inns, just as players had done in London before the purpose-built playhouses. In 1624 the Lady Elizabeth's players got into serious trouble in Norwich for playing at the White Horse Inn despite the mayor having ordered that the inn should not be used in that way. One of the leaders of the troupe, Francis Wambus, was even put in prison.[40] Part of the trouble was perhaps that the Lady Elizabeth, James I's daughter, was living in Holland and had troubles of her own and so couldn't take too much personal interest in the troupe.

Players could end up performing just about anywhere. There are a few accounts of churches being used for performance, although not with permission of those in authority. In fact John Mufford, one of Lord Beauchamp's players, ended up in prison for playing in a church in Norwich in defiance of an order from the mayor. The church house, what we would call a church hall, was often used by players and these premises were even rented out to them on occasion, as in Sherborne in Dorset.[41]

It must have been a luxury for provincial players to work in Bristol, where there was a theatre which was sometimes used by travelling companies. It is the only theatre known to have existed in a provincial town at the time. A cutler, Nicholas Wolffe, who died in 1614, even left money to keep the place running, 'so long only as the same playhouse shall continue as a playhouse that such players as do resort to the said city or inhabit within the same do usually play there and may be permitted and suffered quietly to play there and no longer'.[42]

The playwrights did not find life much easier than the actors. Like actors and musicians, those who managed to achieve financial success did go on to be accepted socially, but in general the profession was not highly regarded. Most of the playwriting of the time was hack work and probably much of it is now lost. It is probably the best which survives, though, as plays were part of a company's financial assets and the best ones were carefully guarded.

The expansion of education in the sixteenth century meant that by Elizabethan times there were more educated men who felt able to produce plays. The theatre was expanding and there was a need for a great number of plays, but unfortunately there were also a great number of playwrights. It was a buyer's market for plays so that the playwrights were in effect the servants of the players.

The playwrights attached to companies did work extremely hard. Shakespeare seems to have produced one comic and one serious play a year throughout his active writing career. Another actor/playwright, Thomas Heywood, who worked with Queen Anne's Men in the early seventeenth century, claimed to have either completely written or at least written the main part of no fewer than 220 plays.[43]

The playwrights attached to companies were the lucky ones. Philip Henslowe, one of the most prosperous impresarios of the time, kept in close touch with several writers whom he employed simply to make alterations to existing plays. Of the twenty-five or so playwrights who made a living by writing for the companies, probably only about eight had regular contracts.[44] The standard method of payment even for contractors seems to have been benefit days, when the playwright took all the profit on a performance. The fact that Heywood's company in the early seventeenth century paid more for the dress worn by the heroine in *A Woman Killed with Kindness* than for the play itself gives an indication of the relative importance of playwrights.[45]

Despite the difficulties of the actors and playwrights, by the end of the sixteenth century the professional theatre was firmly established, so much so that even the eighteen-year suppression during the Interregnum in the seventeenth century was not able to kill it. The theatre, particularly in London, was here to stay.

NINE
Sports, Games and Other Pastimes

In the sixteenth century there was still a strong feeling that men of all classes should be trained and ready for war. Sport was an obvious way of achieving this so wrestling, archery and other sports with martial overtones were very much encouraged. In upper-class circles it was one reason why hunting was so very popular.

Today we may not associate hunting with war but during the Tudor period the two went together in most people's minds. Sir Thomas Elyot in his *Book Named the Governor* talks at some length on the subject. Well-bred young boys should be skilled in hunting because it 'increaseth in them both agility and quickness, also sleight and policy to find such passages and straits, where they may prevent or entrap their enemies. Also by continuance therein they shall easily sustain travail in wars, hunger and thirst, cold and heat.'[1] In fact the type of hunting described by Sir Thomas was not much found in England by the sixteenth century. Sir Thomas describes the hunters going out into the wilds, pursuing game for days at a time. Deer parks were the more usual place for hunting by this time and even though they could be quite large, it was unlikely that the hunters would be forced to sleep rough. There were even some forms of hunting which may have been hard work for the hunt staff, but which can hardly have been so for the privileged hunters, like the bow and stable hunt. In this type of hunting, the ladies and gentlemen were organised with their bows and had the deer driven past them. Bowers were even built out of branches to shelter them from the sun or rain so they scarcely needed to be hardy. Even so, hunting preserved its image as the true sport of the aristocracy.[2]

Why hunting appealed so much to the upper classes is easily understood. This was a time when making a display of wealth and power was the accepted practice. Keeping a full hunting establishment of all the different types of dogs required, plus the horses and attendant staff, was very expensive. Riding out to the hunt, surrounded by all the trappings of wealth, was a good advertisement for anyone's social status.

Hunting was also considered a good way of keeping fit, both mentally and physically. It was a good remedy for idleness and all the temptations which that brought with it. Wealthy young men could spend hours following the hunt. Henry VIII loved it so much that in 1520 he was said to rise daily, except on holy days, at four or five o'clock and then spend the whole day hunting, only returning at nine or ten at night.[3]

The other advantage of the sport was the social status conferred by the venison brought home by the hunt. Andrew Boorde explains the importance of it in his *Dyetary of Helth*. Having explained how healthy and pleasing a meat it is, he goes on to caution his readers that 'I do advertyse every man, for all my wordes, not to kyll and so to eate of it, excepte it be lawfully, for it is a meate for great men. And great men do not set so moche by the meate, as they doth by the pastyme of kyllynge it.'[4] Killing and giving away venison advertised the fact that you were wealthy enough to hunt.

The game roll of Richard Chambry, keeper of the deer park at Framlingham in the late fifteenth and early sixteenth centuries, demonstrates how treasured the deer were. Framlingham belonged to the Duke of Norfolk who used the venison it produced as a way of cementing social relationships. It was presented to various aristocratic friends, to institutions such as abbeys and priories, and to individuals such as Thomas Coke, who received a buck to help celebrate his daughter's marriage.[5] It was a useful way of reminding people of the wealth of the Duke. The importance of the deer as a resource to the Duke of Norfolk is shown by the way that Richard Chambry made careful note of all losses. There were quite a few, through marauding dogs, poachers and disease or accident, like a buck that drowned in the moat. The winter cold could also kill many of the fawns: seventy-one are noted to have died in the winter of 1515.

The social status of a deer park was further enhanced as it was usual to entertain an important visitor by taking them hunting. The owner had a chance to show off his horses and dogs, not to mention his park, in the highest circles. Given the Tudor royal family's love of hunting it was also a good way to entertain royalty. An impressive hunting establishment and its skilled staff were thus well worth the expense. The Percy Dukes of Northumberland were evidently well aware of this as, in 1512, they had no fewer than twenty-one parks in Northumberland, Cumberland and Yorkshire alone, plus others in the south of England.[6]

There was evidently a great deal to learn about hunting, judging from a book called *Hawking, Hunting, Fouling and Fishing with the true measures of blowing* which was published in 1596 by William Gryndall. The book is really a reprint of the *Boke of St Albans* which was written in the fifteenth century, but evidently the information in it must still have been relevant in 1596 if it was thought to be worth reprinting.

One of the first things that strikes the reader is the amount of terminology that had to be learnt. For example, these were the terms used to describe a hart, the male red deer: 'The first yeare he is a Calso, the second yeare a Broket, the third yeare a Spayd, the fouth yeare a Stagge and the fifth yeare a greate Stagge, and the sixth year an hart.' The hart was considered the very cream of game. In England it was the largest animal that was hunted and it was remarkably clever at evading the hounds, making the hunt not only a physical challenge but also a mental one. There was other game, however, such as the hare, although Sir Thomas Elyot was rather dismissive of it.[7] To him, hunting hare with greyhounds was a good pastime for 'them to whom nature hath not given personage or courage apt for the wars'[8] and also for gentlewomen.

Wildfowl, rabbits, etc. could also be hunted with a hawk. Sir Thomas Elyot considered hawking an inferior sport, although many Tudors would have disagreed with him. The trouble and expense of falconry made the sport a status symbol. Henry VII, Henry VIII and Elizabeth I certainly loved the sport as much as they loved hunting with dogs. In the Middle Ages great lords had often kept their favourite falcons in their bedchambers. This was partly out of affection and partly because living surrounded by people helped to make the hawks easier to handle. This was dying out by the sixteenth century, but even so at Greenwich Palace Henry VIII's bedroom was right next to the mews.[9]

Hunting was also a sport that the ladies could join in, and not just hunting the hare as Sir Thomas Elyot suggests. Elizabeth I was not unusual in being a lady who hunted and hawked regularly. Her sister Mary did not share her enthusiasm but that might have been because of her rather delicate health rather than lack of inclination.

Angling was another form of hunting which was practised, although of course it lacked the spectacular display of hunting with dogs. Robert Burton in his *Anatomy of Melancholy* describes it as a 'kinde of hunting by water' and says that it 'yeeldes all out as much pleasure to some men as dogs or hawks'.[10] Henry VIII, despite his love of more lively sports, also enjoyed angling. At The More the mowers were paid to clean the ponds and moat of weed to allow the King to fish. The More was one of the palaces that Henry confiscated from Cardinal Wolsey in 1529, at the same time as he acquired Hampton Court. By this time Henry was no longer a young man, so perhaps the peace and quiet of fishing was very welcome.[11]

Fishing seems to have been quite popular as books were printed on the subject. The 1496 reprint of the *Boke of St Albans* contained a section on angling and another book, *The Arte of Angling* was published in 1577. This was followed by several more, including the famous *The Compleat Angler*, which were published in the early seventeenth century. *The Arte of Angling* takes the usual form of instructional manuals of the time, that of a dialogue between an expert and his pupil. Unfortunately today we have no idea who the writer of the book was as the only copy known to survive has the vital page missing, but he was evidently someone who loved his sport. The author also has the problem common to those obsessed by sport, that of the partner who does not share their enthusiasm. His wife complains bitterly of how the long hours he spends fishing give him the colic, which sometimes leaves him ill for two or three days at a time, something that doesn't seem to bother the sportsman himself at all.[12]

Wealthy Tudors loved hunting so much and celebrated the joys of their sport so enthusiastically that it is easy to forget that most people in the sixteenth century never got the chance to hunt, at least not legally. They were still expected to prepare for possible war, though, so all men were encouraged to practise the much cheaper sport of archery with the traditional English weapon of the longbow.

Archers had been the backbone of the English army since the fourteenth century, so it was understandable that the king was keen to see that people kept in practice. The problem was that Englishmen were happier spending their free time in other ways by the sixteenth century. In 1511 the young King Henry VIII, himself a very fine archer, signed the 'Act concerning the shooting in Longe Bowes' to try to improve matters. The act decreed that all fathers had to provide their sons aged between seven and seventeen with a longbow and two arrows. Masters had to do the same for their male servants, although they were allowed to dock the cost of this from the boy's wages. Men aged between seventeen and sixty had to provide themselves with a longbow and four arrows, although a few classes of men such as justices of the peace and men of the Church were exempted. In order to keep this within everyone's pocket, the bowyers were instructed to make at least two bows of 'wych elm or other wood of mean price' for every bow they made of yew. Every town was to provide butts for practice. Sports such as tennis and bowls were forbidden so that there would be nothing to interefere with archery practice.[13] The act was evidently not as successful as Henry VIII might have hoped. For one thing, as discussed below, the interest in the alternative (and in theory, banned) sports increased rather than decreased. The king was also forced to pass another act in 1541 reinforcing the 1511 act, but even that could not reverse the decline.[14]

Various other attempts were made to stop the decline of archery. Roger Ascham, tutor to the young Princess Elizabeth, tried a different angle by writing his book *Toxophilus* on the subject. In his book Ascham suggests that, like the man who obeyed the Lord Mayor by hanging a lantern in front of his house to help light the city, but who never actually lit the candle in it, men were buying bows and arrows as the law commanded, but never practising their archery. He put this down to a lack of skilled teachers, so the first book of *Toxophilus* was designed to whet the appetite for the sport by explaining the benefits of archery, while the second was a practical archery manual. The book was written in 1544 and presented to Henry VIII in the following year. The king was so pleased that he granted Ascham a pension of £10 a year.

Ascham's book failed to reverse the decline. John Stow, writing in the 1570s, noted the decreased popularity of archery as a pastime in London. 'What should I speake of the auncient dayly exercises in the long bow by Citizens of this Citie, now almost cleane left off and forsaken?'[15] he asks, and goes on to blame the enclosure of common land, leaving the archers with no convenient place to practise. Unfortunately for archery enthusiasts, the decline was not due to lack of knowledge or even to the evils of enclosure, but to the development of the handgun. Sir Thomas Elyot understood this in 1531, when *The Governor* was first published, although he still decried the decline of archery. He describes the introduction of the crossbow and the hand gun as being 'brought into this realm, by the sleight of our enemies, to the intent to destroy the noble defence of archery'.[16]

However strong the affection for archery was, it could not halt the spread of firearms. The importance of the longbow as a weapon of war gradually faded as the century progressed so that its use was gradually phased out of the militia, the trained bands. England did not have a standing army, so the trained bands consisted of men who were given specialist military training so that they could form the nucleus of the army in times of war. They were founded in 1573 and by 1595 the government had tried to rid their ranks of the longbow entirely. The days of English archery on the battlefield were over.

There were other warlike sports to practise though, such as wrestling, which was praised by Sir Thomas Elyot[17] and was another sport much loved by the young Henry VIII. Hall describes him in the second year of his reign 'exercisyng hym self daily in shotyng, singing, dansyng, wrastelyng, casting of the barre . . .'.[18] Wrestling was even part of the entertainments at the Field of Cloth of Gold in 1520, as a wrestling contest took place on a day when it was too windy for jousting. The English royal guard wrestled against the Bretons, who were the most famed of French wrestlers. In England wrestlers from Devon and Cornwall were considered the best. The French eyewitness Robert de la March, Seigneur de Florange also mentions a wrestling match between the two kings. Both Henry and Francis were good wrestlers, but the match was won by Francis. Florange states that losing the match caused Henry to hate Francis ever afterwards, but whether this is true it is impossible to say. None of the English accounts mentions the match and both Henry and Francis were too politically astute to give too much importance to a bout of wrestling.[19]

Another pastime which had originally been training for battle was running at the quintain. The quintain was a target set on a pole on a crossbar that could swing. The target was at one end of the crossbar and a bag of sand at the other. The sport was supposed to take place on horseback and the intention was to ride at the target, hit it with your lance then keep going as fast as you could before the bag of sand whipped around and hit you on the back of the neck. Originally it was training for the joust.

Stow records a quintain 'set upon Cornehill, by the Leaden Hall, where the attendants of lords of merry disports have run and made great pastime, for he that hit not the broad end of the quintain was of all men laughed to scorn, and he that hit it full, if he rid not the faster, had a sound blow to his neck . . .'.[20] The fact that it was the attendants of the 'lords of merry disports' who were enjoying the sport suggests that by Stow's time it was a seasonal sport connected with such things as the May games. Jousting was an expensive luxury for the very few so for most people the quintain was just a game and no doubt an opportunity to poke fun at the upper classes. Another form of mock-jousting took place on the Thames. Stow also records how young men would stand in small boats (wherries) with poles and were 'for the most part one or both overthrown and well ducked'.[21]

Sixteenth-century football should definitely be included among the warlike pastimes practised at the time. It was totally different from the modern game. There were no fixed numbers in a team, and the two teams simply fought over possession of the ball. There were goals but the main point of the game seems to have been the excuse for fighting. Despite the danger, it was very popular and was a common part of Shrovetide games.[22] It was, however, definitely not a game for a gentleman. Sir Thomas Elyot describes it as 'a beastly fury and extreme violence; whereof proceedeth hurt, and consequently rancour and malice do remain with them that be wounded . . .'.[23] People did indeed get hurt and even killed at football but there were also accidents on the hunting field. It was the fact that football was very much the ordinary man's game that made gentlemen like Sir Thomas so wary of it.

War was not the only concern of people in the sixteenth century, even for the upper classes, and many sports and pastimes were simply ways for people to enjoy themselves. The more active of these sports also had the merit of keeping them fit, an advantage that was recognised even at that time. Sir Thomas Elyot was moved to talk at some length about the importance of exercise in maintaining physical and mental health. Exercise improved digestion, made people stronger, made 'the spirits of a man more strong and valiant', among a host of other things.[24] It was no wonder that Sir Thomas approved of tennis.

Tennis was a very old game, even by the sixteenth century. Rackets were not always used and instead players might use the palms of their hands to return the ball, which is why the game was sometimes know as 'hand ball'. Edward III passed an act against the playing of hand ball as early as 1365. The act was, as usual, intended to stop people playing games so that they would concentrate their spare time on their archery. Tennis was therefore not the only game that was banned, but also football, cockfighting and other 'vain games'.

Another act, passed in 1389, was along the same lines but this time regulated the pastimes of servants and labourers, and again banned tennis, showing that even at that time the sport was played by rich and poor alike.[25] In the 1570s John Stow recorded people of all classes playing 'ball', which was presumably either handball or tennis depending on whether or not you had a racquet. He states that 'the ball is used by noblemen and gentlemen in tennis courts, and by people of meaner sorts in the open fields and streets'.[26] The court was obviously the luxury option.

The popularity of tennis was noted by Estienne Perlin, a French cleric who visited England. Perlin commented on what a wealthy nation England was '. . . for here you may commonly see artisans, such as hatters or joiners, play at tennis for a crown, which is not seen elsewhere, particularly on a working day . . .'.[27] This must have been especially surprising to him as in France strenuous efforts had been made to try to ensure that tennis was only played by the upper classes. A decree of 18 June 1530 had ordered all courts in Paris, except those used by the nobility, to be closed down and for no new ones to be built. It does not seem to have been effective so another act forbidding the building of new tennis courts was passed on 24 July 1543. English 'artisans' playing tennis openly and frequently must have seemed odd.[28]

The sixteenth-century game differed somewhat from the modern game. Indoors it involved serving the ball on to the penthouse, which was a kind of small shelf which ran along one side of the court. The ball was then returned across the net, or cord that was often used instead of a net.[29]

Henry VII had tennis courts built at the royal palaces of Richmond, Wycombe, Woodstock, Windsor and Westminster while Henry VIII went on to build several more, including a particularly impressive one at Hampton Court which was turned into lodgings for the Duke and Duchess of York in the seventeenth century.[30] The royal tennis courts were provided with windows covered with protective wire mesh through which people could watch the game.

Tennis at court was a spectator sport, which made it particularly suitable for courtiers in two ways. First of all, it gave the players a chance to demonstrate their skills, an important point at court where everyone was jostling for the limelight and where the king might appreciate a good partner. This idea was not lost on Castiglione, who wrote in his book *The Courtier* that tennis, being played before a crowd, was a good thing to take part in, but that, as was the case with dancing and music, an aristocrat should aim to give the impression that his skills were entirely natural and not the result of hours of practice.[31] The second and more down-to-earth reason for the popularity of tennis at court was the opportunity it afforded for gambling. The Tudors were great gamblers and court life was often dull, so gambling was a way of trying to make it more interesting. The privy expenses show that even the King himself quite frequently lost money betting on the outcome of tennis games.

Edward Hall even dares to record that in the second year of Henry's reign, when he was still only twenty years old, people began to take advantage of Henry's love of tennis. 'The kynge this tyme was muche entysed to playe at tennis and at dice, which appetite, certain craftie persons about him perceavynge, brought in Frenchmen and Lombards, to make wagers with hym, and so he lost much money, but when he perceyved their craft, he exchuyde their compaignie and let them go.'[32]

If tennis was not the game for you, then there were other ways of keeping fit. 'Castinge the barre', one of the sports Edward Hall describes the young Henry VIII taking part in, was one option. It was a bit like modern shot-putting in that an iron bar or some other heavy object would be thrown, each participant trying to throw the object furthest. Running and working with weights were other options.

Bowling was another favourite sport, even if it was unlikely to keep you fit. It was played both in covered alleys and in the open air on bowling greens. Bowling greens were standard in wealthy people's gardens, in the same way that Victorian and Edwardian gardens had a croquet lawn. Bowling alleys were found everywhere from royal palaces to the less salubrious parts of London. Both games involved getting the bowl as close to the jack as possible, but indoors the concave sides of the alley were used to do this. Henry VIII had some very impressive bowling alleys, built of brick and with lead roofs, like the ones at Hampton Court.[33] Bowling would be considered a fairly blameless pastime today, but in the sixteenth century this was not the case. The problem was, again, the gambling that went with it. This was why John Stow disliked it and why he so decried the decline of archery as it caused people to 'creepe into bowling Allies and ordinarie dicing houses, nearer home, where they have roome enough to hazard their money at unlawful games . . .'.[34] Gambling was definitely not confined to the court.

According to Stow, bowling was such a popular pastime that a great number of bowling alleys had been built in the city or in the suburbs that surrounded it. There were so many that there was obviously great competition between them. The gardens of Northumberland House, former residence of the Duke of Northumberland, had been turned into bowling alleys and dicing houses, but 'so many Allies and other houses for unlawful gaming hath been raised up in other parts of the Citie and suburbs that this their ancient and only patron of misrule is left and foresaken of her Gamesters . . .'.[35]

The official disapproval of games such as tennis and bowls was quite understandable when you consider the amount of betting and attendant cheating that went on. An Elizabethan named Gilbert Walker was so annoyed at the dishonesty that he wrote a pamphlet called *A Manifest Detection of the Most Vyle and Detestable of Diceplay, and other practices lyke the same*, revealing some of the ways in which the gullible could be cheated. In bowling alleys a common trick was to draw some idle onlooker into taking interest in a game and laying a few modest bets. One of the bowlers would be very obviously better than the others and he would win constantly, until the unwary onlooker was drawn into placing ever higher bets. Eventually, of course, when the stakes were high enough, the 'certain' winner would lose.[36]

The evils of bowling and dicing seem nothing beside some of the other entertainments chosen by the Tudors. This was an age when public executions were considered a spectator sport. Only a few victims, like Henry VIII's wives Anne Boleyn and Catherine

Howard, were executed in the moderately private confines of the Tower, although even there there were plenty of onlookers.

The idea of making executions public was, of course, to discourage anyone thinking of indulging in crime themselves. In practice people turned up to enjoy the occasion. Thomas Platter, a German who visited England in 1599, watched a public execution in London. This is what he saw:

> . . . every quarter when the law courts sit in London and they throng from all parts of England for the terms . . . to litigate in numerous matters which have occurred in the interim, for everything is saved up until that time; then there is a slaughtering and a hanging, and from all the prisons (of which there are several scattered about the town where they ask alms of passers by, and sometimes they collect so much by their begging that they can purchase their freedom) people are taken and tried; when the trial is over, those condemned to the rope are placed on a cart, each one with a rope about his neck, and the hangman drives with them out of the town to the gallows, called Tyburn, almost an hour away from the city, there he fastens them up one after another by the rope and drives the cart off under the gallows, which is not very high off the ground; then the criminals' friends come and draw them down by their feet, that they may die the sooner. They are then taken down from the gallows and buried in the neighbouring cemetery. . . . Rarely does a law day in London in all the four sessions pass without some twenty to thirty person – both men and women – being gibbetted.[37]

Another of the less pleasant aspects of Tudor life was the use of animals in a number of sports. Baiting various animals, particularly bulls and bears, even had royal approval. There was a royal Game of Bears, Bulls and Mastiff Dogs in Queen Elizabeth's time, which was run by the actor Edward Alleyn and his father-in-law, Philip Henslowe. The Queen herself both watched and enjoyed such baitings.

Thomas Platter, evidently keen to go everywhere and see

everything, watched a baiting while in London. This is how he described it:

> The theatre is circular, with galleries round the top for the spectators, the ground space down below beneath the clear sky, is unoccupied. In the middle of this place a large bear on a long rope was bound to a stake, then a number of great English mastiffs were brought in and shown first to the bear, which they afterwards baited one after another: now the excellence and fine temper of such mastiffs was evinced, for although they were much struck and mauled by the bear, they did not give in, but had to be pulled off by sheer force, and their muzzles forced open with long sticks to which a broad ironpiece was attached at the top. The bear's teeth were not so sharp they could injure the dogs; they have them broken short. When the first mastiffs tired, fresh ones were brought in to bait the bear.
>
> When the first bear was weary, another was supplied and fresh dogs to bait him, first one at a time, then more and more as it lasted, till they had overpowered the bear, then only did they come to its aid.

Platter then goes on to describe how they baited a bull in the same way and finally brought out an old blind bear for boys to hit with sticks. Fortunately for the bear, it knew how to untie itself and so ran back to its stall.[38]

A Spaniard, visiting London in 1544, also wrote a description of a baiting when a pony with a monkey on its back was baited by mastiffs. 'To see the pony kicking at the dogs, and the ape shrieking at them as it hangs on the ears and neck of the pony, is enough to make you laugh.'[39]

Cock-fighting was another unpleasant sport which was considered perfectly acceptable, and was another that Thomas Platter went to see, possibly at the cockpit in Shoe Lane in London. Entrance cost a penny, so, like standing in the yard at the theatre, cock-fighting was cheap entertainment, if you didn't lose too much betting on the outcome. Thomas Platter was told that the stakes placed on a cock could amount to many thousands of crowns so perhaps it wasn't cheap entertainment after all.[40] Like baiting, cock-fighting was taken up by the court, although exactly when is unknown. Henry VIII was probably the first king to build cockpits at royal palaces. He had two, one at Whitehall and one at Greenwich. The Whitehall cockpit was a very fine building indeed, being octagonal in shape and decorated with stone beasts holding iron standards and gilt vanes. Inside it took the form of an amphitheatre, with three tiers of seats. The King had a special seat which formed a cage for the cocks. The Queen watched from a gallery overlooking the cockpit.[41]

Fortunately the Tudors did give the animal kingdom a rest from time to time when they turned to more peaceful pastimes. The long winter evenings had to be filled somehow. Robert Burton in the *Anatomy of Melancholy*, published in 1621, lists suitable winter pastimes as follows: 'cardes, tables and dice, shovelboard, chesse-play, the philosopher's game, small trunks, shuttle-cock, balliards, musicke, masks, singing, dancing, ulegames, frolicks, jests, riddles, catches, purposes, questions and commands, merry tales . . .'.[42]

Many of these pastimes are still familiar today, although the philosopher's game seems to have died out in the seventeenth century. Originating in thirteenth-century France, this was played on a double chessboard and was quite a complicated game as players needed a good head for figures.[43]

'Balliards' or billiards is another old game, not to be confused with snooker which was only invented in 1875. The French King Louis XI, who died in 1483, had a type of billiard table while the unfortunate Mary, Queen of Scots complained that hers was taken away a month before she was executed. In 1588 the Duke of Norfolk is also recorded as owning 'a billyard bord covered with a greene cloth . . . three billyard sticks and eleven balls of yvery'.[44]

Tables may at first sight seem unfamiliar but today it is still played as backgammon. It was a very popular game as is shown by the fact that a board was found on the wreck of the *Mary Rose*, Henry VIII's warship that sank in 1545, as were the inevitable dice and evidence of other board games. In fact board games in general were common pastimes in the sixteenth century. They do not, of course, have to be played on a board. The necessary markings can also be scratched on the ground, or on any convenient surface. A merrills board and another crude backgammon board were found carved into a barrel lid on the *Mary Rose*. In the same way practically every English cathedral of monastic origin has a merrills board scratched in the cloisters somewhere as the monks were keen players. One of these can be found in the cloisters of Westminster Abbey.

Some of the board games enjoyed by the Tudors would be quite recognisable today. Chess and draughts (sometimes called by its French name of 'dames') were both common, although Robert Burton had mixed feelings about chess. He does see it as 'a good and witty exercise of the mind' but warns that it is not a good pastime for someone who is already doing too much academic work. Fox and geese is another game that is still played today, although it is known under a variety of different names. A fox and geese board is carved into one of the stone seats of Gloucester Cathedral, suggesting it was being played in the fifteenth century. The royal household accounts also include payments for 'two foxis and 26 hounds of silver overgilt' purchased to form two sets of the game for Edward IV, 'fox and hounds' being another name for the game.[45]

Another form of indoor entertainment was 'clash', or 'pins'. This was the type of bowling in which skittles are knocked down with a ball, like modern ten-pin bowling. Thomas Elyot thought it far too low class a game for anyone of social standing, although why isn't really clear.[46]

As Robert Burton states, card games were another very popular way of passing the time in sixteenth-century England. The early history of card games is much debated, but they probably developed in China. Chinese cards have a pattern of spots at each end which correspond to the fall of two dice, e.g. 1–3, 5–4 etc. They possibly came to Europe via Egypt as a Mameluke pack discovered in Istanbul, which dates from about the year 400 AD, looks very like the early Italian packs.

Card games are first mentioned in Europe in the fourteenth century. In Spain they are referred to in 1371 and they are first described in detail in Switzerland in 1377. In 1376 they were causing such problems in Florence that the city elders prohibited the playing of a 'certain game called naibbe', 'naibbe' being the early word for cards.

Early cards were hand made and painted individually which did make them expensive, but perhaps old sets of cards found their way down the social scale. The town ordinances of Paris in 1377 and St Gallen in 1379 both prohibit card-playing in such a way as suggests that the ordinances are aimed at the lower classes, so obviously card games were not a luxury for the rich even in the fourteenth century. Perhaps cheap playing cards were produced somehow, but, as is so often the case with everyday artefacts of little value, none have survived.

In the early fifteenth century German and Swiss manufacturers were producing packs of cards in their thousands by printing them from woodblocks. Packs were becoming more standardised by this time, which made mass-production easier. The problem is that, despite the undoubted popularity of card-playing on continental Europe, nobody really knows how it reached England.

The first certain English reference to card-playing comes in a letter of the Paston family thought to date from November 1459. The letter is from John Paston to his wife Margaret. She had asked her husband what entertainments a recently widowed neighbour is going to allow in her house over Christmas. He replied that although 'lowde dysports' such as dancing would not be allowed, chess, tables and cards would be permitted.[47] Cards must have been fairly well established in England by this time as Edward IV's first parliament (November 1461–May 1462) passed an act forbidding dicing or playing of cards in private houses other than during the twelve days of Christmas.

Many of the card games favoured by the Tudors were very simple ones, based on the inevitable betting. In 1564 an Italian named Girolamo Cardano published a book called the *Liber de ludo alae* (Book on Games of Chance) which was more about how to gamble to win rather than about explaining how games were played. He sees gambling as a matter of mathematics rather than luck, but sadly few sixteenth-century people listened to him. As a result, the Tudor love of gambling led not a few people into trouble.

Gilbert Walker had plenty to warn the unwary about, as of course there are always plenty of ways of cheating people of their money once they are persuaded to gamble. Some of the scams were quite elaborate, involving what another pamphlet of 1575, the *Fraternitye of Vacabondes*, called a 'cheator, or Fingerer'. The fingerer dressed like a wealthy gentleman and sometimes even had liveried servants in attendance, as was common among men of social standing. He would promenade in some fashionable part of London, such as the Royal Exchange, looking for gullible young men with money. Favourite victims were young gentlemen who had been sent up to London to study law at the Inns of Court as they had money but lacked experience of the dangers of life in a big city.

The fingerer would make friends with these men, take them back to his house, which would be furnished with all the marks of gentlemanly wealth, entertain them royally and then bring out cards and dice. It was, after all, common for people to play such games at home with their friends, so the young gentleman, who might already have had rather a lot to drink, might not notice anything was wrong until he mysteriously began to lose large amounts of money. Walker reminds the unwary that it is 'the most unfeigned friendship where most deceit is meant'. Gambling with people you don't know well is always a risk.

There were certainly plenty of ways of cheating at both dice and cards. Walker gives a list of the different types of false dice which could be used. 'Gords' were hollowed out on one side, 'fullans' were loaded with lead 'or other ponderous matter', while still others had one face slightly longer than the others. Cards could easily be marked by turning up the corners, marking them with spots of ink or simply making a dent in them with finger nails.

In view of all this dishonest gambling, tennis, bowls and other games were, in theory, forbidden to all but the very wealthy except at Christmas. In practice, though, it was impossible to ban such things and in any case, there was such a lot of money to be made that those in power were unwilling to stamp them out anyway. In 1576 Queen Elizabeth I granted a patent to license gambling houses to Thomas Cornwallis, her Groom Porter. The Groom Porter organised gambling games for the royal household at Christmas, so it was a logical arrangement. From then on, this patent became a very lucrative perquisite of the Groom Porter's office, especially as people were quite willing to pay for a licence to run a gaming house since they were so profitable. The Groom Porter also had the official monopoly on the right to supply playing cards and dice.[48]

The same sort of attitude was taken towards prostitution. In theory it was illegal, disapproved of as a social evil, but there was a ready market and there was money to be made. From time to time the brothels were closed down, such as in Henry VII's time when syphilis first became a serious problem and also during serious bouts of plague, but they always reopened. Stow even records that in 1546 Henry VIII commanded that a certain row of brothels in Southwark should be pulled down but as the area continued to be famous for its brothels these measures obviously had no effect.[49] Too many people were making too much money for anyone to make anything but token attempts to close the brothels down.[50]

The Puritans who wanted to close the theatres down were correct in assuming that there was a link between theatres and prostitution, in that many theatre owners also owned brothels. Edward Alleyn, the actor, and his father-in-law Philip Henslowe were both involved, and Alleyn's wife, Henslowe's step-daughter, was punished for prostitution in 1593. This was probably because she failed to comply when the brothels were ordered to be closed due to plague in 1593.

The prostitutes had ways of earning money other than sex. Gilbert Walker states that they were often involved in gaming fraud, such as by encouraging young men to join in gambling games or to lay ever-higher bets. 'Take this always for a maxim, that all the bauds in a country be of the chetor familiar acquaintance', he writes in his pamphlet. There was, of course, also always the danger that your valuables might be stolen during a visit to a brothel.

From time to time prostitutes were punished. A first offence was likely to lead to the prostitute having her head shaved, after which she was carted about the streets with a paper telling of her offence fastened to her forehead. Hardened offenders were tied to the back of a cart and dragged through the streets while sometimes they would be whipped. Thomas Platter noted that in cases of prostitution the men involved were either fined or imprisoned, but that the women were whipped at Bridewell.[51] In theory those who ran brothels stood likely to be punished in the same way as the prostitutes. The punishments had little effect. Thomas Platter noted the swarms of prostitutes in the taverns and theatres. John Stow even describes how a prison was openly used as a brothel. The prison in question was the compter in Bredstreet. The keeper of the prison was one Richard Husband, who lodged 'theeves and strumpets' at 4*d* a night, while also treating the regular prisoners very badly. Eventually he was dismissed from the prison, but could not be removed from the Bredsteet house as it belonged to him. The authorities were forced to move the prison to another building instead.[52]

Under the circumstances it was not surprising that brothels, gaming houses and bowling alleys continued to thrive. There was too much popular demand for both gaming and prostitutes for either to disappear. Some forms of entertainment never change.

Notes

Introduction

1 *The Illustrated Letters of the Paston Family,* ed. Roger Virgoe (Guild Publishing, 1989), p. 47.

2 Baldesar Castiglione, *The Book of the Courtier,* tr. George Bull (Penguin, Harmondsworth, 1976).

3 B.P. Wolfe, 'Henry VIII's Landed Revenues', *English Historical Review,* LIXXIX (1964).

4 A good summary of the art and ideals of the Renaissance can be found in George Holmes, *Renaissance* (Weidenfeld & Nicolson, London, 1996).

5 Leon Battista Alberti, *On Painting* (Penguin, 1991), p. 60.

6 Simon Thurley, *The Royal Palaces of Tudor England* (Yale University Press, New Haven and London, 1993), Chapter 3.

7 Alberti, *On Painting,* p. 60.

8 Edward Hall, *The Triumphant Reigne of Kyng Henry the VIII* (printed for J. Johnson, London, 1809), pp. 530–1.

9 Castiglione, *The Book of the Courtier,* p. 10.

10 For details of a woman's place in business see Alison Sim, *The Tudor Housewife* (Sutton Publishing, Stroud, 1996).

11 Some of Sabine's letters are printed in Barbara Winchester, *Tudor Family Portrait* (Jonathan Cape, London, 1955).

12 Roger Ascham, *The Schoolmaster* (Cassell and Company, 1909), p. 8.

13 For an overview history of medicine see Charles Singer and E. Ashworth, *A Short History of Medicine* (Clarendon Press, Oxford, 1962).

14 Ibid., pp. 46–7.

15 Nancy Duin and J. Sutcliffe, *A History of Medicine* (Simon and Schuster, 1992), p. 34.

16 Ibid., p. 35.

17 W.S.C. Copeman, *Doctors and Disease in Tudor Times* (Dawson's, 1960), p. 35.

18 Ascham, *The Schoolmaster,* p. 13.

19 Ibid., p. 15

20 A.G. Dickens, *The English Reformation* (Fontana Paperbacks, 1983), p. 80.

1 The Perfect Setting

1 Thurley, *The Royal Palaces,* pp. 113–20.

2 *The Lisle Letters,* ed. Muriel St Clare Byrne (Penguin Books, 1985), pp. 268–9.

3 Ibid., pp. 13–15.

4 Mark Girouard, *Life in the English Country House* (Yale University

Press, New Haven and London, 1978), p. 82.

5   Ibid., p. 103.

6   Sebastian Serlio, 1473–1554, was an Italian painter and architect who worked on Francis I's famous chateau of Fontainebleau.

7   Marcus Vitruvius Pollio, military engineer with Julius Caesar in Africa.

8   'Design and Designers' in Malcolm Airs, *The Tudor and Jacobean Country House* (Alan Sutton Publishing, Stroud, 1995).

9   The plans survive in Sir John Soane's Museum, London.

10 Francis Bacon, *Essayes or Counsels Civill & Morall: Of Building* (The Temple Classics series, J.M. Dent, London, 1899), pp. 161–2.

11 Airs, *The Tudor and Jacobean Country House*, p. 54.

12 M. Jourdain, *English Decoration and Furniture, Vol. 1: Of the Early Renaissance, 1500–1650* (B.T. Batsford, London 1924), p. 17.

13 William Harrison, *The Description of England* (Dover Publications New York, 1994), p. 197. 'East' in this case means the Baltic.

14 Examples of places where elaborately carved panelling was originally brightly painted can be found at The Vyne near Basingstoke in Hampshire and in Paycockes, in the village of Coggeshall in Essex.

15 Thurley, *The Royal Palaces*, p. 89.

16 Ibid., p. 93.

17 M. Jourdain, *English Decorative Plasterwork of the Renaissance* (B.T. Batsford, London, 1926), p. 16.

18 David Gaimster, 'The Supply of

Rhenish Stoneware to London 1350–1600', *London Archaeologist*, 5: 15 (Winter 1987), 339–47.

19 Thurley, *The Royal Palaces*, pp. 104–7.

20 Jourdain, *English Decoration and Furniture*, p. 89.

21 Jourdain, *English Interior Decoration 1500–1830* (B.T. Batsford, London, 1950), p. 10.

22 Airs, *The Tudor and Jacobean Country House*, p. 192.

23 A copy of this still exists in the Royal Collection and hangs at Hampton Court.

24 Thurley, *The Royal Palaces*, p. 208.

25 *England as Seen by Foreigners*, ed. William Brenchley Rye (John Russell Smith, London, 1865), p. 45.

26 Thurley, *The Royal Palaces*, p. 230.

27 Ibid.

28 Ibid.

29 Harrison, *The Description of England*, p. 197.

30 Ibid.

31 Airs, *The Tudor and Jacobean Country House*, p. 127.

32 Ibid., p. 128.

33 Ibid., p. 129.

34 Bacon, *Of Building*, p. 165.

35 Hilary Wayment, 'Stained Glass in Henry VIII's Palaces' in David Starkey (ed.), *Henry VIII: A European Court in Europe* (Collins & Brown, London, 1991), p. 28.

36 Jourdain, *English Decoration and Furniture*, p. 192.

37 Ibid.

38 Thurley, *The Royal Palaces*, p. 223.

39 Rye, *England as Seen by Foreigners*, p. 45.

40   The word 'cupboard' was changing its meaning in the sixteenth century. Originally it meant literally a 'cup board', shelves on which valuable items like cups were displayed, but it was starting to take on the meaning it has today.

41   George Cavendish, *The Life and Death of Cardinal Wolsey* (Folio Press, J.M. Dent, London, 1973), p. 101.

42   Thurley, *The Royal Palaces*, p. 242.

43   Ibid., p. 236.

44   Ibid., p. 130.

45   Maria Hayward, 'The Packing and Transportation of Henry VIII, with Particular Reference to the 1547 Inventory', *Costume Society Journal*, 31 (1997).

46   See Chapter 2 for further information about storage.

47   For information on Renaissance gardens see Roy Strong, *The Renaissance Garden in England* (Thames and Hudson, London, 1979).

48   John Parkinson, *Paradisi in Sole* (London, 1620), p. 54.

49   Francis Bacon, *Essayes or Counsels Civill & Morall: Of Gardens* (The Temple Classics series, J.M. Dent, London, 1899). p. 167.

50   *Thomas Platter's Travels in England*, tr. Clare Williams (Jonathan Cape, London, 1937), p. 200.

51   For more information on banquets see Alison Sim, *Food and Feast in Tudor England* (Sutton Publishing, Stroud, 1997).

52   Mark Girouard, *Robert Smythson and the Elizabethan Country House* (Yale University Press, New Haven and London, 1983), p. 271.

53   Parkinson, *Paradisi in Sole*, p. 610.

54   Strong, *The Renaissance Garden*, p. 46.

55   Ibid., p. 53.

56   *A Journey into England by Paul Hentzner*, tr. Horace Walpole (London, 1757).

57   Bacon, *Of Gardens*, p. 167.

58   Strong, *The Renaissance Garden*, pp. 50–1.

2 Clothing and Fashion

1   Thomas More, *Utopia*, tr. Paul Turner (Folio Society, London, 1972), Book 2, p. 77.

2   Castiglione, *The Book of the Courtier*, pp. 134–5

3   Sumptuary Regulations proclaimed 1533 (24 Henry VIII) printed in *Statues of the Realm* (Records Commission, 1820–8). For the detailed analysis of the regulations I am indebted to Tristan Langlois and to an unpublished paper by Caroline Johnson.

4   Quoted from Janet Arnold, *Queen Elizabeth's Wardrobe Unlock'd* (Maney, Leeds, 1988), p. 159.

5   Jane Ashelford, *The Art of Dress* (National Trust Enterprises, London, 1996), p. 28.

6   A good survey of fashions in the sixteenth century may be found in C. Willet and P. Cunnington, *Handbook of English Costume in the Sixteenth Century*, (Plays Inc, 1970).

7   For more information see Arnold, *Queen Elizabeth's Wardrobe Unlock'd*, pp. 146–8.

8   Taken from Hollybrand's dialogues printed in *The Elizabethan Home*, ed. Muriel St Clare Byrne (Cobden-Sanderson, London, 1930), p. 65.

9   George Whetstone, *An Heptameron of Civil Discourses*, (London, 1582).

10 Hayward 'The Packing and Transportation of Henry VIII', p. 11.

11 This information is taken from wills published in F.G. Emmison (ed.) *Essex Wills 1597–1603* (Essex Record Office, 1990) and *Wills of the County of Essex (England) Vol. 3 1571–1577* (The New England Historic Genealogical Society, Boston, 1986). The analysis of the wills was done by Jane Hugget. Many people did not own enough to bother making a will, so how much clothing such people had is a matter for speculation.

12 Quoted from Arnold, *Queen Elizabeth's Wardrobe Unlock'd*, p. 93.

13 Ibid., p. 190.

14 Ibid., p. 195.

15 Anne Buck, 'The Clothes of Thomasine Petre 1555–1559', *Costume Society Journal*, 24 (1990), pp. 20, 28.

16 Barbara Winchester, *Tudor Family Portrait* (Johnathan Cape, London, 1955), pp. 153–4.

17 For more detailed information about fustian see Florence Montgomery, *Textiles in America 1650–1870* (W.W. Norton, 1984) and glossary of Arnold, *Queen Elizabeth's Wardrobe Unlock'd*.

18 *Lisle Letters*, ed. Byrne, p. 157.

19 Buck, 'The Clothes of Thomasine Petre', p. 16.

20 Information taken from Jane Hugget's analysis of the Essex wills – see note 11 above.

21 Buck, 'The Clothes of Thomasine Petre', p. 25.

22 Peter Erondell, 'The French Garden' in Byrne, *The Elizabethan Home*, p. 88.

23 Winchester, *Tudor Family Portrait*, p. 151.

24 A falling band was a type of collar, often richly decorated with lace, which came into fashion towards the end of the century.

25 'Bootehosen' or boothose were probably designed to be worn with boots, or were perhaps thick hose worn instead of a boot. For more details see Arnold, *Queen Elizabeth's Wardrobe Unlock'd*, p. 206.

26 For the full story see John Stow, *Survey of London* (Everyman, J.M. Dent, London, 1980), p. 173.

27 John Stow, quoted from Samuel Angell, *An Historical Sketch of the Royal Exchange Chiefly Compiled from Stowe* (Robert Jennings, London, n.d.), p. 6.

28 Arnold, *Queen Elizabeth's Wardrobe Unlock'd*, p. 96.

29 For information on Tudor washing and housework see Sim, *The Tudor Housewife*, pp. 44–60.

30 John Stowe, *The Anals or General Chronicle of England*, ed. E. Hawes (London, 1615), p. 96.

31 Philip Stubbes, *The Anatomie of Abuses* (London, printed by Richard Jones, 1583), p. 22.

32 The will in question is that of John Warden, Romford yeoman,

6 June 1600, printed in Emmison, *Essex Wills* , p. 36 (will 177).

33 Stow, *Survey of London*, p. 178.

34 Frize was a coarse napped woollen cloth. See Montgomery, *Textiles in America*, for more information.

35 The 'lace' in this instance would be what we would think of as braid.

36 This is John Warden's will, details as for note 32.

37 *Tudor Secretary Sir William Petre at Court and Home*, ed. F.G. Emmison (Longman, 1961), p. 157.

38 Arnold, *Queen Elizabeth's Wardrobe Unlock'd*, p. 212.

39 Ibid., p. 210.

40 See Michael Roberts, 'Images of Work and Gender' in Lindsay Charles and Lorna Duffin (eds), *Women and Work in Pre-industrial England* (Croom Helm, 1985), p. 127.

41 Arnold, *Queen Elizabeth's Wardrobe Unlock'd*, pp. 207–8.

42 Ibid., pp. 206–8.

43 Alison Weir, *The Six Wives of Henry VIII* (Pimlico, London, 1993), p. 369.

44 Thomas Platter, *Thomas Platter's Travels in England 1599*, ed. Clare Williams (Jonathan Cape, London, 1937), p. 184.

45 A 'crespin' or crepin was a pleated band of silk or lawn worn under the front edge of a French hood.

46 Quoted from Arnold, *Queen Elizabeth's Wardrobe Unlock'd*, p. 205.

47 Ibid., pp. 200–3.

48 Diana Scarisbrick, *Tudor and Jacobean Jewellery* (Tate Publishing, London, 1995), p. 51.

49 See Arnold, *Queen Elizabeth's Wardrobe Unlock'd*, p. 190.

50 Scarisbrick, *Tudor and Jacobean Jewellery*, p. 40.

51 Ibid., p. 75.

52 George Cavendish, *The Life and Death of Cardinal Wolsey*, ed. Roger Lockyer (Folio Society, London, 1962), p. 46.

53 Scarisbrick, *Tudor and Jacobean Jewellery*, p. 78.

54 Buck, 'The Clothes of Thomasine Petre', p. 21.

55 Scarisbrick, *Tudor and Jacobean Jewellery*, p. 80.

56 Ibid., p. 97.

57 Ibid., p. 42.

58 Taken from Erondell, 'The French Garden', p. 94.

59 See Elspeth Veale, 'On So-Called "Flea Furs"', *Costume Society Journal*, 28 (1994).

60 Sumptuary Regulations proclaimed 1533 (24 Henry VIII) printed in *Statutes of the Realm*, (Records Commission 1820–8). For the detailed analysis of the regulations I am indebted to an unpublished paper by Caroline Johnson.

61 *Lisle Letters*, ed. Byrne, p. 96.

62 Arnold, *Queen Elizabeth's Wardrobe Unlock'd*, p. 193.

63 *The Goodman of Paris*, ed. Eileen Power (George Routledge & Sons Ltd, London, 1928), pp. 214–15.

64 Arnold, *Queen Elizabeth's Wardrobe Unlock'd*, p. 194.

65 Ibid., p. 98.

66 Erondell, 'The French Garden', pp. 59–65.

67 The information on the storage

of Henry VIII's wardrobe is taken from Hayward, 'The Packing and Transportation of Henry VIII'.

68 Castiglione, *The Book of the Courtier*, p. 136.

3 Tournaments and Pageantry

1 Calendar of State Papers, Milan (1385–1618) vol. 1, no. 669, quoted from Maria Hayward, 'Luxury of Magnificence? Dress at the Court of Henry VIII', in *Costume Society Journal*, 30 (1996).

2 *Calendar of State Papers Venetian*, ed. R. Brown (9 vols, 1864–98), quoted from David Starkey, 'The Legacy of Henry VIII', p. 11 in Starkey (ed.), *Henry VIII*.

3 For the story of how the red dragon came to represent Uther Pendragon see Geoffrey of Monmouth, *History of the Kings of Britain* (Penguin, 1968).

4 Steve Gunn, 'The Early Tudor Tournament' in Starkey (ed.), *Henry VIII*.

5 Alan Young, *Tudor and Jacobean Tournaments* (Sheridan House, New York, 1987), p. 23)

6 This description is taken from W.R. Streitberger, *Court Revels 1485–1559* (University of Toronto Press, 1994), pp. 35–8.

7 Cavendish, *The Life and Death of Cardinal Wolsey*, pp. 53–4.

8 Sir Thomas Elyot, *The Book Named the Governor* (J.M. Dent, London, 1962), p. 131.

9 Young, *Tudor and Jacobean Tournaments*, p. 54.

10 Hall, *The Triumphant Reigne of Kyng Henry*, pp. 512–14.

11 See Sydney Anglo, *The Great Tournament Roll of Westminster* (Oxford University Press, 1968), p. 4.

12 Letter from Badoer, Guistinian and Pasqualigo (Venetian ambassadors) in Anglo, *The Great Tournament Roll of Westminster*, p. 6.

13 Ibid.

14 Joycelyne Gledhill Russell, *The Field of Cloth of Gold* (London, Routledge & Keegan Paul, 1969), p. 25.

15 Ibid., pp. 28–40.

16 Ibid., p. 126.

17 Young, *Tudor and Jacobean Tournaments*, p. 17.

18 For more information on this theme see Roy Strong, *The Cult of Elizabeth* (Thames and Hudson, 1977).

19 Anne Somerset, *Elizabeth I* (Phoenix, London, 1991), p. 375.

20 Ibid., p. 372.

21 Ibid., p. 373.

22 Ibid., p. 376.

23 Ibid.

24 Strong, *The Cult of Elizabeth*, p. 50.

25 'The Tudor Monarchy and its Critiques' in John Guy (ed.), *The Tudor Monarchy* (Arnold, 1997), p. 81.

26 Young, *Tudor and Jacobean Tournaments*, p. 133.

27 Ibid., p. 154.

28 Ibid.

29 Ibid., p. 153.

30 Ibid., p. 154.

31 Ibid., p. 153.

32 For information on the development of the revels office see Streitberger, *Court Revels*.

33 Young, *Tudor and Jacobean
    Tournaments*, p. 153.

34 Simon Thurley, '*The Banqueting
    and Disguising Houses of 1527*' in
    Starkey (ed.), *Henry VIII*, p. 65.

35 Cavendish, *The Life and Death of
    Cardinal Wolsey*, pp. 54–7.

36 See Thurley, '*The Banqueting
    and Disguising Houses of 1527*' in
    Starkey (ed.), *Henry VIII*,
    pp. 64–6.

37 Strong, *The Cult of Elizabeth*,
    pp. 165–8.

38 John Leland, *Itinerary* (London,
    1770), Vol. IV,
    p. 304, quoted from Anglo,
    'Image Making' in Guy (ed.), *The
    Tudor Monarchy*, p. 18.

39 Ibid., p. 18.

40 Ibid., p. 21.

41 See section 'The Impact of
    Printing' in Anglo, 'Image
    Making' in Guy (ed.), *The Tudor
    Monarchy*.

42 Ibid., p. 25.

43 Hall, *The Triumphant Reigne of
    Kyng Henry*, p. 614.

4 Religion and the Ritual Year

 1 Ronald Hutton, *The Stations of
    the Sun* (Oxford University Press,
    Oxford, 1997), p. 323.

 2 Ibid., p. 191.

 3 Act of Treason 1534: 26 Henry
    VIII, C.13.

 4 A.G. Dickens, *The English
    Reformation* (Fontana, 1964),
    Chapter 5.

 5 Somerset, *Elizabeth I*, p. 73.

 6 Ibid., p. 10.

 7 Eamon Duffy, *The Stripping of
    the Altars* (Yale University Press,
    New Haven and London, 1992),
    pp. 42–3.

 8 Ibid., pp. 416–17.

 9 Ibid., p. 124.

10 Hutton, *The Stations of the Sun*,
    Chapter 10.

11 Ibid., p. 10.

12 Thomas Tusser, *Five Hundred
    Points of Good Husbandry* (Oxford
    University Press, Oxford and New
    York, 1984), p. 62.

13 *A Collection of Ordinances and
    Regulations for the Government
    of the Royal Household* (London
    Society of Antiquaries, London,
    1790), p. 120.

14 David Starkey (ed.), *Rivals in
    Power* (Macmillan, London,
    1991), p. 188.

15 Ibid., p. 190.

16 *The Lisle Letters*, Vol. 2, p. 22;
    *A Collection of Ordinances and
    Regulations*, p. 120.

17 Hutton, *The Rise and Fall of Merry
    England* (Oxford University Press,
    Oxford, 1994), p. 15.

18 Hutton, *The Stations of the Sun*,
    p. 102.

19 Ibid., p. 105.

20 Philip Stubbes, *The Anatomie
    of Abuses in England*, ed. F.J.
    Furnivall (published for the New
    Shakespeare Society by N. Truber
    and Co., London, 1877–9),
    p. 147.

21 Hutton, *The Stations of the Sun*,
    p. 252.

22 Hutton, *The Rise and Fall of Merry
    England*,
    pp. 90–1.

23 Hutton, *The Stations of the Sun*,
    p. 109.

24 *A Collection of Ordinances and
    Regulations*, p. 121.

25 Russell, *The Field of Cloth of Gold*,
    p. 126.

26 Duffy, *The Stripping of the Altars*, p. 13.

27 Ibid., pp. 15–20.

28 Luke 2:21–35.

29 Hutton, *The Stations of the Sun*, p. 29.

30 Hutton, *The Rise and Fall of Merry England*, p. 18.

31 Tusser, *Five Hundred Points of Good Husbandry*, p. 31.

32 Duffy, *The Stripping of the Altars*, p. 111.

33 Hutton, *The Stations of the Sun*, p. 182.

34 Duffy, *The Stripping of the Altars*, pp. 23–6.

35 Hutton, *The Rise and Fall of Merry England*, p. 20.

36 Hutton, *The Stations of the Sun*, p. 36.

37 Ibid., pp. 184–5.

38 Ibid., Chapter 21.

39 Stubbes, *The Anatomie of Abuses*, p. 149.

40 Peter Laslett and Karla Oosterveon, 'Long Term Trends and Bastardy in England', *Population Studies* 27 (1973), p. 259, quoted in Hutton, *The Stations of the Sun*. Also see Peter Laslett, Richard M. Smith and Karla Oosterveon (eds), *Bastardy and Its Comparative History* (Edward Arnold, London, 1980), which showed the same trends in Sweden. The maidens of the sixteenth century were obviously not as stupid as Philips Stubbes thought they were.

41 Hall, *The Triumphant Reigne of Kyng Henry*, p. 582

42 Stow, *Survey of London* , p. 90.

43 Ibid.

44 Hutton, *The Stations of the Sun*, p. 235.

45 Ibid., Chapter 26.

46 Ibid., pp. 279–80.

47 Ibid., p. 280.

48 Ibid., p. 304.

49 Ibid., p. 308.

50 Stow, *Survey of London*, p. 93.

51 Hutton, *The Stations of the Sun*, p. 314.

52 Ibid., p. 311.

53 Tusser, *Five Hundred Points of Good Husbandry*, p. 178.

54 Stubbes, *The Anatomie of Abuses in England*, p. 150.

55 Paul Hentzner, *Journey in England*, tr. Horace Walpole (printed at Strawberry Hill, London, 1757).

56 Tusser, *Five Hundred Points of Good Husbandry*, p. 178.

57 Ibid., p. 124.

58 Hutton, *The Stations of the Sun*, p. 371.

59 Stow, *Survey of London*, p. 124.

60 Ibid., p. 114.

61 Ibid., p. 90

62 Ibid., p. 125

63 David Cressy, *Bonfires and Bells* (Weidenfeld and Nicolson, London, 1989), p. 51.

64 Strong, *The Cult of Elizabeth*, p. 119.

65 Cressy, *Bonfires and Bells*, p. 54.

66 Hutton, *The Rise and Fall of Merry England*, p. 149.

5 *Christenings, Weddings and Funerals*

1 David Cressy, *Birth, Marriage and Death, Ritual, Religion and the Life-Cycle in Tudor and Stuart England* (Oxford University Press, 1997), p. 101.

2 This was such a contentious

issue that licensed midwives were
obliged to swear an oath which
included the type of baptism
they would perform in time of
need. For this oath see John
Styne, *Annals of the Reformation*
(Clarendon Press, Oxford, 1824),
1, pp. 242–3.

3   For more information on the
ceremony surrounding childbirth
see Adrian Wilson, 'The
Ceremony of Childbirth and its
Interpretation' in Valerie Fildes
(ed.), *Women as Mothers in Pre-
Industrial England* (Routledge,
London and New York, 1990).

4   Cressy, *Birth, Marriage and Death*,
p. 151.

5   Ibid., p. 159.

6   Ibid., p. 163.

7   Ibid., p. 277. See also Peter
Laslett, *The World We Have Lost*
(Methuen, London, 1965),
Chapter 6.

8   See 'The Pleasant Historie of
Jack of Newbery' in Francis
Oscar Mann (ed.), *The Works of
Thomas Deloney* (Clarendon Press,
Oxford, 1912), p. 22.

9   Cressy, *Birth, Marriage and Death*,
pp. 366–7.

10 William Vaughan, *The Golden
Grove, moralized in Three Bookes*
(London, 1608), section on 'Of
Matrimony in England at this day
Solemised'.

11 Cressy, *Birth, Marriage and Death*,
p. 427.

12 Ibid., p. 429.

13 Ibid., pp. 429, 433.

14 Somerset, *Elizabeth I*, p. 569.

15 Cressy, *Birth, Marriage and Death*,
p. 440.

16 Ibid., p. 443.

17 Sir Thomas Elyot, *The Castel of
Helth* (London, 1541), p. 65.

18 Ibid.

6 Dancing and Music

1   Cavendish, *The Life and Death of
Cardinal Wolsey*, p. 106.

2   See Chapter 1 for more details.

3   Thoinot Arbeau, *Orchesography*,
tr. Mary Stewart Evans (Dover
Publications Inc., New York,
1967), p. 11.

4   Ibid., p. 12.

5   Walter L. Woodfill, *Musicians in
English Society from Elizabeth to
Charles I* (Princeton University
Press, Princeton, New Jersey,
1953), p. 15.

6   Elyot, *The Book Named the
Governor*, pp. 69–78.

7   Arbeau, *Orchesography*, pp. 15–16.

8   Weir, *The Six Wives of Henry VIII*,
p. 438.

9   Castiglione, *The Book of the
Courtier*, p. 118.

10 Fabritio Caroso, *Nobilita di Dame*,
ed. and tr. Julia Sutton (Oxford
University Press, Oxford and New
York, 1986), p. 19.

11 For information on etiquette in
the ballroom see Caroso, *Nobilita
di Dame*, pp. 134–50.

12 Arbeau, *Orchesography*, pp. 52, 77.

13 Caroso, *Nobilita di Dame*,
pp. 22–3.

14 Ibid., p. 29.

15 A hautboy was a reed instrument,
something along the lines of a
modern oboe. A sackbut was an
early form of trombone.

16 Arbeau, *Orchesography*, p. 51.

17 A shawm is a very loud reed
instrument.

18 For further explanation of some of these difficulties see Caroso, *Nobilita di Dame*, p. 1.

19 For more information about the practicalities of reconstructing Renaissance dance see Julia Sutton's introduction to Caroso, *Nobilita di Dame*, plus her notes to Arbeau, *Orchesography*. Another useful book is Bernard Thomas and Jane Gingell, *The Renaissance Dance Book* (Pro Musica Edition, London, 1987).

20 Arbeau, *Orchesography*, p. 75.

21 Ibid., p. 59.

22 Ibid., pp. 77–8.

23 Ibid., p. 121.

24 Ibid., p. 159.

25 Ibid., p. 161.

26 Caroso, *Nobilita di Dame*, pp. 182–4, 217.

27 Arbeau, *Orchesography*, pp. 182–95.

28 Ibid., pp. 22–46.

29 Elyot, *The Book Named the Governor*, pp. 60–78.

30 Castiglione, *The Book of the Courtier*, p. 120.

31 Elyot, *The Book Named the Governor*, pp. 20–2.

32 For more information on the development of musical literacy see David C. Price, *Patrons and Musicians of the English Renaissance* (Cambridge University Press, Cambridge, 1981), Chapter 1.

33 Ibid., p. 14.

34 Morley, *A Plaine and Easie Introduction to Practicall Musicke* (London, 1597).

35 J.J. Scarisbrick, *Henry VIII* (Methuen, London, 1976), p. 32.

36 Price, *Patrons and Musicians*, p. 12.

37 Woodfill, *Musicians in English Society*, p. 178.

38 Ibid., p. 180.

39 Somerset, *Elizabeth I*, p. 21.

40 Ibid., p. 371.

41 Price, *Patrons and Musicians*, p. 14.

42 Ibid., p. 42.

43 Ibid., pp. 181–9.

44 *The Autobiography of Thomas Whythorne*, ed. James M. Osborn (Clarendon Press, Oxford, 1961). See introduction for an outline of his life.

45 Price, *Patrons and Musicians*, pp. 22–6.

46 *The Autobiography of Thomas Whythorne*.

47 Price, *Patrons and Musicians*, p. 36 and Joan Simon, *Education and Society in Tudor England* (Cambridge University Press, Cambridge, 1966), p. 240.

48 Morley, *A Plaine and Easie Introduction to Practicall Musicke*, p. 179.

49 More, *Utopia*, p. 127.

50 Price, *Patrons and Musicians*, pp. 46–7.

51 Ibid. See sections on 'Private Music and Religious Faith' and 'The Presentation of Music in Worship'.

52 For more information on the Chapel Royal see Woodfill, *Musicians in English Society*, section on the Chapel Royal.

53 Price, *Patrons and Musicians*, p. 52.

54 Joyce Youings, *Sixteenth Century England* (Pelican Books, London, 1984), pp. 282–3.

55 Woodfill, *Musicians in English Society*, p. 136.

56   Ibid., pp. 145–6.
57   For more information on the city waits see Woodfill, *Musicians in English Society*.

7 Reading

1   Simon, *Education and Society*, Chapter 2.
2   James Carely, 'Greenwich and Henry VIII's Royal Library' in Starkey (ed.), *Henry VIII*.
3   Tessa Watt, *Cheap Print and Popular Piety 1550–1640* (Phoenix, London, 1977), p. 12.
4   David Cressy, *Literacy and the Social Order* (Cambridge University Press, Cambridge, 1980), p. 156.
5   Ibid., Chapter 3.
6   Ibid., p. 169.
7   Watt, *Cheap Print and Popular Piety*, p. 260.
8   Cressy, *Literacy and the Social Order*, p. 29.
9   For more information on the education of women see the chapter on education in Sim, *The Tudor Housewife*.
10   Ascham, *The Schoolmaster*, p. 28.
11   Ibid., p. 26.
12   Cressy, *Literacy and the Social Order*, p. 38.
13   Ascham, *The Schoolmaster*, p. 40.
14   For more information on women's reading see Suzanne W. Hull, *Chaste, Silent and Obedient* (Huntingdon Library, San Morris, 1982).
15   Cressy, *Literacy and the Social Order*, p. 59.
16   Philip Gaskell, *A New Introduction to Bibliography* (Clarendon Press, Oxford, 1972), p. 177.

17   Ibid., p. 60.
18   Watt, *Cheap Print and Popular Piety*, p. 261.
19   Ibid., p. 11.
20   Louis B. Wright, *Middle Class Culture in Elizabethan England* (University of North Carolina Press, Chapel Hill, 1935), p. 434.
21   Watt, *Cheap Print and Popular Piety*, p. 2.
22   Ibid., p. 261.
23   Craig R. Thompson, 'The Bible in English, 1525–1611' in Louis B. Wright (ed.) , *Life and Letters in Tudor and Stuart England* (Folger Shakespeare Library, Cornell Press, Ithaca, New York, 1962).
24   George Whetstone, *An Heptameron of Civil Discourses* (London, 1583).
25   *Tell-Trothes New Yeares Gift*, ed. F.J. Furnivall (N. Truber & Co., London, 1876), p. 14.
26   *The Workes of the Reverend M. Richard Greenham*, ed. Henry Holland (London, 1599), quoted from Wright, *Middle Class Culture in Elizabethan England*, p. 233.
27   Wright, *Middle Class Culture in Elizabethan England*, p. 379.
28   Ibid., p. 382.
29   Ibid., p. 297.
30   Ibid., p. 305.
31   Ibid., p. 327.
32   Ibid., p. 140.
33   Gaskell, *A New Introduction to Bibliography*, p. 161.
34   Wright, *Middle Class Culture in Elizabethan England*, p. 354.
35   For more information on female academics in the sixteenth century see Margaret P. Hannay (ed.), *Silent But For The Word* (Kent State

Univeristy Press, Ohio, 1985).

36 Thomas Wilson, quoted from Wright, *Middle Class Culture in Elizabethan England*, pp. 344–5.

37 Elyot, *The Castel of Helth*, Introduction.

38 Wright, *Middle Class Culture in Elizabethan England*, p. 362.

39 For more information on Captain Cox's library see F.J. Furnivall (ed.), *Captain Cox His Ballads and His Books or Robert Laneham's Letter* (Taylor & Co. London, 1871).

8 The Theatre

1 For more information on medieval English drama see Richard Beadle (ed.), *The Cambridge Companion to Medieval English Theatre* (Cambridge University Press, Cambridge, 1994).

2 For more information see Meg Twycross, 'The Theatricality of Medieval English Plays' in Beadle, *The Cambridge Companion*.

3 J.L. Styan, *The English Stage* (Cambridge University Press, Cambridge, 1996), p. 24.

4 Twycross, 'The Theatricality of Medieval English Plays', p. 48.

5 Ibid., p. 53.

6 *The Revels History of Drama in English*, gen. ed. T.W. Craik (Methuen, London and New York, 1980), p. 31.

7 Ibid., pp. 32–3.

8 Ibid., p. 34.

9 Hall, *The Triumphant Reigne of Kyng Henry*, p. 719.

10 Raphael Holinshed, *Chronicles of England, Ireland and Scotland*

(London, 1586), p. 1028.

11 *The Revels History of Drama in English*, Vol. II, p. 20.

12 Ibid., pp. 27–8.

13 Andrew Gurr, *The Shakespearean Stage 1574–1642*, 3rd edn (Cambridge University Press, Cambridge, 1992), p. 73.

14 Quoted from E.K. Chambers, *The Elizabethan Stage* (Oxford, 1923), Vol. IV, pp. 273–4.

15 Gerald Eades Bentley, *The Profession of Player in Shakespeare's Time, 1590–1642* (Princeton University Press, Princeton, 1984), p. 3.

16 Gurr, *The Shakespearean Stage*, p. 215.

17 Andrew Gurr, *Playgoing in Shakespeare's London* (Cambridge University Press, Cambridge, 1987), pp. 23–6.

18 Youings, *Sixteenth Century England*, pp. 148–50.

19 Gurr, *Playgoing in Shakespeare's London*, p. 55

20 Gurr, *The Shakespearean Stage*, p. 213

21 Platter, *Travels in England*, pp. 166–7.

22 Gurr, *The Shakespearean Stage*, p. 104.

23 Letter from Philip Gawdy to his brother, quoted from Gurr, *Playgoing in Shakespeare's London*, p. 67.

24 *The Autobriography of Anne Lady Halkett*, ed. John Gough Nichols (Camden Society, London, 1875) p. 3.

25 Gurr, *Playgoing in Shakespeare's London*, p. 77.

26 Thomas Dekker, *The Gull's Hornbook*, ed. R.B. McKerrow

(Kin's Classics series, Alexander Moring, London, 1905), p. 63.

27 Quoted from Gurr, *Playgoing in Shakespeare's London*, p. 47.

28 Platter, *Travels in England*, p. 167.

29 Quoted from Gurr, *Playgoing in Shakespeare's London*, p. 38.

30 Platter, *Travels in England*, pp. 170–1.

31 For more information about Kemp's feat see William Kemp, *Kemps Nine Daies Wonder* (London, 1600; reprinted Lark's Press, Norfolk, 1997).

32 Gurr, *Playgoing in Shakespeare's London*, p. 35.

33 Bentley, *The Profession of Player*, p. 184.

34 Ibid., p. 5.

35 Ibid., p. 35.

36 Ibid., p. 304.

37 Quoted from Ibid., p. 195.

38 Ibid., p. 191.

39 Ibid., p. 201.

40 Ibid., p. 196.

41 Ibid., p. 198.

42 Ibid., p. 200.

43 Gurr, *The Shakespearean Stage*, p. 19.

44 Ibid., p. 20.

45 Ibid., p. 82.

9 Sports, Games and Other Pastimes

1 Elyot, *The Book Named the Governor*,) pp. 66–7.

2 For information on different types of hunting see John G. Cummins, *The Hound and the Hawk: The Art of Medieval Hunting* (Weidenfeld & Nicolson, London, 1988).

3 Letter to Cardinal Wolsey from *Letters and Papers Foreign and Domestic of the Reign of Henry VIII* (catalogued J.S. Brewer, revised and enlarged R.H. Brodie, 21 vols, London, 1861–3). Quoted from Thurley, *The Royal Palaces*, p. 191.

4 Andrew Boorde, *A Dyetary of Helth*, ed. F.J. Furnivall (Early English Text Society, Keegan Paul Trench & Trubner & Co., London, 1870), p. 274.

5 Cummins, *The Hawk and the Hound*, pp. 62–3. Richard Chambry's game roll is reproduced at the back of the book.

6 Ibid., p. 58.

7 Ibid., p. 32.

8 Elyot, *The Book Named the Governor*, p. 68.

9 Thurley, *The Royal Palaces*, p. 193.

10 Robert Burton, *The Anatomy of Melancholy* (Longman, Rees, Orme & Co., London, 1827), p. 405.

11 Bodleian Library Rawl. MS D 776f 224; Rawl. MS D 780 f 155v. Quoted from Thurley, *The Royal Palaces*, p. 193.

12 *The Arte of Angling*, ed. Gerald Eades Bentley (first published 1577; Princeton University Press, Princeton, 1958).

13 Statutes of the Realm, Vol. 3, Henry VIII, Record Commission, London, 1817, p. 25, 3 Hen VIII c 3, *An Act concerning the shooting in Longe Bowes*.

14 Ibid. p. 837. 33 Hen VIII c 9, *An acte for the Mayntenance of Artyllarie and debarringe of unlawful Games*.

15 Stow, *Survey of London*, p. 104.

16 Elyot, *The Book Named the Governor*, p. 93.

17 Ibid., p. 60.

18 Hall, *The Triumphant Reigne of Kyng Henry*, p. 151.

19 Russell, *The Field of Cloth of Gold*, p. 131.

20 Stow, *Survey of London*, pp. 86–7.

21 Ibid., p. 87.

22 Hutton, *The Stations of the Sun*, pp. 154–5.

23 Elyot, *The Book Named the Governor*, p. 92.

24 Ibid., p. 59.

25 Julian Marshall, *The Annals of Tennis* (The Field Office, London, 1878), pp. 52–8.

26 Stow, *Survey of London*, p. 86.

27 Estienne Perlin's experiences of London can be found in James Beeverell, *The Pleasures of London* (Witherby & Co., London, 1940). His comments on tennis appear on p. 66.

28 Marshall, *The Annals of Tennis*, pp. 14–15.

29 For more information on how the game was played see Thurley, *The Royal Palaces*, p. 185.

30 Ibid., p. 186.

31 Castiglione, *The Book of the Courtier*, p. 118.

32 Hall, *The Triumphant Reigne of Kyng Henry*, p. 520.

33 Thurley, *The Royal Palaces*, p. 189.

34 Stow, *Survey of London*, p. 104.

35 Ibid., p. 149.

36 Gilbert Walker, *A Manifest Detection of the Most Vyle and Detestable of Diceplay, and other practices lyke the same* (Percy Society, London, 1850), p. 39.

37 Platter, *Travels in England*, p. 174.

38 Ibid., pp. 168–9.

39 Quoted from C.L. Kingsford 'Paris Garden and the Bear Baiting', *Archeologia*, 2nd series, Vol. XX, (March 1920), p. 161.

40 Platter, *Travels in England*, pp. 167–8.

41 Thurley, *The Royal Palaces*, p. 190.

42 Burton, *The Anatomy of Melancholy*, p. 413.

43 For more information see H.J.R. Murray, *A History of Board Games other than Chess* (Clarendon Press, Oxford, 1952), p. 84.

44 Clive Everton, *The Story of Billiards and Snooker* (Cassell, London, 1979), pp. 9–10.

45 Murray, *A History of Board Games*, p. 101.

46 Elyot, *The Book Named the Governor*, p. 92.

47 *The Paston Letters*, quoted from David Parlett, *The Oxford Guide to Card Games* (Oxford University Press, 1990), p. 46.

48 Gamini Salgado, *The Elizabethan Underworld* (J.M. Dent & Sons Ltd, London, 1977), pp. 36–7.

49 Stow, *Survey of London*, p. 362.

50 For more information on the London brothels see E.J. Burford, *Bawds and Lodgings: a History of the London Bankside Brothels* (Peter Owen, London, 1976).

51 Platter, *Travels in England*, pp. 175–6. See also Salgado, *The Elizabethan Underworld*, pp. 52–3.

52 Stow, *Survey of London*, pp. 350–1.

Further Reading

The subject matter of this book is so wide that there is no one other book that covers all the topics. Anyone interested in finding out more about any of the individual subjects should see the notes given for each chapter.

Here are a few particular suggestions for books that are well worth a read.

On the subject of daily life in Tudor England:
William Harrison, *The Description of England* (Dover Publications, New York, 1994).

The Lisle Letters, ed. Muriel St Clare Byrne (Cobden-Sanderson, London, 1930).

The Lisle Letters, ed. Muriel St Clare Byrne (Penguin Books, 1985) gives a good feel for life in courtly circles at the time of Henry VIII.

On the subject of religion and the ritual year:
Eamon Duffy, *The Stripping of the Altars* (Yale University Press, New Haven and London, 1992).

Ronald Hutton, *The Rise and Fall of Merry England* (Oxford University Press, Oxford, 1994) and *The Stations of the Sun* (Oxford University Press, Oxford, 1996).

On the subject of the stage:
Andrew Gurr, *The Shakespearean Stage* (Cambridge University Press, Cambridge, 1992) and *Playgoing in Shakespeare's London* (Cambridge University Press, Cambridge, 1987).

There is much less information on drama in the early part of the sixteenth century but Richard Beadle (ed.), *The Cambridge Companion to Medieval English Theatre* (Cambridge University Press, Cambridge, 1994) gives a good overview.

There is a wide range of reading on the subject of literacy and literature, but one of the most interesting, despite its age, is Louis B. Wright, *Middle Class Culture in Elizabethan England* (University of North Carolina Press, Chapel Hill, 1935).

On the subject of clothing, I suggest Janet Arnold, *Queen Elizabeth's Wardrobe Unlock'd* (Maney, Leeds, 1988).

On the subject of houses:
Mark Girouard, *Life in the English Country House* (Yale University Press, New Haven and London, 1978) is a good guide to the social history of large-scale houses.
Malcolm Airs, *The Tudor and Jacobean Country House* (Sutton Publishing, Stroud, 1995) is an excellent guide to their planning and building.

For an idea of just how basic life was for the less fortunate a visit is recommended to the Weald and Downland Museum near Chichester, where actual houses from the period are on display.

Index